Racing Romance

Racing Romance

*Love, Power, and Desire among
Asian American/White Couples*

KUMIKO NEMOTO

RUTGERS UNIVERSITY PRESS
New Brunswick, New Jersey, and London

Library of Congress Cataloging-in-Publication Data

Nemoto, Kumiko, 1970–
    Racing romance : love, power, and desire among Asian American / white couples /
    Kumiko Nemoto.
        p.   cm.
    Includes bibliographical references and index.
    ISBN 978-0-8135-4532-5 (hardcover : alk. paper)
    ISBN 978-0-8135-4533-2 (pbk. : alk. paper)
    1. Interracial marriage—United States. 2. Interracial dating—United States.
    3. Asian Americans—Psychology. 4. Asian Americans—Race identity.
    5. Race awareness. 6. Race relations. I. Title.
HQ1031.N45 2009
306.84'608995073—dc22

                                                                            008038708

    A British Cataloging-in-Publication record for this book is available from the
    British Library.

Visit our Web site: http://rutgerspress.rutgers.edu

Manufactured in the United States of America
Composition: Jack Donner, BookType

For my mother

Contents

Acknowledgments

This book is a result of my long personal and intellectual journey. Many persons have helped to make the work possible. I thank all the couples and individuals who endured my questions and allowed me to explore their personal experiences. Composing the stories about each individual required an enormous amount of reflection on my part, viewing each account from my perspectives as a researcher, a feminist scholar, and a Japanese woman; accomplishing this task would not have been possible without the genuine and kind assistance of the people I interviewed. Parts of this book were previously published in the *Journal of Asian American Studies* and in *Gender Issues*.

The book began while I was at the University of Texas at Austin. I am especially indebted to Christine L. Williams for her long-term mentoring and role-modeling as a scholar and a teacher. On a number of difficult occasions during and after my graduate school career, Christine consistently offered me encouragement and helpful suggestions. Her guidance as a feminist scholar was invaluable in my completing this book. I thank Debra Umberson and Pauline Strong for engaging with my project with positive affirmations and suggestions. I am indebted to Art Sakamoto and Sharmila Rudrappa for their generosity, warm support, and continuous friendship. Several colleagues further helped me with the volume. I am grateful for the insightful comments and warm friendship of Karen D. Pyke of the University of California, Riverside. I am indebted to Erica Chito Childs for providing generously of her time and for her helpful comments. I thank these other colleagues who also provided helpful comments and suggestions: Rebecca Klatch, Jyoti Puri, Sharon Bird, and Katrina Bell McDonald. I am grateful to my editor at Rutgers University Press, Adi Hovav, whose patience and thoughtful suggestions have also made this book possible.

I am grateful to friends who supported the process of writing, over the years, and provided insights in innumerable ways—particularly Esther Alston and Andrea Braendlin, who have taught me much and helped me with love and care. I owe a special debt of gratitude to Lynne F. Chapman, who gave generously of her time to read manuscripts, and who helped my writing through her thoughtfulness and wisdom. I thank my friends in Japan, particularly Murasato Tadayuki, Simada Tatsuhiro, and Naoko, who have always taken my questions seriously and provided philosophical and intellectual affirmation of my ideas.

Finally, this book would never have been written without my parents, who have affected my career and life tremendously. I thank my mother for cultivating my early intellectual curiosity, and for her unfailing strength and sustaining support. I also thank my father, who lived and worked in three countries and taught me to question the meaning of the boundaries of nation, race, and ethnicity.

Racing Romance

Introduction

Wʜʏ ᴅᴏ ᴡᴇ ғᴀʟʟ ɪɴ ʟᴏᴠᴇ? What are the components that constitute love and desire? How do we develop and sustain feelings of love for another person?

Having an intimate relationship with another person is seen as a decidedly private activity in our culture. Yet desire and passion for other people is shaped socially and culturally, and often reflects a person's desire for self-realization and a social identity, and by extension a person's craving for certain social and cultural powers. The promise of self-realization can be seen fleetingly in one's identification with another person, who is seen both as a source of pleasure to identify with and as a power to possess. Intimacy is a cultural and social device of self-making. One's views of oneself transform through the exchange and confirmation of one's recognition. Intimacy allows us to fashion ourselves and determine our futures through identification with others, and these others' powers and identity are constituted by race, class, and gender.

Many social theorists have pointed out the paradox of sex and love—they can bring a person simultaneously empowerment and conformity. Michel Foucault discusses the powerful nature of sex as an essential part of individual identity, as sex has historically been under the modern state's management and control:[1] "It is through sex, an imaginary point determined by the deployment of sexuality—that each individual has to pass in order to have access to his own intelligibility, to the whole of his body . . . to his identity."[2] Elizabeth Povinelli similarly writes that modern love is a project critical to modern enlightenment, providing a liberal subject with a sense of freedom and sovereignty, and simultaneously inculcating the subject with social ideologies.[3] Judith Butler describes the sublimation of our desire as "the desire to be known, to come into being through the look of the Other,"[4] and this is precisely the moment when "liberation paves the way for new power relationships."[5] In this book, I explore these two sides of intimate relationships: their potential for empowerment and their ability to instill conformity to social and cultural discourses. The book is not so much a collection of "love stories" as a collection of stories about making sense of the power structures surrounding racialized and gendered desires, and about the current cultural milieu that regulates and disciplines the exchange of desires in interracial relationships. How do gender, race, and class form the shape of love relationships, and how do the discourses of nation, family, and multiculturalism also constitute the patterns of gender and race?

In this book, I focus specifically on interracial relationships between whites and Asian Americans. Interracial relationships have recently become more popular than everbefore in the United States, despite the fact that, where they have historically been far from the social and cultural norm. The noticeable increase in interracial couples gives an impression that racism is on the decline in America. Popular multicultural imagery sells racialized bodies and fashions as exotic sexual signs in the marketplace; an interracial relationship similarly attracts public attention as some exotic commodity. A color-blind view of race emphasizes race as a cultural symbol and a cultural marker of the body, rather than as as a reminder of inequalities and discrimination.[6] Under the guise of color-blindness and the commodified culture of intimacy, the issues surrounding social inequalities in interracial relationships—such as a couple's race consciousness, the couple's gender dynamics, or the couple's social reception—have rarely drawn public attention.[7] Focusing on the context of black–white intermarriage, Patricia Hill Collins criticizes the color-blind view of intermarriage, which portrays the growing rate of interracial relationships as rebellious or revolutionary. She writes, "Crossing the color line to marry interracially challenges deep-seated American norms, yet such relationships may not be inherently progressive."[8] In discussing the higher rate of intermarriage among black men versus that among black women—a rate often associated with popular images of black hypermasculinity—Collins argues that black men can enhance their standing within the system of American masculinity, but prevailing images of black men and women in U.S. culture continue to be internalized by black individuals and simultaneously to reify the lack of race consciousness among whites in their pursuit of "hypersexual" black men and women. Similarly, Erica Chito Childs points out the black community's gendered tension regarding intermarriage, in which black women often view a black man's choice to be with white woman as betrayal or rejection of black women.[9] Both Collins and Childs point out that the problem with a color-blind view of interracial relationships is that it lacks critical engagement with the complexity of racial and gender dynamics and inequalities inherent in relationships.

Just as in black–white interracial relationships, racial stereotypes have long played crucial roles in Asian American–white interracial relationships.

Asian Americans' interracial relationships have long been portrayed in the media, often in conjunction with popular images of Asian American women as submissive, as hypersexual, or as "dragon ladies," or with images of Asian American men as emasculated laborers or hypermasculine martial artists. In regard to Asian American women, the word *Asian* conjures images of a racialized femininity (of women who are extremely feminine and concerned with pleasing men), which corresponds well to what Michael Kimmel has called "emphasized femininity." A woman who displays emphasized femininity appears to embody stereotypical masculine desires: she is willing to be social (rather than to be competent), to accommodate men's desires and interests (rather than her own), and to comply with men's desire to be titillated and have their egos stroked.[10] In keeping with such stereotypes of Asian American women as the embodiment of hypersexual femininity, and of Asian American men as lacking in American ideals of masculinity, many studies have reported a strikingly higher number of Asian American women married to white people than of Asian American men married to whites.[11] However, the link between such racial stereotypes and the actual Asian American experience has rarely been explored. If Asian American women have been construed as hyperfeminine, and if Asian American men have been seen as lacking masculine traits, how have such images become reflected in individual relationships? How do Asian American women and men negotiate their own racialized images in the context of intimate relationships? How does race matter in the gender dynamics of relationships? How do white men and women engage with the race of their partners? In chapter 1, I provide a deeper discussion of stereotypes of Asians and Asian Americans, and I explore how these stereotypes have historically mirrored ideologies about Asian American–white intimacy.

Many of the stories in this book highlight individual exchanges of racialized and gendered images in relationships. Some white men I interviewed explicitly pursued Asian women as their ideal partners for marriage and intimacy, and many men referred in their comments to stereotypical "model minority" traits ascribed to Asian women (traits such as docility, domestic femininity, and upward mobility). White women discussed racialized images of Asian American men both positively and negatively, some describing these men as domineering, some seeing them as possessing model minority traits.

Just as whites often employ racial stereotypes of Asian Americans in spousal selection, it is also known that Asian Americans often pursue whites for their "Euro-American"–looking or "aesthetically pleasing" characteristics, such as "tallness, round eyes, 'buffness' for men, and 'more ample breasts' for women."[12] A couple of Asian American men I interviewed described white women as the people who embody the highest standard of beauty. Most Asian American women also chose white men as ideal partners, citing their large physical size, their potential as breadwinners, and their "knightly" masculinity. But intimate relationships do not consist only of racialized images—they also have their own gender dynamics, which differ in accord with generation, education, social class, and even national immigration discourse.[13] My interest is in tracking the flow of these images and their psychological implications, and exploring their interplay with issues of gender and class in actual relationships, rather than in merely pinpointing static exchanges of racialized images.

I am also interested in addressing how Asian American–white intimacy has been shaped by certain gender hierarchies and inequalities inherent in the discourses of nation and family in America, discourses that are juxtaposed with discourses of multiculturalism and color-blindness. Gender inequalities entangled with issues of race, class, nation, and citizenship have often been masked by the celebratory tone of interracial relationships. When I speak of gender inequality, I do not simply mean men's explicit physical dominance or financial control over women, but rather refer to the system of femininity and masculinity, and how it is culturally constructed as imagery, scripts, and discourses. Power dynamics in relationships can be generated by projection and exchanges of racialized images, even though such acts can be mutual. Scholars of postcolonial studies have been interested in Fanon's classic work on the black desire to be white, and have discussed whiteness as an unobtainable norm and a psychological object of envy and mimicry for the colonized. Alfred Lopez writes, "The idea of whiteness as a cultural aesthetic norm combines with the idea of whiteness as a desirable and even necessary trait for colonized subjects who wish to achieve class mobility and financial success in a colonized society."[14] David Eng also points out Asian American men's identification with or submission to whiteness.[15] Similarly, Anne Cheng discusses the social system in which racial minorities' psychological submission to white authority is normalized as "racial melancholia."[16] Racial melancholia creates a sense of loss and grief in the racial minority as a result of "failed" identification with the white as the ideal. Thus, "irreversible loss as well as amnesia" among racial minorities' psyches is inevitable.[17]

How does such psychological conformity resulting from the structuring of race follow certain gender patterns? Feminist psychoanalyst Jessica Benjamin discusses how male dominant culture produces female psychological submission to, and identification with, male authority in intimate relationships. She writes: ". . . submission to authority is itself is an erotic experience" because such submission to a powerful other is often "understood as a means, however problematic, of securing or freeing the self and, at the same time, finding recognition."[18] How does such a psychological process intersect with understandings of social class? Or, how do the discourses of ideal family and nation play a role in the maintenance of such gendered conformity? Rather than viewing gender and race separately, I want to find the intersection of these ideas in the self-making of individual women and men and in the maintenance of their own relationships. Finally, I will explore what these processes tell us about social discourses and the ideals of family, nation, and love in America.

The act of falling in love can include a "moment of freedom," in which one might imagine one's own agency in the situation; in this moment a person's desires may follow certain "scripts" learned from one's culture with the goal of attaining the ideal relationship and self-identity. Investing one's past in a relationship and exploring one's future self with another individual is what transforms a mutual impulse of attraction into a strong bond in a relationship.

In my interviews, when an Asian American woman chose white men as ideal partners, her psychological attachment included her desires to attain self-realization in the form of upward mobility, to attain the "American dream," to be free from the negative stereotypes that label Asian Americans as second-class citizens, or to be free from the ethnic patriarchy in which she grew up. Exploring the individual meanings people invest and associate with interracial intimacy helps us understand the hegemonic scripts and narratives through which Asian American women desire to transform their identities, and thus helps us address the social structures that led them to employ such hegemonic discourses. A few Asian American men I interviewed attempted to repudiate negative stereotypes of their supposedly marginal manhood, by gaining recognition and power through relationships with white women. Their desire to repudiate these stereotypes or attain normative masculinity is rooted in emotional investment in certain issues, such as their desire to reconcile their conflicting cultural notions of masculinity, free themselves from racist stereotypes against Asian Americans, and distance themselves from the ethnic disciplining they grew up with. Asian Americans' psychological and emotional investment also follows gendered patterns. For example, some young Asian American women I interviewed often discussed their own images, or their image of Asian American women in general, through the lens of white male desire—that is, in terms of being a desirable object for a white male, rather than as the subject of desire. Some emphasized their view of Asianness as a desirable feminine cultural signifier, in the same way that white males described them. On the other hand, some Asian American men viewed white men either as the objects of rivalry or as the norm they feel they should attain. They also saw positive responses from white women as a sign of the transformation of their marginalized masculinity, but they did not view white women as the liberators of their racialized selves. They derived their masculine confidence from their ability to possess white women, or from white women's compliments of their masculinity.

Although so-called whiteness of a partner can be seen as cultural capital, Asian American women and men's identification with a white partner's race demonstrates gendered patterns. To highlight these gender patterns, I have divided this book into two parts: (1) Asian American Women and White Men, and (2) Asian American Men and White Women. I have framed the stories of the couples by highlighting instances of gendered patterns in which Asian American women and men explored and managed their womanhood and manhood in relation to their white partners.

Racial concerns and tensions toward Asian American–white couples in Asian American families and in white families appear to be less severe than those occurring in black–white relationships. In the context of black–white relationships, Childs' study reports white families display "nuanced" opposition toward black–white marriages: whites elude to racist remarks, and black families are distrustful of white partners.[19] Much as Childs found in regard to black–white couples, some white families, neighbors, and friends, in cases of Asian American–white couples, expressed negative views of Asian American partners indirectly by ignoring the partner or by showing discomfort toward the issue of intermarriage. But gendered patterns also emerged in these white people's views of interracial couples: the negative public reception of Asian American men having relationships with white women differs from the reception of Asian American women dating white men. Some Asian American men faced overt racism for dating or marrying white woman; one man's white wife was disowned by her family. Some white women reported their white friends' disinterest in, hostility toward, or racist views of their partners. However, many Asian American women, along with white men, did not believe that their racial difference had ever created problems or made them a target of suspicion among whites. Thus, it is crucial to understand how and why public perceptions of Asian American–white couples are gendered, and how historical images and stereotypes of Asian American–white marriage have influenced public reception of such couples. Such an understanding will demonstrate how social receptions of interracial couples differ from popular notions of color-blind multiculturalism.

Race, Gender, and Subjectivity

Due in part to the difficulty of examining and evaluating desire and intimate relationships in their full complexity, very few ethnographic studies have been undertaken on these topics. The study of interracial relationships may also have been seen by some as an inappropriate subject of scholarly study, since it entails investigation not only of dominant groups but also of racial minorities and their racialized desires, ambivalence, or alienation (including some aspects of internalized racism).[20] Karen D. Pyke and Tran Dang, citing Russell, Wilson, and Hall, argue that the topic of racial minorities and their internalized racism is an "intellectual taboo," potentially embarrassing and disconcerting to discuss.[21] Pyke notes the inherent difficulty in discussing internalized racism, in that such discussion is often understood to place the blame on victims of racism, or to treat the victims as mere dupes who lack the agency to resist the injustice of racism.[22]

Similarly, discussing racialized desires among racial minorities might be seen as a futile or even damaging endeavor, one that could endanger the formation of political coalitions. However, examining the emotional and affective dimensions of intimate relationships enables us to see the complicated machinations of race and its effects upon individual psyches. According to Anne Cheng, studies of race tend to have a political agenda and often dismiss the importance of analysis of the psychological complexities of the racialized subject.[23] Cheng states, "beyond the strategic issue lies the psychical issues." She emphasizes the critical study of subjectivity and "the complexity of identification as a psychical process."[24] She suggests that we examine the complicated or even contradictory dimensions of the race structure that often emerge in one's identity or subject formation:

> What would it mean *not* to look at the subjective dimension of race for fear of its unwieldiness? . . . We do not know yet what it means for politics to accommodate a concept of identity based on constitutive loss or for politics to explore the psychic and social anchoring points that keep us chained to the oppressive, wounding memories of love and hate that condition the mutual enmeshment of the "dominant" and the "disempowered." To refuse to contemplate these aspects of racial dynamics, however, has not been productive either, as is evidenced by the ongoing national drama of racial repudiation and reprisal. . . . What has been missing in much of the critical analysis of race relations and representations has been a willingness to confront the psychic implications of the haunting negativity that has not only been attached to but has also helped to constitute the very category of "the racialized."[25]

Examining racialized desires and the outcomes of these desires may not lead to the instant correction of racial inequality, but it may lead to an awareness of the ways in which racial ideologies interact, along with gender, class, and nation, with one's psyche and emotions, and thus are deeply tied to one's conformity to structural inequality.

In this book, I will analyze the directions of individual affection and desires as observed in the interviews. This focus on the "subjectivity" or "psychology" of individuals is uncommon in traditional sociology. Sociological models often fail to take into account the roles of desire, affection, imagination, and the complexity of psychological dynamics in the social actor's creative and reflective processes. For example, Giddens stresses the "rational individual" model, which assumes that subjects act according to their own capability, will, and knowledge, since "to be a human agent is to be a highly knowledgeable and skilled individual."[26] This notion of rational and calculating agency excludes the actor's affective and emotional engagement in the processes, because such engagement is not reflexive. Since many gendered images and desires include "pre-reflexive aspects of masculine and feminine behavior,"[27] and since many structural inequalities generate ambivalent emotions and contradictions, and not rational actions, in individuals, analysis based only on rational and utilitarian models is inadequate to address issues of race and gender emerging at the emotional level.

A psychoanalytic perspective is useful in looking at specific emotional patterns that reflect the structure of gender and race. Certain emotional patterns experienced within intimacy, such as desire, anxiety, and repulsion, are gendered and racialized. The formation of these emotional patterns in intimacy should be explained sociologically, rather than be merely attributed to the general human need for "basic trust" and "ontological security."[28] Feminist psychoanalysis has suggested that the gender socialization process is more than individual intention and role-taking. Chodorow argues that the structure of male–female contrasts, informed by a pattern of male dominance, privilege, and superiority, is not only experienced as the symbol of gender structure, but also accordingly produces emotions such as rage, envy, excitement, fear, guilt, and submission.[29] Psychoanalysis has been criticized as an ahistorical and culturally universalized approach.[30] It has been argued that psychoanalysis reduces gender inequality to its psychological processes and therefore ignores social structure. But psychoanalytic theory does not consider any social relationships as given; instead, it reveals the internalization of social norms and conformity at psychological levels.[31] Connell sees the psychoanalytic perspective as a map of one historically possible pattern rather than as a normalized scheme.[32] This map thus provides insight into exploring the structure of gender and racialized masculinity and femininity in subjective experience. McNay writes that psychoanalysis "adds depth to an account of agency and guards against voluntarism by showing how action may be subverted or intensified by unconscious motivations,"[33] making it possible to grasp larger social and cultural patterns of gender.

The psychoanalytic perspective is also useful in examining race as a factor that influences imagination and desire. A person's identification with another occurs when one *imaginatively* identifies with this "object" but experiences feelings of grief or loss since one cannot *be* the ideal object. Cheng says that the psychoanalytic concept of *identification* refers to particular experiences of identification with the lost or abandoned object,[34] such as whiteness.[35] I have analyzed the structure of race, not only as material or visible inequality, but also as the process by which Asian Americans negotiate their lack of, and desire for, whiteness, and incorporate these psychological experiences into their identities and relationships. Some Asian Americans expressed strong resentment and repulsion concerning race, while others denied such emotions and remained silent. I have recognized these responses, rather than eliminate them as unconscious and unreliable data, and have tentatively and speculatively examined them in the context of the social implications of race. The psychoanalytic perspective on gender and race in life-history narratives enables research to portray a broader range of agency than current sociological theory allows. Through this perspective, we can grasp the social actor's imaginative and emotional practices; we also gain a greater understanding of how this "affective residue"[36] can be a crucial social process through which the human actor may creatively transform and project an already learned structure of thought and action onto the future.

With this methodological emphasis on psychology of individuals, I have constructed many of the interviews around events that have caused emotional and psychological changes in the subjects, events and changes such as trauma, loss, and alienation. Benjamin writes, "The deadening of emotions in mourning can produce a pathological state, but this state, it will turn out, will characterize our relation to history."[37] I have highlighted the personal and relational crises of Asian American men and women as the locations of reconfigurations of masculinity and femininity. In considering the subjects' "relation to history," I have included the social conditions to which they are subject, including their own immigration history, the global economy, ethnic patriarchy, and racism, as well as their capability to reconfigure these conditions within the current gender and racial structure.

Defining Terms

Although Asian American history has never been homogeneous,[38] the category of *Asian American* has historically played a critical role in resisting exclusion,

violence, and racism against Asian American immigrants and laborers.[39]
However, the political, ethnic, and cultural definitions and usage of this term
have not yet been settled. Due to the enormous increase in Asian immigrants
after the Immigration Act of 1965, there has been a further diversification of
Asian American history; it has become increasingly difficult to understand
the experiences of Asian Americans without considering the increasing
transnational flow of capital and labor between the United States and Asian
countries. As the Asian American population has become more diverse, the
category of *Asian American-ness* has broadened to create a sense of panethnicity.[40] Many recent works have defined *Asian American* as the site at which
multiple Asian American experiences should meet to form a dialogue that will
serve as a basis for a social coalition.[41] However, as Susan Koshy points out, such
panethnicity remains "a vexed, conflicted and incomplete process, especially in
the recent past, and is further complicated by the fact that no readily available
symbols or grounds of cultural commonalty exist within such a heterogeneous
formation."[42]

I have sometimes encountered criticisms from Asian American scholars
that I should not conflate Asian Americans with Asians. By saying that, these
scholars implied that Americans who are Asian immigrants (at least if they
immigrated after childhood) are not really Asian Americans. Some suggested
that I should not consider the experiences of highly educated American-born
Asian Americans alongside those of poor immigrant women who entered
the United States to marry whites. Others suggested that I should just study
Japanese because I am not really an Asian American. Even though these
comments are correct in suggesting that it is difficult to discuss all the wide-
ranging demographic and immigration differences within Asian American
experiences, these criticisms correspond deeply to Asian American exclusion of
Asian immigrants from the status of *Asian American,* as well as to the exclusive
emphasis on U.S.-born Asians in Asian American studies. Indeed, binary divisions between foreign-born Asian Americans and U.S.-born Asian Americans,
mostly in the form of the latter's exclusion of the former, has remained strong in
Asian American scholarly works and community perceptions. Asian American
studies' dismissal of foreign-born immigrant Asian Americans, and its exclusive
focus on American-born Asian Americans, has sometimes been criticized
as a cultural nationalism of Asian America that internalizes "American
exceptionalist, xenophobic, imperialist, exclusive, nationalist, and essentialist
politics . . . ,"[43] which could lead to "right-wing arguments about the difficulty
of incorporating Asians into American nationhood."[44]

My study, which intentionally includes both foreign-born and American-
born Asian Americans as Asian Americans, is a challenge to existing tensions

in Asian American communities. However, what is most important in this study is not the question of employing either a nationalist view or a panethnic ideal of Asian America, but rather the question of how the issues surrounding interracial relationships can be examined most effectively, and how to address racialized and gendered patterns in the current Asian American experience. Since Asian American–white interracial relationships have remain shaped by both colonial history and U.S. racial politics, both American-born Asian Americans and foreign-born Asian Americans have been influenced by these regimes. Thus I use the term *Asian American* to refer to the varying experiences of both American-born and foreign-born Asian residents in the United States. I do not use the term *Asian* for the individuals I interviewed, because the term refers to those who live in Asian countries.[45]

In determining the racial and ethnic grouping of Asian Americans, I have relied on past empirical studies of Asian American intermarriage. In those studies, *Asian American* was used as an inclusive research category, usually including those of Chinese, Filipino, Japanese, Korean, and Vietnamese descent in America.[46] My interview subjects included a sampling from each of these ethnicities. The individuals ranged in age from their early twenties to their early fifties. All subjects were heterosexual. They all had U.S. citizenship, except two Asian American men who had the status of permanent residency at the time of their interviews.

Methodology

To find my interview subjects, I contacted local Asian American organizations, cultural groups, and multiracial student organizations by email on a single university campus in September 2000. After I was given the opportunity to talk about my project at a meeting of a local Asian American organization, one member told me that he and his close friends would be happy to meet with me. After I placed an advertisement in a local Asian American paper, another person contacted me by phone. Following a first interview in October, a couple who were members of a local Filipino American organization introduced me to three more couples. I interviewed one student couple in November who called after hearing about my project through friends who were members of the campus multiracial organization. One person contacted me after I gave a talk on my project in an Asian American Studies class; he introduced me to more couples. This sort of referral from respondents yielded most of my sample. I also used multiple public spaces, such as gyms, grocery stores, and coffee shops, to approach interracial couples and ask about their interest in being interviewed. From October 2000 to January 2002, I conducted interviews with sixteen couples and ten individuals. All names and other identifying factors have been changed to protect the anonymity of interviewees.

Interviewing Individuals and Couples

I conducted two types of in-depth interview: one with the husband or wife individually, the other with the spouses together. The purpose of conducting two types of interviews with each couple was to examine two aspects of an individual's view of the relationship: one as an intersubjective self, and the other as a more reflexive self. Since this study frames intimacy as a project of self-making, each interview of a single individual was used to examine how that person integrates his–her relationship reflectively into his–her past experience and his–her current view of self. In the couple interviews, I tried to observe power dynamics that were not revealed in the individual interviews.

The interviewing of a couple challenges the traditional assumption of social science that each person is a coherent and self-determined individual. As anthropologist Henrietta Moore argues, the self is not "self-contained and autonomous, but is intersubjective and depends on its relations with the other."[47] The self is never static, but rather is subject to social context and to the influence of the partner. Thus, the experience of self or "I-ness"[48] shifts fluidly between self-affirmation and submission to the other's recognition. My analysis of the couple interviews aims particularly to observe how race and gender affects each partner's position as either dominant or subordinate in the couple interactions.

Feminist-studies scholars argue that intimacy is the site of gender inequality—the man arrogates subjectivity only to himself, and the woman accepts her lack of subjectivity.[49] As a result, these authors state, women's alienated desire takes the form of submission to, envy of, and idealization of men. The couple interviews I conducted enabled me to observe how gender is played out concurrently with race in the interactions of these couples, and how power patterns emerge in the interview: one person dominating the conversation, belittling the other partner, and the other partner blaming her- or himself, compromising, engaging in silent acceptance of the other partner. In addition to gender and race, a person's social and cultural resources (such as having a good job and speaking English) in comparison to those of his–her partner, seemed to play important roles in determining the degree of the partner's passivity.

My methodology of constructing a subject's narrative in the context of his or her life history fits well with my approach to interracial intimacy as a project of selfhood and with my emphasis on agency within the space of intimacy.

A life history allows "sociologists to observe the process of 'structuration' by moving analytically between personal accounts and institutional histories."[50] Narratives constructed in this way provide "maps of action."[51] By looking at the social and cultural contexts that form a person's life experiences, we can grasp what has shaped an individual's experiences and what options the individual had in each situation. A life-history method also enables us to find the trajectory of multiple actions within a certain period of time, allowing us to avoid generalizing from a single action in time. By locating the patterns of engagement within varied contexts, the researcher can discover the ways in which the individual has transformed his or her relationship to the social structure. Feminist researchers have regarded the life-history methodology as a useful one, especially as a means of addressing the *survival* of women and racial minorities. By *survival*, I mean the subject's creative utilization of social forces to get through everyday life. Kaplan argues that life-history methodology is an outlaw approach that "renegotiates the relationship between personal identity and the world, between personal and social history."[52] It ties the "narrative invention to a struggle for cultural survival."[53] I am interested not only in how gender, racial, and class structure have operated within the subjects' lives, but also in how the subjects exploit and transform these social forces inventively. I have read the interviews closely, looking at themes and patterns of gender and race; for the book, I selected those interviews that overrepresented patterns of inequalities surrounding Asian American–white intimacy.

Analyzing a small number of cases collected through life-history interviewing is not an atypical approach to the study of sexual relationships or gender. Connell's study of gay masculinity is based on his interviews with eight gay men in Australia,[54] and Chen's paper on Chinese American manhood relies on interviews with nine men.[55] But there are limitations to analyzing such a small number of cases, especially when including information on sexual relationships. Connell points out that the condensation of findings and the difficulty of faithful representation of data are major constraints on the life-history method.[56] My analysis of desires and relational dynamics relies largely on the personal views and the memories of the respondents. The life-history method enables me to hypothesize about possible social and cultural patterns of gendered and racialized desire and interactions. Nevertheless, I face constraints in my analysis of the data because the information is limited. This study aims only to offer plausible interpretations of interracial relationships between Asian Americans and whites; there are certainly alternative explanations for my findings.

My status as an academic researcher and as a Japanese woman has created a unique dynamic in my interviews. The fact that I was a student at the time, and a Japanese woman who spoke English with an accent, may have given most respondents the impression that I was a nonthreatening interviewer. This is probably why some white men did not hesitate to express to me explicitly sexist views and beliefs about their partners, as well as some resentment toward white women. Listening to a personal account, especially a man's story, closely and attentively put me into the position of playing a traditional feminine listener role, and thus some men may have found it very comfortable to talk to me. One white man thought the interview was a good opportunity to initiate an affair with me, an offer that I repeatedly declined. Interviewing white men in general was somewhat difficult, I should note, because I had preconceived notions about their views of "Asian" women.

As an immigrant woman, I found that many Asian Americans' stories, especially those that dealt with individual survival, family bonds, the patriarchal emphasis in one's childhood, and coping with racism and sexism, became a crucial opportunity for me to develop rapport with the interviewees. One woman sobbed openly during the interview, possibly from recounting the difficult life she has had or marriage she endured, which she might not have discussed before. Some Asian American women and men talked about their mothers' lives and immigration experiences as if these were their own; many had mothers who had endured much suffering in their marriages, had struggled with ethnic patriarchy, and had faced a lack of opportunities upon immigration. My listening to the interviewees' strong emotional bonds and love for their families, especially for their mothers, not only served to develop a rapport, but also greatly motivated me to delve into their stories, especially in terms of gender, family, and nation.

I was initially concerned that my being a Japanese person who was born in Japan might hinder second-generation Asian Americans from talking openly and honestly with me. A couple of Chinese Americans mentioned that their parents or grandparents disliked Japanese people because of Japanese colonization of China in the past. But all respondents, especially young Asian Americans, were eager to talk to me about their views, beliefs, and upbringings. Some, especially young Asian American women, perceived the interview as an opportunity to try to understand why they have only dated white men. If the subjects asked me, I would mention some of my own experiences with dating white men, but I did not detail my stories or discuss my personal views of interracial relationships. On the other hand, my focus on gender and race was sometimes threatening for some interviewees, who denied that race and gender were factors in their selection of partners and said they only saw their partners as individuals. In particular, one Asian American woman was reluctant to discuss any issues of race or gender in her relationships, and she did not let me tape record our conversation.

The oversampling of second-generation Chinese American women and Filipino American women was not intentional, but the overrepresentation of Filipino American and Chinese American women strongly affected the conclusions of my study. It was more difficult to find Asian American men paired with white women than it was to find Asian American women paired with white men; out of the fifteen couples, there were only five in which Asian American men were coupled with white women. Also, Asian American men coupled with white women showed reluctance toward being interviewed. For example, in the case of two pairs of Asian American men and white women whom I planned to interview, both white women immediately showed willingness to participate, but the Asian American men declined.

Outline of This Book

Chapter 1 looks at how the American public has culturally imagined Asian American women and men in the context of interracial intimacy throughout the twentieth century. I especially look at political and cultural discourses of gender as shaped by colonial–postcolonial relationships between the United States and Asia, as well as by the model-minority myth and whiteness as hegemonic ideologies. Discussing the historical and ideological contexts of military brides, mail-order brides, the model minority myth, and globally circulated images of *Asians* and *whites*, I discuss how white men's and Asian American women's gendered positions and desires have been historically produced within these discourses, and how such historical backgrounds make relationships between Asian American women and white men culturally and socially unique. I also look at the historical and cultural milieu in which Asian American manhood has been marginalized. By introducing the framework of *masculinity* to explore relationships between Asian American men and white women in terms of the making of the men's masculinity, I question how the marginalization of masculinity has influenced the images and the realities of Asian American men's interracial relationships. The final part of the chapter overviews previous studies of interracial relationships, particularly those focusing on race, gender, and Asian American–white intimacy, arguing that further study of gender and race is necessary.

In chapter 2, I draw on my interview data to explore foreign-born Asian American women's marriages with white American men. Placing six different marriages within the contexts of the United States' postcolonial–neocolonial regime, I examine how the gender and racial dynamics of these couples have been shaped by ideological tropes. In particular, I focus on white men's view of foreign-born Asian American wives as "masculinity maintenance." Some of the white men who were married to foreign-born Asian American women intentionally chose "Asian" woman because they are known to be "good wives." I consider, along with the white men's expectations of "Asian" women as "model minority wives," how limited socioeconomic resources, language barriers, and the culture of ethnic patriarchy that these women grew up with are linked to the women's views of marriage as a sure bet to survive in the United States.

In chapter 3, I look at second- or higher-generation Asian American women's relationships with white American men. I focus here on how "successfully assimilated" Asian American women negotiate ideologies of race and gender in their interracial relationships. By contrast to stereotypes of subservient Asian women, second- or higher-generation Asian American women presented themselves as the independent, career-driven, and egalitarian partners of white men. Some saw their relationships with white men as a means to overturn negative stereotypes and to free themselves from ethnic patriarchy and achieve modernity. I examine how Asian American women employ hegemonic views of race and gender, including color-blind views of race, idealization of white hegemonic masculinity, and identification with model minority feminine subjects.

Chapters 4 and 5 discuss Asian American men's interracial relationships in the context of the formation of masculinity.

In chapter 4, I look at three marriages and discuss middle-age professional Asian American men's views of white women as possessors of ideal femininity who enable these men to assimilate into mainstream society and approximate the normative white manhood. I also look at how white women actively maintain the construction of white middle-class family. Observing the couples' experiences of racism and of traditional gender divisions in marriages, I discuss how interracial marriage conforms to the discourse of family, nation, and assimilation.

Chapter 5 examines three young Asian American men's relationships with white women, and their aspirations toward hegemonic masculinity. Whereas chapter 4 focuses on the marital dynamics of professional Asian American men, this chapter looks more at young nonprofessional Asian American men and their views of what they see as white manhood. Attaining white manhood becomes a strategy of their identity formation, especially in their attempt to ascend through the masculinity hierarchy and gain white women's validation of their racialized manhood. I explore how the class status of these Asian

American men and the deployment of gender sensibility shapes the gender dynamics of their relationships and shapes white women's views of them.

By contrast to the previous two chapters, wherein Asian American men strived to ascend up the masculine hierarchy, chapter 6 discusses two second-generation Asian American men who decided to date or marry women of their own ethnic group. I will explore how Asian American men experience aversion to racism and sexism in their socialization processes, and how their desire to belong to an ethnic community shapes their ambivalent views of interracial marriage. Asian American men's marginal masculinity makes the socialization of young Asian American men highly susceptible to the scrutiny of people of their own race, ethnicity, and class, and I also ask how such socialization processes affect their ambivalent aversion to "interracial relationships" and in turn stimulate a desire to consolidate ethnic masculinity.

In the conclusion, I discuss the portrayal of interracial relationships in the contemporary media; I also overview the major points of my findings and refer to the current patterns of Asian American–white intermarriage. Focusing on the patterns of "gender" that emerged in the interviews, I take a closer look at how ideologies of marriage, family, and nation, along with the logic of patriarchy–gender, have shaped the exchanges of racialized images and power dynamics within Asian American–white interracial couples.

I then look at how whiteness operates in the gender orders in couples' stories, and I argue that the discourses of color blindness and multiculturalism obscure not only the racial issues, but also the gender inequalities, embedded in interracial relationships.

Chapter 1   Interracial Relationships

Discourses and Images

RELATIONSHIPS BETWEEN ASIAN AMERICAN WOMEN and white men have historically been shaped and organized around three ideological constructs, which have also played a critical role in America's maintenance of its national identity: (1) colonial/postcolonial U.S. imperialism; (2) discourse about *model minorities* and multiculturalism; (3) global and locally maintained desires for whiteness. The next three sections discuss how these three ideological structures have shaped the discourses and experiences of Asian American women's relationships with white men. I focus especially on gender in these ideological structures and gendered effects on the relationships.

From early in the history of the United States, Asian American–white interracial relationships were shaped by American imperialism in Asia, national security issues, immigration regulations, and domestic racial politics. The United States' involvement in three wars—World War II, the Korean War, and the Vietnam War—created a large influx of military brides from these countries. Existing studies indicate that many of these relationships reflect colonial/postcolonial gender dynamics, wherein a woman's legal status and life is entangled with her subordination to the American patriarchal order.[1] In the post-Vietnam period, the image of Asian women as docile and sexually available became pervasive as a result of the U.S. military presence in Vietnam, the development of the sex industry there, and the mail-order bride industry in Southeast Asia.

With the rise of the Asian economy, especially in the 1970s and 1980s, multiculturalism and the idea of the model minority have reshaped and transformed the dominant image of Asian American women from that of the docile wife to that of the economically mobile woman. The concept of the model minority puts an interesting twist on the issue of gender. Feminism among white women, which has generated cultural anxiety among American men, has interested these men in Asian American women, who are marked not only as possessing economic mobility, but also as possessing traditional femininity.[2]

In addition to these two historical periods that have helped to mark Asian American women as desirable objects, the notion of *whiteness* has generated the popular narratives of Asian–white intimacy on the global marketplace. Racialized desires among Asian Americans in the United States have similar dynamics to the colonial/postcolonial desires that occur globally, but in this chapter I argue primarily the notion of racialized desire among Asian Americans, and I discuss how racialized desires reproduce the process of disempowerment and inner struggle for, specifically, Asian Americans. As the Asian American experience becomes increasingly diverse and transnational, we find that examining the notion of desire in the context of colonialism/postcolonialism and U.S. racialization enhances our understanding of the complex histories and backgrounds behind these Asian American experiences.

In the final section, I shift my focus to the issue of Asian American masculinity, often marginalized and stereotyped negatively in the United States. These popular images have affected Asian American men's relationships with white women. I draw out the historical and cultural contexts that have shaped current images of Asian American manhood; finally I suggest looking at relationships between Asian American men and white women from the larger perspective of American masculinity.

Brides from Asia

Although the image of Asian military brides became widely popular after World War II, Asian American–white interracial relationships were already being influenced by American immigration policy (like America's colonization of the Philippines and the Chinese Exclusion Act) in the nineteenth and early twentieth centuries. In the 1800s, Chinese female immigrants were suspected by the U.S. government of being a demoralizing threat to whites. In the late nineteenth century, due to concerns generated by the growing Asian population and the resulting fear of miscegenation (seen as the "Yellow Peril"), various federal legislatures passed exclusion laws and antimiscegenation laws.[3] Heightened public anxiety over immoral and contaminated Chinese "prostitutes" led to passage of the Page Law in 1875, which restricted Chinese and Japanese female immigration, as well as to passage of the Chinese Exclusion Act of 1882, which banned the immigration of all Chinese laborers.[4]

Two distinctive images of Asian American women, as military brides and as prostitutes, derived from the long history of American military presence in Asian countries, where Americans established a stereotype of Asian American–white interracial relationships. As clear from reception of the opera *Madame Butterfly* (1904) and the Hollywood movie *Shanghai Express* (1932), stereotypes of Asian American women as submissive, sexual, and/or treacherous were already popular in America at the beginning of the twentieth century. When a large influx of military brides entered the United States in the 1950s as a result of the United States' wars with Japan and Korea, sexual encounters and marriage between white men and Asian women became far more visible.[5] The first War Brides Act, passed in 1945, provided temporary permission to soldiers to bring their Asian wives to the United States, and later the McCarran-Walter Act repealed the legal prohibition against bringing these women into the United States, a prohibition included in the 1924 Immigration Act.[6]

Relationships between Asian American women and white men were often depicted, through images of military brides either as submissive wives or as foreign prostitutes, in either case rescued by America's paternal discretion and international power. The subordination of military brides in the colonial/post-colonial gender order translated into national racial politics, in which white men emphasized the overfeminized characteristics of Asian American women to maintain the racial privileges of whites and patriarchal ethos of family and nation. Because of U.S. relations with Japan, Japanese military wives served as a symbol of emancipation from oppressive Japanese patriarchy.[7] In the context of U.S. racial politics, they were welcomed as "compliant wives and mothers" and as representatives of a model minority, images that at that time successfully masked the past internment of Japanese Americans and the worsening racial tensions between whites and blacks.[8]

Military wives were thought of, not only as loyal and docile wives, but often as tied to military prostitution. Encounters between Asian women and American men often occurred on the U.S. military bases in Okinawa, South Korea, Vietnam, and the Philippines in which local women catered to the American soldiers as sex workers. Ji-Yeon Yuh's extensive study on Korean Camptown women demonstrates that these Asian countries' colonial dynamics and gender order influenced the marriages between these women and the U.S. servicemen. Korean women in Camptown not only served the American soldiers sexually, they also "serve[d] to symbolize all the humiliation that Korea suffers at the hands of the United States."[9] Korean Camptown women often married American men because they associated American servicemen with prosperity and freedom. Even during the 1980s, long after the Korean War, American soldiers "remained the primary symbol for American material abundance and the luxurious life of plenty."[10] Approximately four thousand Korean women married U.S. soldiers and arrived in America in the 1970s and 1980s.[11]

Popular culture can reproduce and reinforce hegemonic narratives of race and gender. The military brides may have struggled with racism, isolation, and low-wage jobs in the United States,[12] but Hollywood films of the 1950s and 1960s, such as *Japanese War Brides* (1952) and *Sayonara* (1957), portrayed Asian American–white intimacy as evidence of white America's acceptance of Asian brides (who were exemplars of submissiveness, domesticity, and quiet endurance) and as the precursor of the multicultural and multiracial household of the future.[13] Hollywood movies of this era also depicted romantic love between Asian American women and white men as a white-knight assimilationist love story—a white man is depicted as the ideal knight for an Asian woman, who is the Cinderella figure, to attain material prosperity, spiritual transcendence, freedom, and salvation—and thus such narratives perpetuate her subordinate position to white men.[14]

In the 1960s and the decades that next followed, post-Vietnam America continued to exploit colonial/neocolonial images of Asian–white sexual relationships. During the Vietnam War, Asian women, not only from Vietnam but also from Thailand and Cambodia, were supplied to American military bases; further, the U.S. military and the World Bank promoted and supported sex industries and sex tourism as a means of developing the economy of Thailand during the Vietnam War.[15] During this era, images of Asian women as sex objects became widely popular, and the industry that still supplies Asian brides today began to become prosperous in the United States. Even today, on websites for sex tourism and in the mail-order industry, finding a marital partner in Asian countries is often conflated with engaging prostitutes and enjoying sex tours.[16] On many of these sites, large pictures of half-naked or swimsuit-clad Asian women are provided, with comments emphasizing their "traditional femininity." Many sites sell Asian women as the brides of the future, who provide men with both sexual pleasure and feminine domesticity. As Robert Henderson mentions, in his book *The Secrets of Dating Asian Women*,[17] there are so many Asian women who want to marry Westerners[18] that the mutual desires between American men and Asian women, which are often based on economic inequality, have become a common transaction in the global economy.

In popular culture, the image of Asian women as submissive prostitutes of white men has emerged both as an alluring spectacle and as a cause of political uproar. The 1989 megahit musical *Miss Saigon* represented a Vietnamese prostitute, Kim, during the Vietnam War. The musical recycles "the familiar Hollywood themes"[19] of the Asian female as passive, domestic, and having a tragic yet transcendent love for a white American man. Kim devotes her love to a white American G.I., and when he eventually goes back to his white wife in the United States, Kim gives birth to their biracial son. After singing of her ardent hope for her son to go to the United States and attain the "American Dream," she shoots herself. Eleanor Ty argues that Western-centered masculine images of Vietnamese prostitutes as disposable and temporary substitutes for white women legitimizes not only these stereotypes of Asian American women, but also the economic and sexual exploitation of third world women.[20] As Dorinne Kondo writes,[21] "No matter how seductive the spectacle, racism is still racism." The show prompted hundreds of protests for its stereotypical representation of Asian women.

Colonial narratives with white-master and native-maid/whore themes remain transnationally circulated in postcolonial Asia, and they have affected Asian American–white relationships far beyond the contexts of the American military in Asia.[22] As Ling notes, the popular narrative sells "the wild sexual adventures of white men with seductive, available 'native women'" in Asia (playing into the mail-order bride industry in Asian countries), wherein an Asian woman appears with "her below-the-waist black hair, projectile-like breasts, tight dress, and sexual insouciance" and aims to "trap a high-salaried white expat."[23] Transnational imagery of Asia mirroring the Western and American gaze returns to, and recirculates within, the United States. Transnational images of Asian women easily mesh with racialized images of Asian Americans. As Celine Parreñas Shimizu points out, "Asian women remain live under the sign of the prostitutes in the U.S. popular representation from *Shanghai Express* (1932), *The World of Suzie Wong* (1960), and *The Deer Hunter* (1978), to lawyer Ling Woo (Lucy Liu) owning an escort service in *Ally McBeal* (1997–2002)."[24] Asian American women have been represented as hypersexual individuals, measured against the white female norm in the United States,[25] and these stereotypes have been consumed and reinforced in the context of colonial/postcolonial gender orders.

The Model Minority and Asian American Femininity

The model minority myth that became popular in the 1960s and 1970s has often been known as an ideological reflection of American public anxiety over Asia—a concept that encompasses Communist China, the Vietnam War, and Southeast Asian refugees.[26] The myth of the model minority is also a conservative ideology of the Civil Rights era that lifted the blame for inequality from institutional racism and placed it upon the supposedly inherent shortcomings of African Americans themselves.[27] The large influx of middle-class Asian immigrants after the 1965 Immigration Act, the rise of multiculturalism, and the growing impact of Asian economies augmented the visibility of highly educated middle-class Asian Americans who were no longer subordinate laborers for

whites but rival agents of whites. The model minority discourse emerged with
such demographic, cultural, and economic change in the United States. It also
transformed the image of Asian American women from that of the embodiment
of colonial femininity to that of the upwardly mobile middle-class woman.

Susan Koshy argues that images of Asian American women as hypersexual,
combined with the model minority myth, has played a critical role in the
popularity of Asian American women since the 1970s.[28] Koshy claims that
long-existing images of these women's supposed subservience and domesticity,
along with the images of them as hypersexual, have enhanced Asian American
women's "sexual capital" and their status as a "sexual model minority."[29] She
notes that the femininity of Asian American women has become popular
precisely because it is perceived as a substitute or replacement for traditional
white femininity, perceived as receding due to the rise of feminism among white
women; thus, images of Asian American women as "traditionally" feminine
became a cultural and sexual remedy for white men's masculinity crises in the
face of white feminism. Koshy writes:

> Asian American women's sexuality—earlier defined as extra territo-
> rial because the sexual license it represented had to be excluded from
> the moral order of the nation and marriage—is by the late twentieth
> century domesticated to mediate a crisis for a white bourgeois sexual
> order. . . . As a sexual model minority, the Asian American woman
> cannot entirely displace the white woman, whose appeal is reinforced
> by racial privilege and the power of embodying the norm, but she does,
> nevertheless, represent a powerfully seductive form of femininity that
> can function as a mode of crisis management in the cultural contest over
> different meanings of America.[30]

The transformation of Asian femininity, from the subordination of the
colonial era to its more recent status as an indication of sexual capital, also
explains how femininity in present-day America is not merely about docility or
"emphasized femininity" per se, but is tied to a particular physical appearance
and body physique. As Patricia Hill Collins notes, "evaluations of femininity are
fairly clearcut. [S]kin color, body type, hair texture, and facial features become
important dimensions of femininity."[31] Asian American women have been able
to attain the ideal "feminine" body because "the Asian beauty of reputedly
slender and petite doll-like bodies was extolled in terms of soft skin and silky
hair, and contrasted with images of repudiated and coarser African hair and
skin."[32] Such cultural imagery of gender marks the physical appearance of Asian
Americans with racialized notions of hyperfemininity and hypersexuality.

With the rise of the model minority discourse, professional Asian American women have become more visible in the media. In the 1980s, the appearance of the successful female newscaster Connie Chung "embod[ied] a new bent on racist representations of Asian Americans as the 'model minority.'"[33] The 1985 film *Year of the Dragon* also features a Chinese American female newscaster, who is depicted as a model minority who has class privileges.[34] However, as Marchetti notes, the interracial relationships in this film follow a script of patriarchal anxiety, characterized by white racism, gendered privileges, and class anxiety, a script that metaphorically portrays the white man's conquest of Asian American women and America's conquest of Asia. The emergence of upwardly mobile Asian American women certainly marked the progression of the cultural signifiers of Asian American femininity, yet these markers remained subordinated to white men.

Like the model minority discourse, Asian American–white interracial relationships served to mitigate tension between multiculturalism and anti-immigration sentiments in the 1980s and 1990s. Interracial relationships were often presented as the multiculturalist solution that confirmed the hegemonic orders of American national identity. Palumbo-Liu discusses how the utopian multicultural narrative of interracial marriage stands upon white anxiety about hegemony.

> Intermarriage can now be a spectator sport. . . . Yet the very obvious-ness of this erasure of not only race, but the politics of race, belies an anxiety over the actualization of multiracialization and an ardent desire to leap beyond such concerns to a future time of reconciliation, wherein, somehow, those concerns have already been sorted out. . . . While one can understand and sympathize with that utopianism, this positive view of multiracialization masks deeper anxieties over national identity and privilege that must be attended to in the present.[35]

Lauren Berlant writes that the multiculturalist image is born of "fantasizing the future as what will happen when white people intermarry,"[36] and that it masks white hegemony and reluctance to acknowledge historical and existing racial problems. The image of interracial marriage is built on heterosexuality and the patriotic ideals of family and nation; thus it consists of hegemonic orders of gender and race; interracial relationships have become acceptable or even "revolutionary" that is, when they embody hegemonic orders of gender, nation, and family. It is in precisely such a context that Asian American women have been designated as the sexual model minority for the reconstruction of America's masculine and heterosexual national identity.

Meanwhile, some critics have argued that contemporary popular images of Asian American women have changed, and are no longer limited to depictions of submissive and passive people. Recently, Asian American women have appeared more frequently as symbols of independence and power, and as figures transgressing previously existing images of gender and race. Shimizu discusses some Asian American actresses who play stereotypical hypersexual roles transgressively: Annabel Chong engaged in a gang-bang shooting as part of her self-proclaimed feminist project in the late 1990s; Lucy Liu played a dominatrix for the Chinese mafia in the film *Playback* in 1999. [37] Liu won an MTV Movie Award for Best Movie Villain for her performance in Quentin Tarantino's *Kill Bill* in 2003; her roles in this film as a fighter, assassin, and avenger against male authorities strongly contest the traditional images of Asian American women. The increasing popularity of Asian American action stars during the 1990s has been thought to have contributed to a new vision of Asian American femininity, as seen in *Crouching Tiger, Hidden Dragon* (2000); in this film, Chinese women do not fit the model of traditional passive and submissive womanhood, but rather embody a heroic brand of womanhood that, arguably, can be seen as successfully incorporating a Western feminist perspective. [38] Others, however, argue that the success of Asian action films in the United States, and the view of Asian female heroes as being subversively "masculine" are deeply embedded in the discourse of American-centered globalization and cultural imperialism, since Asian female warriors are not new to the Asian martial arts genre. Also, the characters in these films are able to fight only under traditional male authority, and their sexuality is subject to constant control and scrutiny under conventional gender norms. [39]

The "new" or transgressive images of Asian American women seem, then, to at once reinforce and contest familiar stereotypes. For example, America's model minority myth, which, as Palumbo-Liu notes, is a "fetishized ethnic dilemma" that promotes "healing" through self-affirmation, [40] reproduces the image of Asian American women as both independent and submissive subjects both globally and locally; the popular reception of the Academy Award–winning movie *Memoirs of a Geisha* (2005) exemplifies Hollywood's still popular depiction of Asian women as submissive and hard-working—exemplars of the sexual model minority. Yet the emergence of relatively diverse popular images of Asian American women, including many characters who are strong and independent and not constrained within the boundaries of domesticity, is easily explained by the important roles of East and South Asia in the global economy, as well as by the accomplishments of Asian Americans in the United States in terms of income and education. However, it is highly questionable to what extent the economic mobility and strength of Asian American women depicted in these media images challenge or destabilize patriarchal logics of gender, race, and family.

Whiteness as Object of Desire

Interracial relationships between Asian American women and white American men have been shaped by colonial/postcolonial U.S.–Asian relations and racism in the United States. With transnational exchanges between the United States and Asia increasing in frequency all the time, Asians with colonial/postcolonial desires enter into transnational romances, come to the United States, and become a part of the Asian American–white interracial experiences. Whiteness, as an object of desire, makes the divisions between the colonial/postcolonial subject and the racialized subject unclear, since both colonial/postcolonial subjects in Asia and racialized subjects in America desire whiteness as the norm to emulate and identify, especially when increasing numbers of Asian Americans experience both postcolonial regimes in Asian countries and racialization within the United States. Asian and Asian American women are both vulnerable to hegemonic white images and discourses, and they internalize these influences and in turn aspire to be the ideal partners of white American men. These two subjects, Asian women and Asian American women, are different, and the differences between them may lessen as time goes on. But it is important to distinguish between two kinds of desires shaped by two different contexts of race, the context in Asia and the context within the United States.

Local Asian women emulate what Ling calls "colonial scripts with white-master and native-maid/whore narratives" in Hong Kong and Singapore,[41] and women in Japan are also eager to consume and appropriate the white American men who have been associated with a global phallic authority.[42] Japanese women equate the pursuit of the American man with the mastery of Anglo-Saxon standards of behavior—as a means of self-invention through the fetishization of the white American man or the possession of whiteness. The Western/U.S. version of orientalism is reappropriated and reinvented among local Asians as a means of approximating the desirable modern citizen in the global marketplace. Colonial/postcolonial desires for, and identification with, white men in Asian countries also reproduces American images of Asian women who are willing to submit to the white American male.

In the context of racialization or racial dynamics within the United States, whiteness reigns as the desirable object that represents the esthetic, the modern, and the superior. Local Asian Americans' identification with whiteness as a source of self-fashioning overlaps somewhat with colonial/postcolonial desire for whiteness. One study on Asian Americans' images of white partners discusses the fact that foreign-born and American-born Japanese Americans and Chinese Americans associated white standards of beauty and power with their desire to "outmarry" white Americans.[43] Those Asian American men and women who have dated whites criticized each other for "being overly serious, having pragmatic occupations or narrow interests, being rather lackluster and not a part of the dominant or counterculture."[44] The study of American-born Chinese and Japanese Americans found that they desire the esthetic appearances of whites "such as tallness, round eyes, 'buffness' for men, and 'more ample breasts' for women."[45] Identification with whiteness occurs among young Asian Americans who grow up in the United States. The study shows how Asian Americans who grew up in the United States discussed difficult experiences trying to "fit in," and reveals how they went through a "white phase" or "time of wishing they were white," which was "a reaction to experiences of exclusion and negative stereotyping."[46]

However, within the United States, individuals with racialized desires in local contexts have always contested and struggled with constant, long-term racism. Different from the notion of whiteness that exists in postcolonial Asia as a pure object of desire and fantasy, whiteness in the United States has also occurred as a trope of powerlessness, contestation, and ambivalence among Asian Americans. It is not uncommon for Asian Americans who grow up in the United States to develop unhealthy self-images as a result of internalizing the white appearances and behaviors from which they have been excluded.[47] Asian American identification with whiteness has operated as a social system of self-regulation and self-domination that serves as a source of physical and psychological oppression.[48] Anne A. Cheng refers to the resulting condition as "racial melancholia," in which racial minorities' unattainable desire for whiteness is perpetuated inside their psyches. Racial melancholia is "the condition of having to incorporate and encrypt both an impossible ideal and a denigrated self."[49] David L. Eng and Shinhee Han discuss the increasing occurrence of depression and the high rate of suicides among Asian Americans, arguing that these result from attempts to approximate unattainable white norms and white expectations of Asian Americans as a model minority.[50] Among women aged fifteen to twenty-four, of any race or ethnicity, in the United States, Asian American women have the highest suicide rate.[51] Their high rates of depression and suicide are often explained as a result of family pressures along with social pressures to succeed at school; Eng and Han argue, however, that such an understanding of Asian American's mental health problem as stemming from specific familial issues is itself embedded in America's refusal to see Asians as part of the mainstream.

Within the context of race relations, the internalization of whiteness does not mean only that Asian Americans identify whiteness as an ideal. Rather, Asian Americans often exhibit ambivalent aversion to the subordinate notion of *Asianness* that results from identification with dominant racial ideology.

Karen D. Pyke and Tran Dang have reported on the existing internal racism among second-generation Korean and Vietnamese American men and women who, with their more "whitewashed" status, look down on fellow ethnic Asians by mocking their accented English, fashions, styles, and friendship choices, referring to them as FOBs (an acronym for "fresh off the boat").[52] Similarly, Asian Americans' emulation of whites generates mixed states of ambivalence among second-generation Asian American women—they desire white partners, they are averse to being seen as stereotypical Asian women, and they are averse to their fellow Asians. Pyke and Johnson report that the second-generation Asian American women they interviewed viewed whites as self-confident, independent, assertive, egalitarian, and successful, and thus as superior to Asians, whom they saw as submissive and constrained. Pyke and Johnson discuss the Asian American women's ambivalence towards identification with whiteness and dominant racial ideology:

> Racialized expectations can exert pressures to display stereotyped behavior in mainstream interactions. Such expectations can subtly coerce behavioral displays that confirm the stereotypes, suggesting a kind of self-fulfilling prophecy. Furthermore, as submissiveness and passivity are denigrated traits in the mainstream, and often judged to be indicators of incompetence, compliance with such expectations can deny Asian American women personal opportunities and success. . . . As they are forced to work against racial stereotypes, they must exert extra effort at being outspoken and socially gregarious.[53]

Those outside the United States, with their colonial/postcolonial desires, lack this identification with U.S. racial ideology and American experiences of racialization, but racialized subjects within the United States have no way to avoid the racialized images of themselves that they encounter in U.S. culture or the racial hierarchy under which they struggle. The process of racialization in the Asian American experience shares some similarity with the colonial/ postcolonial desire for whiteness, in its desire for whiteness as its highest goal. However, racialized desire entails constant scrutiny of, and negotiation with, racial hierarchy and racism through the mastery of hegemonic discourses. Thus, resistance by a racialized person in the U.S. context differs from that of a colonial/postcolonial subject, whose resistance may be directed and bound by his or her home country's and postcolonial position relative to the United States. Global and local images of whiteness as a signifier of self-fashioning shape important aspects of Asian American–white interracial relationships, but the ways in which Asian American women engage in racialized or colonial/postcolonial imageries and hegemonic discourses differ vastly, just as their immigration histories and ethnic histories greatly vary. The distinction I have explicated here between colonial/postcolonial desires and racialized desires may not be clearly recognizable in one person's life. But the distinction is helpful in order to read and understand the negotiation of the desires of Asian American women, desires shaped by tropes of race, gender, nation, and personal history.

Asian American Masculinity

By contrast with the social perception of Asian American women as possessing sexual capital, Asian American men have been seen as lacking attractive masculine traits. In Hollywood films, Asian American men have been portrayed historically either as enemies of white men, or as the devoted but impotent servants of white men.[54] In early twentieth-century Hollywood movies, the Asian man was often portrayed as a rapist, villain, or sadistic sexual deviant.[55] Although Chinese martial artists have attained popularity as hypermasculine characters, they are rarely seen as romantic partners of American women. Asian American men are even feminized in popular culture, a tendency that stems from the general feminization of Asian cultures. Cliff Cheng argues that hegemonic masculinity in American culture, which is characterized by aggression, rationality, and dominance, inevitably categorizes Confucian-oriented traits, such as conformity, cooperation, absence of open ego displays, and the tendency to honor tradition, as feminine.[56] Many critics have argued that the desexualization of Asian American men in mainstream culture is used to justify racial discrimination against these men[57] and negatively affects these men's view of themselves. Eng describes Asian Americans' internalization of negative images of themselves as "racial castration," a process by which self-contempt and self-rejection affects Asian American men's manhood.[58]

Mainstream society has lumped Asian Americans into one category. But each Asian ethnic group has a different immigration history; thus the concept of Asian American manhood has been shaped quite differently in each of these ethnic groups. Filipino men have been exploited as low-wage laborers in Hawaii and on the West Coast, and have been seen as sexually dangerous "breeders."[59] Chinese immigrant men who entered the United States as railroad construction workers were both "desexed" and seen as oversexed.[60] As Nyguyen notes: "The asexuality of Chinese immigrants, an aspect of their inhuman dedication to work, threatened white labor, while their contradictory voracious sexuality threatened white womanhood and white patriarchy. In neither case did Americans see the Chinese immigrants as 'real' men."[61] The absence of Chinese women (banned from entering the United States by the Page Law of

1875), as well as the concentration of Chinese immigrants in feminized jobs at laundries, restaurants, and in the service sector, fed the stereotypes about these Chinese "bachelor" communities.[62] Nguyen argues that America's violent treatment of Chinese men not only maintained their subordination to white American men, but also continues to affect Chinese Americans' perception of themselves.[63]

The Asian American population became much more diverse after the 1965 Immigration Act. Greatly increased numbers of immigrants came from South Korea, the Philippines, Vietnam, and Cambodia, all countries directly affected by U.S. imperialism and wars.[64] The 1965 Immigration Act also increased the population of Asian American immigrant professionals and skilled workers; their middle-class status further complicated the identities of these Asian American groups. More recently, thanks to the rise of East Asia and of globalization, the identities of Asian American men and the formation of their families have become more transnational and global than ever. For example, some diasporic Chinese men Ong writes about travel fluidly and adjust to global capitalism as possessors of "flexible citizenship."[65] It is not uncommon for Asian American men to have romantic relationships and families beyond the borders of the United States.

The negative stereotypes of Asian American men as desexed and foreign remain strong. Popular media continue to depict only unsuccessful heterosexual relationships between Asian American men and white women—perhaps in part as a result of the still-pervasive view of "the larger society's taboos against Asian male–white female sexual union."[66] In the 2000 film *Romeo Must Die,* Chinese martial artist Jet Li is portrayed as "the castrated yellow man"; depicted as "an errand boy," he serves only to mediate the white men's desire for black masculinity.[67] While this popular Hong Kong martial artist is embellished and hybridized with stylistic black hip-hop music, the main theme of the film concerns white male authority and its alliance with black masculinity. The film repeats the belief that "Asian American masculinity must be deleted."[68] In his interracial romance with an African American woman, the Asian protagonist is portrayed more as a platonic friend than as an intimate partner. Interracial intimacy is a representation of the Asian American man's deficiency of heterosexual prowess.

Previous studies have argued that men of color with high socioeconomic status (SES) often marry white women with low socioeconomic status, which would make interracial relationships between minority men and white women be exchanges of high socioeconomic status for whiteness.[69] However, recent studies have refuted this exchange theory,[70] arguing that "white females who marry minority group males are not educationally disadvantaged,"[71] and that "racially intermarried individuals and their partners have always had similar levels of status."[72] Yet society still associates the economic successes and inter-marriages of minority men as signifiers of power that could complement their race. That is, race remains operative as a symbolic dimension of power.[73] As minority men's sexualities are labeled deviant, their socioeconomic status is portrayed as the acceptable form of masculine compensation for such devi-ance. For example, Asian American men's model minority characteristics have often been portrayed positively as traditionally masculine breadwinner traits, which have the potential to romantically attract white women. Esther Pan's 2000 *Newsweek* article "Why Asian Guys Are on a Roll" ascribes the rising popularity of Asian American men as romantic partners to the men's high economic and educational status.[74]

It is also important to note how white women have been seen by men of color as a source of symbolic and cultural capital. In the context of interracial marriage between African American men and white women, Collins argues, for an African American man to marry a white woman is to commit a status-enhancing act—an essential component in a racial minority man's achievement of honorary membership in hegemonic masculinity.[75] The ideology of white femininity as the embodiment of supreme beauty "operates as a tool of white supremacy and a tool of patriarchy by elevating men and whites in importance and status."[76] As Michael Kimmel argues, "Women become a kind of currency that men use to improve their ranking on the masculine social scale."[77] In a study of black men who date interracially, Kelina M. Craig-Henderson reported that black men expressed an aversion to black women, and a desire for white women, based on their physical appearance.[78] Her study does not extend discus-sion of these black men's attraction to white women into a discussion of the issue of their manhood, but certainly it is worthwhile to analyze how minority men, whose access to white women is still limited by prevailing negative stereo-types, contest or appropriate racialized masculinities through relationships with white women.

Minority men's views of interracial relationships are also associated with images of gendered power. Jachinson Chan notes that Asian American men's interracial relationships are equated with their disempowerment.[79]

[S]o many Asian American men feel disempowered within America's cultural landscape that the gender conflicts between men and women have become exacerbated by the interracial relationships some Asian American women entered into and in response, the urgent need for some Asian American men to reassert their manhood or masculinity according to a hegemonic model of masculinity.

How are racism and sexism manifested in the actual dynamics of Asian American men's interracial relationships with white women under historical and current ideas of masculinity? To inquire about the social structures of gender and race as they intersect with issues of social class requires not just a discussion of Asian American men's empowerment or disempowerment, but also an analysis of white women's participation in the hierarchies of race, class, and gender. Indeed, in my interviews, I found that the socioeconomic resources of the Asian American men I interviewed complicated the racial hierarchies among whites and Asians Americans. Also, the white women I interviewed were not passive objects of desire but active participants in Asian American men's negotiation of their masculinities. These women's participation varied from being either actively desiring subjects who provided recognition to Asian American men, to desired subjects who presented themselves as ideal feminine objects for Asian American men.

Studies of Interracial Relationships

Interracial relationships have often been an indicator of the assimilation of racial minorities.[80] High rates of intermarriage have been interpreted as a sign of "the amalgamation of different racial groups" into white America.[81] Thus, increasing rates of intermarriage have been seen as an *erosion* of racial sensibilities and a lessening of the social distance between the races. Although this utopian view of intermarriage has served to enhance the image of America as a melting pot, it has also been criticized for its implicit imperative requiring racial minorities' conformity to the white authority. This celebratory view also prevents our discussing frankly issues of race, gender, and class that underlie the interracial relationships.

Recent studies have examined interracial relationships historically as racialized and gendered processes shaped by the state, by laws, and by social inequalities. Randall Kennedy addresses how interracial relationships have been controlled legally by the state,[82] and Rachel F. Moran discusses historical changes in legal regulations surrounding interracial relationships.[83] Joan Nagel looks at how intersexual borders in the United States have been constantly regulated by formal and informal means of control, including state antimiscegenation laws, lynching, castration—and even today, through Internet-circulated images of interracial sex.[84] Previous studies have also criticized "color-blind" views of interracial relationships. Moran writes that the idea of romantic love "permits individuals to rely on love to explain their marital choices without ever thinking very hard about the characteristics that make their partners lovable."[85] Thus, this concept allows Americans to easily "embrace a color-blind ideal."[86] As Patricia Hill Collins points out, the growing number of racialized images sold in the media constitutes, itself, a "new racism,"[87] undeniably the source of Americans' impulse for interracial sex. Farman points out the contradiction between popular culture's commodification of race and its disguise of racism, asking "how much of our own desires are fed by racism" when our private lives "indulge in the racial-sexual culture of the past more unabashedly."[88]

For Asian Americans in interracial relationships, the high income and education of Asian Americans are often cited as significant reasons for their high rate of intermarriage with whites,[89] since these factors allow them to approximate whites or to be "honorary" whites.[90] Yet this seemingly positive portrayal of Asian Americans as ascending to the status of honorary whites through marriage obscures the underlying complexities of the gender, racial, and sexual politics of America (wherein Asian/Asian American men and women are often stereotyped as either hypersexual or desexed). The portrayal cloaks large gender imbalances, imbalances revealed in the significantly higher numbers of Asian American women marrying white men than of Asian American men marrying white women.[91] Thus, some critics do not see Asian American intermarriage patterns as indicative of an *erosion* of racism; rather, they argue that a racist sensibility in fact *promotes* interracial relationships. From this perspective, the high rate of Asian American intermarriage is a "material outcome of an interlocking system of sexism and racism."[92] Because of the overly feminized image of Asian American women and the desexualized portrayal of Asian American men, the Asian American woman "is marrying 'up' (and therefore 'out' of) the racial and gender hierarchy in which white males occupy the superordinate position"[93]; this problem is compounded by the fact that Asian American women often perceive Asian American men as undesirable partners in romance. However, few studies have empirically investigated how Asian Americans' racialized femininity and masculinity influence the actual dynamics of relationships, and how racialized images intersect with gender and class and play out in actual interracial relationships.

An obvious weakness of this perspective is that it does not explain why white American women sometimes date or marry Asian American men. In fact, few empirical studies have addressed issues of race and gender in Asian American women's marriages with white men. Paul Spickard, in his study of

Japanese military brides, notes that white men's attraction to these brides stemmed from stereotypes of Asian women as submissive and domestic. Yet how such stereotypes actually shaped marital dynamics and individual race consciousness remains unknown. In her book on diverse interracial couples, Maria Root argues that Asian American women's marriage to white men has historically provided Asian American women with racial upward mobility by *transforming* their racial status. She argues, "White male involvement in this transformation has been critical; their privilege had facilitated a subtle change in Asianness from a caste to a class."[94] Such a statement is problematic since it provides little historical or social context for couples involved in these dynamics. Her views, including the idea that "love and democratic ideals" have increased intermarriage,[95] as well as the notion of the white man as "willing to give up some aspects of white male privilege,"[96] line up closely with the views that characterize the current hegemony of race and gender.

Racialized images of Asian Americans apparently have been seen as important characteristics of interracial relationships, but the actual effects of gender and race have rarely been touched on. For Asian American–white interracial relationships, gender and race are complicated by social class as well as generational differences. For example, many second-generation Asian American professionals with high education and income levels (often surpassing those of whites) have little sense of themselves as belonging to "racial minorities" or as subordinate to whites.[97] It is extremely critical to inquire about social, historical, and cultural contexts in which diverse Asian American–white relationships have been formed, including the relevant histories of colonialism, immigrations policies, and racial politics. Further, since previous empirical studies of U.S. interracial relationships rarely delve into the gender inequalities beneath the racial dynamics, the intersection between gender and race needs critical attention.

In addition to looking at racial and gender dynamics, we must examine how Asian American–white couples engage in the discourses of color-blindness. Existing studies have discussed how couples and individuals in interracial relationships employed "color-blind" strategies. Ruth Frankenberg's book *White Women, Race Matters* explores how white women engage in the discourses of race, within their interracial relationships.[98] Frankenberg points out white women's "lack of attention to the areas of power imbalance that in fact generate hostility, social distance, and 'bad feeling,'" and that lead to color-evasive and power-blind views of relationships.[99] In her book *Navigating Interracial Borders: Black-White Couples and Their Social Worlds*, Elica Chito Childs argues that some black–white couples in her study downplayed race as putting "constraints on their individualism and ability to be successful or happy."[100]

In contrast to the assimilationist view of intermarriage, in which interracial marriage is seen as an erosion of racial lines, these studies illustrate that the discourses of race, especially the color-blind views of interracial relationships, are maintained by both social structures and individuals' participation. If Asian Americans who intermarry are perceived as assimilable honorary whites, how and why do they resist or conform to color-blind views of themselves? How does their participation in the discourse of color-blindness intersect with the model minority discourse?

Part I

Asian American Women
with White Men

Chapter 2   The Good Wife

From the beginning of the twentieth century to the present day, the image of the Asian woman as subservient, loyal, and family oriented has been popular. During the period of U.S. political and economic dominance over Asia after World War II, overfeminized images of Asian women became a catalyst for the rising visibility of intermarriage between Asian American women and white men. Studies of military wives and correspondence marriage (also known as mail-order or pen-pal marriage) have reported that such stereotypes are pivotal to white American men in choosing Asian women as wives over American women.[1] However, the image of Asian women as "good wives" operates far beyond such marriages. Images of Asian femininity, along with those of idealized white masculinity as a sign of modern middle-class manhood, have been a major part of intimate transactions in postcolonial/neocolonial Asia–U.S. territories. The image of postcolonial and model minority femininity has served not only to stimulate white men's attraction to Asian and Asian American women, but also as part of the self-image of the women and to generate certain patterns of marital dynamics.

In this chapter, I examine how colonial/neocolonial mores, along with stereotypes of Asian women, have shaped marriages between Asian American and white people. I focus in particular on these men and women's investment in their ideas of masculinity and femininity. I differentiate marital experiences of foreign-born Asian American women who immigrated to the United States upon marriage, and those of young second-generation Asian American women who grew up in the United States, because the former group's unfamiliarity with American culture, its language barriers, and its diversity of immigrant histories had a large impact on the gender dynamics in the members' relationships and in their male partners' tendency to overfeminize them.

To explore gender dynamics and its link to ideological tropes and political economy, I have divided this chapter into three parts.

In the first, "The Asian Woman as a Good Wife," I discuss three marriages, one that took place in the 1950s, one in the 1970s, and one in the late 1990s. The historical period of each marriage places it within a particular postcolonial/neocolonial context of American–Asian relations. The marriage that took place in the 1950s points up considerations of gender and race in the context of post–WWII relations between Japan and the United States. The 1970s marriage shows the cultural climate of marriage under the influence of the American military presence in South Korea. The 1990s marriage explores marital dynamics as shaped by neocolonial views of the Philippines and by conservative masculinity ideology. The Asian American women in these relationships, upon marrying, immigrated to the United States from Japan, South Korea, and the Philippines. In these three marriages, I explore how the white husband racializes the characteristics of subservience and domesticity of his wife, and how he controls marriage by viewing his masculine authority as sustainable only through his possession of his Asian wife.

In the next section, "The White Man and Upward Mobility," I shift focus to, exclusively, Filipina American women's marriages that took place in the 1980s. Focusing on these women who grew up under the heavy influence of neocolonial/postcolonial images of America created by the American military presence in, and economic deprivation of, the Philippines, I explore how the women's desires for and views of marriage with white American men unfolded and how their patterns of subordination followed.

In the last section, "A Different Kind of White Man," I question how the Asian American woman can be free from the neocolonial/postcolonial subordination, and I explore an egalitarian marriage occurring in the 1990s. I explore how the earning power of the woman in this relationship and the couple's race consciousness make the relationship distant from stereotypes of marriage between foreign-born Asian Americans and white men.

The Asian Woman as a Good Wife

Having been married in three distinct periods, three couples I interviewed had entirely different personal, ethnic, and social backgrounds. Sachiko married George in the 1950s and entered the United States as a military bride from Japan. Soonja met Gary in South Korea, and they married in the 1970s. Melissa met Patrick in the 1990s, at a large corporation that had a branch in the Philippines, Melissa's native country. Regardless of the differences among these individuals, the husbands all commented repeatedly about their Asian wives being good wives and about their strong association of such qualities with their being "Asian"—Japanese, Korean, or Filipina. In the following stories, I explore how such white men's racialization of Asian women as "good wives" or "model minorities" shapes the gender dynamics of the couples, and how these men's employment of such discourses associates with their aversion to American women. I also discuss how gender dynamics and the racialization of Asian women by Americans were shaped by the postcolonial/neocolonical contexts of post–WWII America, by the strong influence of the American military in South Korea, and by the neocolonial position of the Philippines.

JAPANESE MILITARY BRIDE

The War Brides Act of 1945, allowing exceptions to the antimiscegenation laws then in place, led to about 150,000 Asian American military brides' entrance into the United States between 1947 and 1975.[2] The Japanese military bride was often marked as the subservient wife of an American serviceman, and symbolically contributed to the ideal of American pluralism. Yet the actuality of her new life in white suburbia served to contradict this ideal,[3] and many of these women experienced isolation and self-blame for their marital problems, while gaining only minimal work experience.[4] The following story illustrates a Japanese American woman's role as a wife and mother, shaped by limited options and by the social and cultural imperatives of assimilation.

George Green, a sixty-six-year-old former military serviceman, tall and quiet, was talkative when describing his forty-four-year-long marriage to Sachiko, a very soft-spoken sixty-six-year-old Japanese American. Describing himself as "bossy," George took over the couple's interview. Having served in the Philippines, Hong Kong, and Japan, George met Sachiko and married her in Japan in 1956, a decade after the War Bride Act was passed. By the time they married, George said, "that kind of . . . interracial marriage was accepted in all but six states." Sachiko worked at a restaurant near the American military base near Tokyo. When she and George decided to marry, Sachiko's father opposed her marriage to their former WWII enemy and disowned his daughter. The American military also strongly discouraged servicemen's marriages to Japanese women, and it took Sachiko two years to pass the military's background check. After those two years had passed, Sachiko and George moved to his home in St. Louis, Missouri, and Sachiko was not allowed to see her parents for the next ten years.

George grew up in a lower-middle-class family, with little idea of his father, who had been killed in a car accident early in George's life. After his father's death, his mother remarried four times. Her second husband supported George and his mother as a pressman, and George looked back on him as "the only man who had any influence on me at all." At some point once he was grown,

George went back to his hometown and worked at an optical laboratory for a while; then he worked as an engineer at a large computer company.

George always liked "short, dark-haired women with brown eyes." When he mentioned this, he pointed to the large picture of young Sachiko on the wall; she was twenty-two at the time of their marriage. "I thought, 'Hey, she is cute, I like her.'" He described her as a good listener: "I fell in love with Sachiko because she wasn't pushy." He claimed her lack of forcefulness or aggression was unique to Japanese women and a contrast to Chinese woman, whom he described as "pushy and loud." Several times, George mentioned Sachiko's ability to "handle adversity," including problems they encountered in the course of their marriage. "She is not a weak person, she is so strong," he said, stating that many people mistakenly assume a lack of pushiness signifies weakness.

Sachiko grew up in a traditional family in Japan, where her father was a professional architect. The gender division was extremely strict in her family. Her father was a "very authoritative" patriarchal man, "hard for children to be close to." He always clapped his hands two or three times to summon his wife, rather than call her name, to ask her to do such things as serve tea for him. Because Sachiko was a woman, he did not allow her to ride a bicycle or talk in front of other people. In her own marriage, Sachiko, like her mother, took on all responsibility for the household and child rearing. After she moved to St. Louis, she worked as a waitress in local restaurants, and later started a small food catering business.

In the couple interview, the conversation, inspersed with a lot of laughs and jokes, centered on their lives in Japan, his views of Japanese culture, and their parenting of three children. In his individual interview, George talked mostly about how Sachiko was supportive of him in "giving" and "caring" ways. He talked about his past drinking problem, which started when he was in the U.S. navy in Japan. "I used to fight a lot. . . . I was not very nice. . . . I was very selfish." His drinking lasted twelve years from the time they married. This, for a time, was the major problem in their marriage. At one point in the interview Sachiko raised her voice, looking at George, and said, in reference to the drinking, "I would have gone back to Japan immediately if I had no children!" She also repeated this in her individual interview. But she did not leave. George explained why: "She was trapped. She couldn't divorce me. What could she do? Try to live in Japan with half-breed children? They would be treated like the handicapped there. . . . So she couldn't leave me. Physically, she could leave me. Logically, she couldn't." After she was disowned by her Japanese family, that is, Sachiko did not have the option to go back to Japan, where there was still adamant discrimination against women who married American servicemen, as well as against their biracial children. So Sachiko stayed in the half-broken marriage. Continuing to hold a restaurant job, she raised three children. Meanwhile, George never wanted a divorce. "Watching my mother's marriages and divorces tore me apart. Each one tore me up. So, I knew getting one would have torn me apart and ripped me off." Thus, George's fear of divorce and Sachiko's lack of options kept their marriage alive. "If I had married an American woman, she wouldn't have been trapped. I'm sure she would have divorced me. . . . That would have torn me apart. . . . Sachiko is the best thing that ever happened to me."

In George's individual interview, his story unfolded as a tale of recovery in which he overcame his depression and drinking, seemingly parts of his working-class masculinity, by growing trust in and love for his wife. The discourse of the Japanese woman as traditionally feminine persisted throughout his story of their marriage. Sachiko's "choice" to stay in the marriage as a good wife, regardless of her hardships and George's description of her as "strong," also reinforces the popular image of military brides as women loyal to their husbands, husbands who had offered them protection and a good life in America. In George's interview, such racialized characteristics as Sachiko's subservience thus merge to form a picture of "a good woman."

Throughout the interview, when George and Sachiko talked about race, they regarded it as a problem of blacks versus whites. The couple remembered very little racial animosity directed against them. Growing up with the de facto segregation of blacks and whites in his hometown, George was aware that his marriage might not have been as easily accepted if Sachiko had been a black woman: "If she were black, I would have given it serious thought. Especially back in the 1950s, the marriage of a white man and a black girl would have been hard to be accepted. . . . But, me marrying a Japanese never gave me any second thoughts." Sachiko described the couple's two sons and one daughter as "Eurasian" or "Amerasian," as did George. However, George also referred to their children as "white." He described his daughter's being married to a black man as an issue of "white–black marriage." He said: "It is about a black marrying a white. She is a white. . . . It wasn't that I had a problem. It is about prejudice here against blacks marrying whites. Probably we will always have it. Because it is easiest to recognize the difference . . . because the oldest one [of their grandchildren], she is the darker of the two." Thus George viewed black–white biracial children (such as his grandchildren) as a potential problem due to the possibility of darker skin, while viewing his own children as white, apparently as a result of their seeming racial invisibility in comparison to blacks'. Likewise, Sachiko was seen as assimilate-able or as a potential white person because she was not a black.

However, Sachiko remembered how their biracial children "would cry as they were called 'Chinaman' in school." She encouraged her children to be proud of their half-Japanese racial origins, and taught them her language and culture. But she also learned that sometimes Japanese women are not welcomed by white society. She told me about a Japanese woman friend of hers whose son was ashamed of his mother's race. "This boy whose mother was Japanese, like me, told his mother not to come to school and asked his white father to come to school. Her son was ashamed of his mother." Race was also a factor in Sachiko's parenting style, which needed to be tailored to emulate the white middle-class standard. A psychiatrist to which her oldest child was referred by the school advised Sachiko to hug and kiss her son frequently and tell him "I love you" as other white mothers did. Otherwise, he said, her son would not feel he was loved. "I never thought about my son having a thought of me not loving him. So I was really upset and started giving hugs and kisses. . . . Japanese don't do that," Sachiko said.

It was thus through her parenting that Sachiko learned her place as an unwelcome minority in white middle-class communities, and the necessity to emulate "willingly" white middle-class standards. Although the American government had accepted Japanese military brides, because of the nation's ideological embrace of cultural pluralism and its post-WWII expansionist project, Sachiko and the other brides were expected to measure up by adhering to the patriarchal imperative of being the good wife and mother of an "American" family.

THE MODEL MINORITY WIFE FROM SOUTH KOREA

Some white men I interviewed, such as Gary Morris and Patrick Bennett, intentionally chose foreign-born Asian American women as their marital partners because of their perception that these women would be traditional and family oriented. Gary, a man with a high education and a good job, wanted a strong family based on traditional gender roles. His emphasis, throughout the interviews, on the "Asian woman" as a good wife illustrated his belief in such a wife's race and nationality marking her out as a subservient laborer for a white American man.

Gary was a fifty four-year-old Jewish male, born in New York, who was a vice president of an insurance firm. He had been married to his current wife, Soonja, a fifty-eight-year-old Korean American, for twenty years. Soonja, welcoming me into their huge house with a warm smile, went immediately into the spacious kitchen that was custom-designed for her. She started peeling fruit for me and talking about her two sons in college. Gary, on the other hand, was eager to finish the interview as quickly as possible, and sat in his office checking his computer even as he told his story.

In 1970, Gary went to South Korea as a member of the Peace Corps, where, he remembered, he witnessed massive poverty and hostility toward the American military as a result of the Korean War. Gary taught English for a year and a half at the school where Soonja was also teaching. "I think I was attracted to her values—rather conservative, family-oriented, strong family," he said. A week after Soonja lost her mother to a sudden illness, Gary, who also had lost his mother at a young age, asked her to marry him.

Soonja's father disapproved of the marriage at the beginning, and told her he would disown her. His reaction was typical of Koreans' negative perceptions of "international marriages" between Americans and Koreans. Said Soonja, "People in Korea, they don't respect international marriage. Because usually international marriage, more like American GIs go to prostitutes. . . . We have nothing to do with military people. . . . We were different. That's what my husband told my father—that he is different from military people in Seoul. 'I'm different than military people, so just trust me.' . . . And also he speaks Korean."

Soonja strongly expressed her embarrassment at being subjected to the stereotype of the international marriage, and also revealed her strong disapproval of what are seen as typical Korean-American relationships. Her husband's ability to speak Korean showed Gary's interest in communicating with Soonja and understanding Korean culture, unlike the stereotype of the military man who had temporary sexual relationships with local women. Noticeably visible in the couple's house was a big wedding picture showing Gary and Soonja beautifully draped in Korean formal dresses, further evidence of Gary's willingness to respect his wife's culture.

Gary also stressed the couple's distance from "typical intermarriage" between military servicemen and Korean women, saying of such stereotyped women, "They are poor, they are poorly educated, and divorce rates were very high. Once in the United States, sometimes husbands would beat them up or throw them out. In order to survive, they had to become prostitutes again." Gary and Soonja emphasized their class and education as markers of difference setting them apart from these couples.

Ji-Yeon Yuh discusses Korean military brides who have been "despised for what is seen as their immorality and corrupting influence," and notes that most Koreans dismiss them as outsiders in Korean society.[5] In her study, Yuh argues that the Korean wives of Korean men believed that the Korean wives of American soldiers were unclean and not fit to prepare food. Koreans would reject the offer of military brides to help prepare food for church events. This condemnation and dismissal of military brides served to bolster Korean national pride in the face of Korea's subjugation to America. According to Yuh, this logic of gender embedded in U.S. imperialism and Korean nationalism allowed Korea to maintain its image of the United States as savior and liberator rather than colonizer. Soonja and Gary's negative responses to American servicemen and their Korean wives verified that this ideological narrative of the moral corruption of military brides is maintained not only by Korean American immigrants but also by some American men.

Gary's father "just accepted [his] marriage" to Soonja even though "he probably wanted to say, you know, why didn't you marry a nice Jewish girl?" Gary also remembered how his cousin reacted to the couple when he introduced Soonja. "She said, 'It looks funny, it looks odd.' It was strange for them." Despite this awkward beginning, Soonja soon overcame his family's suspicion and developed a good relationship with them.

Gary believes that the maintenance of the intact family is only possible through the traditional gender order, in which men are breadwinners and women are housewives. Also, he had a pragmatic view of marriage as "like a business partnership," based on trust. He said, of the loyalty and subservience alleged of Korean women, "That's one of the reasons why I wanted to marry a Korean woman." He sees race as a marker of ideal femininity. He said, "I just liked that family system . . . the relationship between parents and children. Respect . . . taking care of the family, taking care of the children, taking care of the house." Gary was also attracted to the idea that a woman in Korea was subject to her father or to her husband as the head of the family. Soonja added, "In Korea, parents are first, rather than the husband first. . . . In America, no matter what, the husband is the first." Soonja, as she grew up, looked at female subservience to husband and father as the normative feminine obligation. The male authority in the Confucian tradition of the extended family would be replaced by the male authority of the husband in the more individualistic context of U.S. marriage.

Gary employed his ethnicity as a justification for his preferences for gender division and strong family ties: "It has to do with the history of the Jewish people, survival. People try to kill us . . . so we learned to survive. One of the ways we survive is to have a very close family life." As Gary was growing up, his father treated his mother "like a slave," a behavior that, as Gary noted, was "similar to [that of] a Japanese or Korean husband." A pharmacist, Gary's father owned a store and expected his wife to work both at the store and at home. Gary, while never getting along with his father, saw in himself a similarity in terms of the expectations both held for their wives. He looked back to the time when Soonja worked at an assembly factory and a motel to support their family while he was working on his graduate degree. "She went out and took a very low-class job. She was working in the motel, cleaning the beds and toilets and things like that. I did appreciate it. We needed money. We had to get it somehow. She didn't finish college. She couldn't get a very high-paying job. So she had to take a minimum-wage job. . . . She was very loyal, very faithful." Soonja also grew up in a family subject to the strong dominance of her father. It was not uncommon in Korea at that time for a married man to have several mistresses and children outside his marriage. Soonja's mother endured a similar situation. Soonja, like her mother, considered such sacrifices a part of a woman's obligation to serve her husband and strive to be a "good wife" with little or no support. She constantly blamed herself for being inadequate. Soonja described this struggle:

> I was very unhappy. . . . He [Gary] complained that I didn't cook very much. He complained a lot to me about everything. . . . [When I first came to the United States], I didn't know what to cook for dinner. I didn't know what the breakfast was like. . . . I didn't know what to cook in America. . . . He bought me some cookbooks. . . . I made plenty of mistakes, millions of mistakes. . . . At the beginning, I didn't know anything. It's natural that he complained to me. I understood. . . . What I expected life to be in America was quite different from what it is.

This pressure to find her place as a good wife kept her from having children for seven years. Soonja also had a hard time getting a job. As she said, "I never had any skill," and "My English wasn't good," and these barriers made her options very limited. Yet such obstacles never really limited her as a manager of the family. As she says, "We have an old saying that a good cook never gets kicked out of the house in Korea." Her devotion to her family's maintenance and daily cooking in order not to be, as it were, laid off kept her family and marriage strong and solid and pleased Gary.

In Gary's view, Soonja's race became a positive signifier of family loyalty. From his perspective, the characteristics associated with being a good wife and a good mother contributed to social capital that benefited his traditional male authority. "In fact, many of my friends, non-Asian friends, actually say that they envy me because they understand that Asian women are very good wives and very nice ladies. They exhibit qualities that a lot of American women don't seem to have. . . . [They are] family oriented, they are good mothers and good parents. Loyal to the families. . . . I think Korean ladies have a reputation here for being very graceful, gracious, gentle, kind. That's why I want to tell people my wife is Korean. . . . Japanese, too." Similarly, he saw their children's racial identity as not a problem but an advantage, because their choices were multiple. His elder son claimed to be Caucasian Jewish, and the younger one Asian American.

Gary placed American women in opposition to Asian women, criticizing them as lacking the quality of domesticity. "Most Americans don't understand that [cooking and serving good food is a way to attract men]. They like to be waited on by the men, really spoiled. . . . I meet women who brag that they don't like to cook or they can't cook. I would never marry such a woman. I don't care how sexy she is, I am not interested. . . . So I couldn't find an American woman. I had to find a woman from another country." Gary considered American women too individualistic or selfish. He mentioned the problems of the American family, such as the high divorce rate, and attributed these to the decline of the traditional division of labor, and exercise of male authority in the household, resulting from American women's egotistical desertion of traditional gender roles. Both Gary and Soonja believed that the economic and public spheres were the man's world and the domestic sphere the woman's world.

Gary and Soonja's marriage worked well partly because Soonja believed that American husbands treated women better than Korean husbands did. Soonja said she observed how Americans tended to stereotype Asian women as oppressed by their husbands. Soonja briefly mentioned a time when her neighbor, a white woman, asked her about Korean culture. "She didn't understand how Oriental women put up with their husbands' behavior, coming home late, anytime, any day, they are drinking. She said, 'How do you tolerate men like that?' I never thought about it. I never thought about the wife putting up with that kind of behavior." She said, "I am not married to one like that," but such encounters seemed to make her think about the cultural differences, thoughts that may have contributed to her gladness not to have married a Korean man. "I'm glad that I didn't marry a Korean, who ignore his wife, drink a lot, and come home late." Gary interrupted immediately and stopped the conversation from going further into a criticism of husbands as oppressors. "American women are very egotistical! They think everything is revolving around them. They can't put themselves in the shoes of Asian women. They just can't!" (What Gary was defending strongly here, under the guise of supporting Asian women, was men's taken-for-granted privileges as husbands.)

THE CULT OF TRUE FILIPINA WOMANHOOD

Even in recent years, the idea of the "Asian woman" as a loyal wife remains strongly attractive to many young American men such as Patrick Bennett. From the 1970s, the ideal termed the *sexual model minority* by Susan Koshy became popular, and Asian femininity became associated with not only domestic subservience but also professional success and upward mobility. Asian women, in the eyes of white men such as Patrick, embodied fashionable agents of global consumer culture, with, in addition, traditional submissiveness traits. Patrick appreciated his wife, Melissa, for possessing "sexual purity, piety, submissiveness, and domesticity," a list of traits that bears a striking resemblance to that encompassed by the Victorian ideal of white femininity, the so-called cult of true womanhood. Patrick's description of his wife focused exclusively on Melissa's devotion as a loyal wife, her appearance, and her shopping habits; he expressed little interest in her culture, family, or profession.

During the couple's entire interview, Melissa and Patrick Bennett, married only two months, sat with a wide space between them. Patrick talked most of the time, the result partly of Melissa's weak English and partly of his role as decision maker for the household. A tall, soft-spoken, and very quiet young man, Patrick mentioned repeatedly how much he loved watching sports and how much he missed seeing football games since he got married. During Patrick's interview, Melissa, tall and very slender, with long hair, prepared dinner, going back and forth between the living room and kitchen.

Patrick, a twenty-eight-year-old engineer, met Melissa, also a twenty-eight-year-old engineer, about a year ago when Melissa visited the United States for a training session at the company where Patrick works. Patrick recalled his first impression: "It struck me that she was the tallest Filipina girl I'd ever seen." He had been on several business trips to different Asian countries, including the Philippines; "That really introduced me to Asian women. . . . I kind of acquired a taste or the inclination for Asian women." Patrick claimed he could distinguish among Chinese, Korean, Japanese, and Filipina women. He had gone out with several Asian women, mostly Filipinas, and his last girlfriend was a Filipina whom he met in the Philippines. When I asked why he preferred to date Asian women, he responded, "Asian women are just something different" and, "It's weird. Black women and Mexican women, they are different, too. But for some reason, I've never been attracted."

After six months of working in the United States, Melissa returned to the Philippines and the couple kept in contact over the phone. Several months later, Patrick decided to marry Melissa. Patrick recalled his parents' reaction: "I think it was kind of a shock for me to bring home an Asian girl" because of "the way they grew up. They live in a white neighborhood. Mainly because they don't know any Asian people. . . . No, I don't think it's a bad reaction." After the couple started living together, "they really accepted her" and his parents learned to enjoy driving Melissa around town and spending time with her.

Having worked in Dallas and having visited Japan in the late 1990s, Patrick thought of "Asian people" as cosmopolitan consumers who were willing to spend on clothing, accessories, cars, and food. "In Dallas, there were a lot of Asians who work there. It wasn't uncommon to see them drive a Lexus or a Mercedes. I knew that I was making a lot more money than they would but somehow they would drive a Lexus." When he married Melissa, a friend of his joked about how "Asian women love to shop." He said that I "would have to get a second job to support her shopping," laughed Patrick. "It is true," Patrick added with some frustration. Patrick said Melissa would go to have her nails done at least twice a month or pay someone to do her makeup in the Philippines. "That's hard for me. Here, it is very expensive." Patrick said this caused the couple "small tension."

In both their individual and couple interviews, Patrick praised Melissa's loyalty to her role as wife. Although Melissa was a professional engineer, Patrick's description of her centered on her devotion to him. Interestingly, in the entire interview Patrick did not make a single comment about her skills or her talents as a co-worker or as a person who shared the same intellectual interests as he. He briefly mentioned their similar work ethics: "we had similar intensity for our schooling" and " we have very good jobs." Yet, his affection toward her was shown more in his teasing comments about her shopping habits or her fashion consciousness. His mind seemed to unconsciously confine her to the private sphere, where she liked shopping and strived to be beautiful. "Melissa likes to have the highest quality stuff or good name brands. She always looks for the highest price!" Two other husbands married to Asian American women similarly confined their thoughts of their wives to the private sphere.

Patrick believed that the willingness with which Melissa performed her domestic tasks derived from a "natural" essence that American women did not possess. "About Melissa . . . it is important for her to be a good wife. Like she's motivated to do things, to make me comfortable or whatever. I know there are lots of good American women, too, but I think that American women are. . . . I think what it is, is that Melissa, not because of anything that I've ever asked her to do, but her nature is to try to take care of her husband. I don't think that most American women that I've met have been that way." Patrick compared his wife to American women who, he says, lack femininity and devotion, though he notes that "even to say this to American women would make them mad." He took care to express that he did not mean to offend American women, or me. He went on to explain what Melissa's feminine devotion meant to him. "She just does things like, she cooks good food . . . or she would make sure that my clothes are in a certain place so I will be ready in the morning. . . . I was really disorganized, messy. . . . We are opposite in that way too. She is really clean and neat. Everything has its own place. I'm totally the opposite. Now she is here. I appreciate the order that she kind of put in our lives. . . . Now I have that order, I appreciate it. I appreciate it whenever things are in order." To Patrick, Melissa's work, such as cooking and providing order for the house, was part of her "nature," and his disorganization was justified as an aspect of *his* natural characteristics. By presenting her as essentially "neat and clean," of course, Patrick diminishes the value of her labor.

All three men I have discussed—George, Gary, and Patrick—idealized Asian American women as maternal figures. Adrienne Rich discusses the maintenance of the mother-son relationship between women and men as characteristic of compulsory heterosexuality, in which male-female relationships center on male needs, male fantasies about women, and male interest in controlling women.[6] Patrick compared Melissa to his mother, whom he described as an "old-fashioned type of woman." His mother would wake up at five each morning to prepare breakfast for the family and sack lunches for him and his brother; she also worked as a full-time teacher at an elementary school. Patrick desired and expected to find the same self-sacrificing devotion to the family in his wife. He wanted to maintain his control over her, just as had his father over his mother. "[My mother] would do a lot of things for my dad. So one of the reasons I was attracted to Melissa was because she's a lot like my mother." Patrick added, "It's weird to say that about someone who came from the other side of the planet." He, like George and Gary, desired and found a mother-son relationship in his relationship with his wife. Even though Patrick's description of Melissa as a maternal figure might have been intended as a genuine compliment, his childlike, one-sided expectations and idealization of her emerged as an aspect of his control, signifying a taking advantage of his gender and cultural privileges over Melissa, who had little knowledge of gender sensibilities within American culture.

Patrick's and Melissa's religious backgrounds seemed to play an important role in their relationship. Having grown up with traditional Protestant parents, Patrick was adamant about his wife's conversion, saying "the agreement is that Melissa will go to the Protestant Church with me." At the time of the interview, however, he was attending the Catholic Church with Melissa "for a while" until Melissa felt comfortable enough to convert. Even while exhibiting a paternal tolerance toward his wife's "adjustment" to his value system, Patrick regarded her choice of faith as his decision.

Patrick explained that what tied the couple together was not religion, but common morals and a common set of values. Patrick referred to the male control of female sexuality in the Philippines as the "old-fashioned ways of her culture," and saw it as a sign of Philippine women's loyalty to their husbands. "In the Philippines, it is common for ladies to remain virgins until they get married," he noted. It was not only Melissa's domesticity that Patrick marked as a sign of Filipina femininity, then, but also her sexual purity. This, again, is in line with the idea of True Womanhood," which Patrick wanted in his marriage—a value that, he lamented, could not be found among American women, but that was common among women in the Philippines. Raised with strict Catholic discipline, Melissa also placed a high value on Patrick's conservative attitudes toward sexual commitment. "I learned he is a really conservative guy, who is very different from most American guys I met before," she says.

Like George and Gary, Patrick expressed a deep fear of, and aversion to, divorce, and he admitted that he decided to marry Melissa because he thought she would never divorce him. "One of the reasons I was attracted to Melissa is her confidence in herself and her culture [so] that I felt . . . she would never divorce me. Where, with American girls, even if she loves you and you love her, it's like a year or two. I don't think that American women, or even American men, have the stick-to-it [capacity]. That's one of the reasons that I was not hesitant to pursue her so quickly. Basically I do have the idea that Filipina women are very loyal." A Filipina woman would be more likely not to leave him, allowing him to maintain more control over the marriage. Unlike American women, who lacked patience and faithfulness, he felt Filipina women were loyal, possessing a controllable and desirable femininity. This loyalty is not earned in the development of a relationship but is expected from the beginning.

Melissa, who had started life in the United States only two months before our interview, described the difficulty of doing everything alone, and noted that "adjusting into a different culture" was a solitary process. She started by joining a local Filipino American group, cooking Filipino food and speaking in her native language with other Filipina American women whose husbands were also white. Patrick, however, showed explicit indifference to her culture. He sometimes went with her to parties with other Filipinos, but said of them, simply,"[They're] all right." Melissa talked about her desire to teach her language, Tagalog, to their children, but Patrick responded, "I don't particularly care if they can speak her language. If they can, that's fine." His responses to these topics were strikingly different from his excited descriptions of how she cooked, cleaned, and organized the house for him.

Patrick's lack of interest in these cultural matters important to Melissa was also striking when compared to his interest in sports. Changing the subject with a suddenly exhilarated tone, he said, "You won't believe this! We went to a Nascar race!" He became animated when he described football and car races, adding "I like sports a lot. That's too foreign to Melissa. So we haven't been able to share that experience," he said in a frustrated tone.

Except to object to what he saw as Melissa's habits of overspending on her appearance and shopping, Patrick had no complaints and was happy in his marriage; Melissa embodied the traits marked desirable in the Cult of True Womanhood and the model minority. But her language barriers, lack of family, and lack of knowledge about American culture constrained her from acting otherwise; once Melissa acquired a work permit and started working as an engineer, Patrick's control over the relationship perhaps would be threatened.

WHITE MASCULINITY AND RACIALIZED FEMININITY

Although the historical and cultural contexts in which theese marriages took place differed, the three men—George, Gary, and Patrick—expressed similar views of their wives as loyal and subservient wives and mothers. With the United States being the world's largest economic and political power and having a military presence in Japan, South Korea, and the Philippines, these white American men unquestionably enjoyed social and economic privileges over their marriages with these women, who had language barriers and few skills for maneuvering in American culture. Sachiko, who entered the United States after WWII and after America's long prohibition on Asian immigrants, had few options other than being a "good wife" to George. In the context of South Korea, the military wives' subjugation to their own nation and to the authority of American men was clear in Soonja and Gary's marriage. Gary and Patrick intentionally employed the stereotype of loyal and subservient Asian women in their descriptions of their wives. Soonja, as a Korean, was identified as a model minority wife and laborer who would serve white male authority. Besides loyalty, Patrick also wanted "sexual purity," which he saw as common among Filipinas; though George and Gary expressed appreciation of their wives' household labor, Patrick viewed Melissa's domestic work as among a Filipina wife's "natural" traits. Patrick also described Melissa as consumed with shopping and appearance, which he saw as new signs of Asian femininity, yet he took little interest in her actual culture.

As Susan Koshy points out, having foreign-born Asian American wives allows some men to enhance their sense of their masculinity, which has felt threatened by white women—whom the three men discussed here described as assertive, self-centered, and threats. These men also expressed an attraction to the gender hierarchy and collectivism of Asian families, under either Confucian or Catholic models in which women's subordination to male authority was normalized. Asian cultures' family collectivism sharply differs from mainstream American culture's individualism, self-sufficiency, and egalitarianism,[7] and it is precisely because of this cultural and national gap that the Asian family system is idealized, and unassimilated foreign-born Asian women become racialized as feminine, inclined to serve men as in their home countries.

Using a foreign-born Asian American woman to maintain conservative masculinities can become problematic. First, Koshy describes how Asian American women's racialized femininity "counter[s] modern feminist challenges to white masculinity," as "when white American men were assailed by growing demands for equality made by white American women, the Asian American woman came to stand in for the more traditional model of family-centered femininity challenged by feminists."[8] Second, as seen in Patrick's view of Melissa, such men's motive of masculine enhancement could inadvertently exploit foreign women's disadvantages or vulnerability, such as unfamiliarity with the English language and American culture, and might serve to justify the men's decision to remain ignorant of their wives' culture and family and, in the name of love, to impose their own preferences and stereotypes regarding marriage.

The White Man and Upward Mobility

Marriage between white men in America and Asian women from developing countries, such as the Philippines, has been a popular trend since the 1980s. In such marriages, images regarding mutual spousal expectations are distinctly gendered. Nicole Constable writes: "Modern and rapid forms of communication and transportation and relationships between nation-states make marriage between U.S. men and Asian women more practical and more imaginable than ever. Women may desire wealth, opportunity, freedom, citizenship, marriage, or a better way of life. Men's desires are also complex and varied, involving visions of domestic order, enduring relationships, modesty, femininity, sexuality, and an old-fashioned division of labor."[9] Asian–white intimacy that takes place in post-colonial/neocolonial territories including the Philippines, Japan, South Korea, and Southeast Asia, and that is not limited to correspondence or mail-order marriages, often includes exchanges of similar gendered and racialized images of Asian femininity and white masculinity. White American men have not only been associated with the material notion of a so-called better life; they have also been seen as potential liberators to free women from the patriarchal constraints extant in these Asian countries. Thus, many of these marriages, rather than being unequal transactions, are built on material and psychological reciprocity. As Constable rightly points out, "stereotypes of Asian women (willing to do anything for the green card) and of Western men (taking advantage of their vulnerability) seem far too reductionistic, simplistic, and misleading."[10] Still, these brides end up paying the price for these supposedly reciprocal marriages, because they must be subordinate to their new husbands. Giddens describes intimacy as "paradoxically . . . a means of achieving a measure of autonomy" and "a gamble against the future"; that is, an intimate relationship can be a vehicle for attaining self-realization through a high-stakes investment.[11] For the foreign-born Filipina American women discussed here, love with white men is a risky gamble, but one they take hoping to overcome the gendered subordination and economic deprivation that they have grown up with and endured.

A WHITE HUSBAND AS A MIDDLE-CLASS INVESTMENT

Angelina Brown, a short thirty-nine-year-old Filipina American with a very warm smile and a quiet demeanor, showed me pictures of herself and her mother at a younger age. She told me she had always wanted to be beautiful like her mother. Angelina had been married to Thomas for fifteen years. Thomas Brown, a thirty-eight-year-old computer engineer, was, in contrast with Angelina, big, talkative, and bellicose. Although often expressing his affection for Angelina with expressions such as "I'm true to her" and "I can't really imagine myself without Angelina," Thomas did not hesitate to take over the interview by frequently interrupting Angelina and presenting his own views as the couple's views, or by teasing her. In her individual interview, Angelina talked much more confidently and freely about her ambition, her mother, her upbringing, and her children.

Angelina's mother ran away from her first husband, a Filipino and Angelina's father, because of his serious physical abuse of her. "She left bleeding, literally bleeding. That's how bad it was," said Angelina. "She jumped out of the window and she went to the neighbors." When Angelina was about two years old, her father, who had already abandoned his wife and nine children, stopped contact with the family completely.

To raise her large family, Angelina's mother worked at an American military base as a waitress "all day and night." Angelina was cared for mainly by her grandparents. "My mom . . . only visited us twice within seven years. She sent us support. . . . She hated the entire place because that was the hometown of my father, who abused her and all that. She had no choice." Over the years, Angelina tried to come to terms with why she saw her mother so rarely.

As the eldest child, Angelina helped take care of her brothers and sisters. By the age of six, she had already begun to earn money as a member of the choir in her church. When she turned sixteen, Angelina started working as a waitress at the military base where her mother worked. Soon after, her mother told Angelina that she was leaving her and the family again. Her mother went to the United States and married an American serviceman, who, like her first husband, soon started abusing her. "She has been abused forever, she's still abused now with her second husband. . . . For some reason, she wants to stick with that kind of abusive relationship."

Americans. "This couple, who are both Filipino, I tended not to invite them to the parties," because "they don't belong to us," she said.

In her individual interview, Angelina told me that she chose to marry Thomas because she thought marriage would provide emotional as well as financial security. "I think I did that for security reasons, to be honest. . . . He's like an investment. I was like, you buy this mutual fund in the beginning, and it gets bigger and bigger, and at the end, you know, you get all of this and you get to enjoy it."

It took Angelina a long time before she could spontaneously say she loved her husband. Perhaps, she said, this was because she had witnessed her mother suffering in three marriages. Although she frequently expressed some doubts about her trust in Thomas, she said, "Because he loves me so much, we are going to be all right. Those negative things are going to be just overshadowed by the positive side." Much of her concern centered on Thomas's open infidelity, or what he referred to as the couple having been "swingers." In my individual interview with Angelina, she did not mention specific conflicts between her and Thomas, but in my interview with Thomas, he mentioned that he had been with a few women since he was married. He defended this behavior by saying that "Angelina was always there," or that she knew about all of the other women, so he viewed such behaviors as based on mutual agreement, "not [as] cheating." He raised his voice when he said, "I am true to her, in a certain sense."

Both Angelina and Thomas regarded building a solid family as the primary goal of their relationship, which they believed should be based on a traditional division of labor. Angelina took care of their two sons, a five-year-old and an eleven-year-old, whom she called "Caucasians." She and Thomas went to soccer games on the weekend. Angelina often cooked two or three different meals for Thomas, herself, and the children. "He likes steak and I'll fix steak, but then I'll cook something else for me, a Filipino dish that no one else cares about. And I cook something like macaroni and cheese for the kids."

Thomas believed in playing the traditional masculine role of breadwinner, with Angelina to be solely mother and wife. Although acknowledging the changes in women's roles in American society, Thomas identified with the conservative "white guy" who supports so-called family values. "The cultural influence says that the mother should raise the children. For me, as a white guy, my culture would have me keep my wife at home. . . . It's recommended that the woman stays home and raises the kids." He also believed that having a wife who did not work was a demonstration of class privilege as well as evidence of a man's success. Thomas resisted the social and cultural messages for men to change. He felt he had to uphold traditional masculinity as the "dominant male," ignoring the "confusing messages" from the feminist movement. "Then there is women's liberation. But men are still taught to be gentlemen. So men are taught to react a certain way toward women. But at the same time, we are told not to be chauvinistic. It confuses us. We are supposed to be the dominant male, protecting women and providing for the family. . . . If we are equal partners, then what are we? Aren't we important anymore? I think there are a lot of mixed messages sent to the guys. It's tough." He did not feel that an alternative mode of partnership, in which he would not dominate but would rather build an equal partnership, would work for him. He thought this would risk his masculinity too much.

Although both aspired to lead an upper-middle-class American life and strongly valued family, Thomas and Angelina showed cultural differences in their views of family. In the couple interview, Thomas talked about spending money on family trips to Disneyland and on American holidays with "thousands of presents." Thomas said, "When I was growing up, my mom would fill a whole room with presents. I like my children to have that." But Thomas expressed reluctance about continuing to send money to Angelina's family in the Philippines. He resented this obligation and could not understand why Angelina's family remained dependent on his support. Thomas believed in the U.S. conservative rhetoric regarding individual effort as a solution for poverty, and he looked at Angelina's family's request for money as a sign of their lack of effort. Angelina tried to diminish his resentment by insisting on the close kinship system in the Philippines. "We have a different culture. . . . We tend to be close as a family," said Angelina. But Thomas interrupted her: "Part of it is culture. But part of it has been individuals who we're dealing with. My perception is sometimes that the less industrious ones are the ones who ask for money. Then they're offended when we don't give them money. Because they think we are very rich. I'm not rich. . . . I have a lot to pay for. . . . They kind of expect people in the United States to buy for them. You know, that's not our culture, you know, so that's a compromise for me." Angelina tried to make him understand how difficult it was for her brothers to thrive, given the weak economy of the Philippines, but ultimately she resorted to a different defense, one relying on gendered obligations. "Once you marry a Filipino, you marry into the family. Because the man, if he is a white guy, always ends up supporting not just the wife but also the wife's family. Maybe it's a one-time thing, or it could be a monthly or annual thing. It's very common." Giving to your family, for Angelina, was far more important than gift giving or holiday celebrations. It was what you did to help one another survive.

MARRIAGE AS FAMILY REUNION

Linda Miller, a petite, thirty-four-year-old Filipina American woman with straight black hair and brown eyes, and wearing a tight mini skirt, informed me in a quiet but serious tone that her husband was not interested in participating in the interview. She had been married to her husband, Jack, a forty-one-year-old computer engineer, for ten years, and the couple had two children, whom she described as "white." Linda first met Jack through what she called a "pen-pal relationship" while she was employed as a domestic worker in Hong Kong.

In the living room of the couple's apartment, Jack was working intensely on his laptop when I arrived. He glanced at me without stopping his fingers and said "Hi" very curtly. His silent absorption with the computer seemed designed to prevent any social contact. According to Linda, Jack worked mainly at home, using his laptop "from 7 to 7." We decided to go to the children's bedroom for the interview.

Linda told me about her childhood. Her father worked at an American military base as a maintenance man, and her family ran a small store. Linda started working as a maid for an American serviceman's family when she was twelve years old. She always gave half of her income to her family. Among people in the Philippines, it was very common to work from childhood on. Linda said, "We just work because work is there." At twenty-one, Linda had few choices available. She could either go to Hong Kong to work as a domestic worker or go to Japan to work as a waitress or a singer. She chose to go to Hong Kong. "All I did was just to clean the house and cook." At that time, she earned the equivalent of $250 US per month.

The family she worked for owned a small house, but they did not give her a private room, and they fired her when she expressed a desire for one. "I said, 'I need space even though I am a domestic.' But in Hong Kong, you don't have that choice unless your employer is really rich." Fortunately Linda found another family willing to employ her. Linda looked back on the American family for whom she had worked at an early age as being particularly friendly. She preferred working for Americans in the Philippines to working for Asians in Hong Kong: "For Asians [in Hong Kong], you have to work for what you get paid. Americans are very pleased by what you've done, and they give you money because they are pleased with what you did. . . . You are not feeling like you are a slave or anything. You just go to their house like a friend and wash the dishes and you get money. That's what you feel. They are just like a friend, not a boss. That's what we felt."

Around the time Linda went to Hong Kong, her Filipino friends were circulating lists of American men who were looking for Filipina brides. Linda chose Jack because he was the youngest of all the Americans on the list, which mostly included men in their sixties and seventies. She went back to the Philippines, and Jack came over to meet her. Although Linda did not have any romantic feelings toward him, she accepted his offer of marriage, which took place four days after his arrival in the Philippines. "He was a quiet, simple person. That's it. I can't think of any other words . . . but I thought he was okay, a macho man, a big guy." Linda said this without a smile or any facial gesture. Asked about any concerns she might have had about marriage, Linda expressed a combination of disassociation and irritation. Her attitude toward her husband was distant and mechanical. "It's just, this is my man. I am going to be with him. . . . I didn't feel anything about him. Not excited. Not fear." Marriage was the survival investment she chose and committed herself to, bravely and deliberately.

Linda never dated American men before she married Jack. She saw many Filipina women mistreated by American servicemen around the U.S. military base, and she knew those American men were never serious about the Filipina women there.

> They [American servicemen] are all playboys. They all just want some-thing from you . . . one-night thing. That's all. All American people I know do like that. They just do, you know, one-night stand and all that. . . . I saw how they end the relationship with Filipina. . . . I don't want American boyfriend because they're just going to treat you like, you know, bad. Or maybe they will love you for a year, and that's it. They can't care for longer relationship. I wanted a longer relationship. . . . So in my mind back then, that's the reason I just didn't even care, or think about or dream about marrying American. They are all the same.

In expressing strong resentment toward American servicemen's treatment of local Filipina women, Linda added, "I'm not a one-night stand! Back off!" She knew not to become one of these women who had short relationships with American men and were then discarded with no financial or emotional support. But she ended up resorting to another way of finding an American, a "different kind" of man who would guarantee her a long-lasting marriage. However, she still seemed in denial about the contradiction between her aver-sion to American men in the Philippines and her choice to marry one. "I didn't know that I would marry American," she repeated.

For Linda, who had worked all her life as a maid, marriage to an American man was a high-stakes gamble. She hoped to end up serving a husband who would treat her with warm gratitude, and possibly as a friend and an equal. But the marriage could not begin immediately; it took Linda about two years before she could get permission to emigrate and start her new life in America. During this period, Jack supported her financially by giving her a credit card as well as by supplying enough cash that she did not have to work. "When he came to the Philippines, he told me I didn't have to go back to Hong Kong," Linda said. At the time of the interview, Jack still sent $150 per month to her family in the Philippines. She sighed, "That's not enough for them. It's not enough to support them. . . . It's still a poor economy." Linda appreciated her husband's financial support of her and her family, but her words could not conceal a huge emotional distance underneath, especially when she talked about Jack showing no interest in her family and culture. "He doesn't ask how my brothers and sisters are doing. I'm getting used to it. It doesn't matter anymore. I don't care . . . I talk to his family. But he doesn't talk to my family. I just accept it. I can't do anything. You are not expecting him to talk more or be happy about what he hears from you. I wish he were. I wish he could commit more to my family and my background. Yeah . . . it bothers me. But I can't make him do that."

Jack was not required to know anything about her culture or her family, and even disregarded her background, but Linda was required to know all about his family, his job, and his life. He expected her, it appeared, to serve him in the traditional sense as a docile, good wife in exchange for financial security. Linda cooked, every day, and had never heard Jack say anything about her cooking. "He doesn't show any, you cannot hear any, you just cook and put them on the table. He puts them in the sink. It's like your kid. You don't want to wait for a kid to say thank you." Linda barely finished her sentence and seemed about to cry. She did not move or speak for a while.

Describing her marriage and housework, Linda repeated many times such phrases as "I accepted more" and "You just have to live with it, just do it." Her marriage seemed to require the same endurance and adjustment as the domestic work of her earlier days. Linda's distraught voice suggested that she was afraid to admit that this marriage was just another long-term contract.

In contrast, when Linda talked about her desire to go out to work, her voice became strong. "I want to work," she said. But she followed her husband's suggestion she not do so because "it is not worth it," since she had no skills or higher education and this would prevent her getting a job that paid well. However, before giving birth to her first child, she had worked at a grocery store and also as a nursing aide, which she enjoyed. She hoped to study to be a nurse someday.

Linda said she followed her husband's suggestions except when he yelled at her. When he yelled at her loudly, she even threatened to leave him. Linda described this very poignantly in a small, barely audible voice. However, divorce was the last thing she wanted, given its cultural unfamiliarity and the consequent loss of support she would suffer. She never knew about divorce until an American serviceman who was married to her friend left the friend and their children in the Philippines. "When I was a teenager, I heard about this divorce thing. It happens to anybody in America. It could happen to you. In the Philippines, Filipinos, my family, you get married 'til death. That's what we are. So it just stays in my mind that American people will divorce you in two years. A year or two years. The relationship doesn't last long. They get married and if they don't like it, they get divorced. . . . If your husband is American, you will get there. You will get a divorce in a few years."

Having barely avoided material deprivation in the Philippines and Hong Kong, Linda finally acquired upward mobility by coming to the United States. However, like the Filipinas already discussed, she had little power to transform her husband's perceptions or the dynamics of the marital relationship. At the time of the interview, Linda's only hope for happiness was to live one day with her parents, who had been waiting in the Philippines for ten years for legal permission to emigrate to the United States: "Here in the U.S., when they get old, you just throw your parents into the nursing home. But me, my kids, we don't do that. You take care of your parents when they get old." Five years after my interview with Linda, a friend of hers told me that Linda's parents and siblings from the Philippines had arrived in the United States.

HAPPY TOGETHER

With the rise of globalization in the 1980s and 1990s, marriage with American men became a widely popular survival strategy for Asian women from Third World countries such as the Philippines. The American military presence and American economic prosperity played important roles in the women's ambitions and imaginations regarding marriage with American men. Angelina's childhood dream of experiencing American prosperity was realized when her mother married an American and when she later did the same. Similarly, Linda's husband appeared, through a bride importation service, as a savior figure; he assisted her leaving the Philippines and saved her from the necessity of working in Hong Kong as a domestic worker to help support her family. However, their lack of economic, social, and cultural resources inevitably made these women dependent on the husband and marriage. Uma Narayan, in a study of domestic violence and mail-order brides in the United States, notes that "women with dependent immigration status are often more economically, psychologically, and linguistically dependent on their spouse,"[12] and even "susceptible to prolonged physical abuse."[13] Angelina and Linda concealed the unhappiness and humiliation resulting from their dependence, the price they paid for their security.

In situations such as this, the Asian American woman can be seen as a colonial subject. Ann Stoler, citing Franz Fanon, suggests that colonialism "uses sex as a vehicle to master a practical world."[14] Marrying the colonizer gives the colonized access to privileged schooling, well-paying jobs, and desirable residential quarters. Fanon's insight about colonial desire, that "to marry white culture" is "to grasp white civilization and dignity and make them [hers],"[15] describes Angelina's desire to attain the "highest standard" by marrying the powerful other. Also, such desires for upward mobility are gendered. Feminist psychoanalysts have argued that women often seek to fulfill their desires by identifying with the power of an idealized lover.[16]

Although Angelina idealized white Americans as symbols of material prosperity and avenues of access to mainstream America, she also had a pragmatic or detached view of marriage as an "investment." Through her pragmatism, or detachment, she was able to disassociate herself from such negative aspects of the marriage as Thomas's open infidelity, his dominance over most of the decision making, and his blaming of her Filipino family. Linda, too, explicitly detached herself from affective or romantic views of marriage, and dealt with her unhappiness by "adjusting herself" as she had during her time as a domestic worker. She did not express much ambition to assimilate into the white mainstream, with its, to her, foreign values. Attaining a "better life" for her Filipino family was her main goal in marriage.

How were these marriages different from the marriages of typical white Americans? Do race and culture matter? Were these women, because they were Filipina, more oppressed than white American women who endure similar marriages? These women's personal histories need to be understood within the contexts of racial, global, economic, and cultural subjugation. Factors to be taken into account include the women's having grown up and worked under the governance of the U.S. military, their having seen American servicemen abuse local women, and their managing their double consciousness of race and culture as well as their monitoring their speech and behaviors as "immigrants" and "non-Americans"—none of which native-born white American women must go through. Such multiple forms of subjugation could easily deprive these women of confidence and the power to sustain and build their individual identities, thus leaving them dependent on their husbands and constraining their marriages. But, ironically, it is precisely the constraints on, and dependence of, these women that make their marriages work.

A Different Kind of White Man

Although I have discussed several cases in which mutual racialized desires substantiated the traditional gender roles in marriage, it is erroneous to say that all marriages between a white man and a foreign-born Asian American woman are bound by gender inequalities or marital tradition. Among five such marriages that I looked at, one couple did engage in egalitarian marriage. This Filipina American woman had more financial power than had her white husband, and her husband agreed with her in her assessment of the racism and sexism that foreign-born Filipina women often experience. The couple's views of typical Filipina female–white male marriages also further illustrate how common it is for Filipina women to bury their sense of inequality or their unhappiness in their lives in the United States.

A COUPLE AVERSE TO RACISM AND SEXISM

John Anderson, a tall, blond thirty-eight-year-old pharmacist, had been married to Amy, a toned and assertive thirty-eight-year-old Filipina American, for six years. Both John and Amy joked and laughed throughout the interviews. In their couple interview, they talked about their exercise regimen (running together), John's favorite international food recipes, parenting two children (whom they called "Amerasian"), and their shared aversion to racial stereotypes of Asians in general and Filipinos in particular.

John had just finished a graduate program and had started working as a pharmacist. He said his ideal woman was dark-skinned and has black hair. (He was attracted to Tina Turner when he was a boy.) John described his first impression of Amy: "I thought, she's really cool. She's very relaxed. She was very mysterious. Alluring, it's kind of inviting and attractive, you know, makes you want to pursue it more. She's not shy. Don't get me wrong. She's not shy, right? It's just her personality, coupled with her beauty, was very intriguing. . . . With Amy, if you want to go ahead and operate on this stereotype that Asian women are shy, demure, and submissive, well, Amy is everything but that. She is not that at all."

When they met, Amy was working as an accountant in the same building where John was working as a musician. They were invited to the same party, where Amy first heard John play. John was in his late twenties and was starting to feel the limitations of his life as a musician. He was becoming tired of the lifestyle, full of parties and casual relationships that went nowhere. "It was a period of self-reflection and self-analysis for me," he said. After a year, John and Amy started living together, and they married in the fourth year of their relationship.

In her early twenties, while still living in the Philippines and unmarried, Amy had become a single mother. Her son, Jay, fifteen years old at the time of the interview, was fathered by a Filipino man. Amy came to the United States (twelve years before this interview) when she married a white American, a friend of her sister's. The marriage lasted only two years, and her ex-husband felt that he had provided her with legal status in the United States and therefore should have the power to deport her from this country. Amy reflected on her ex-husband: "He was threatening me when we were fighting, 'I'm getting immigration to have you deported.' I'm like, you know what, why don't you go right now to immigration because I would really love to go back to the Philippines. In the Philippines, I had a career, I don't really need this, yes please let's go to immigration, I want to go back home. But he never did. But what happened was divorce."

Amy received her green card in the same year that she got her divorce. Even though Amy was a chief accountant in the Philippines, she could not easily get a job as an accountant in this country. "I was a CPA in the Philippines. But I got here, and nobody wanted to hire me, even for a much lower position in accounting." Amy had to apply for welfare to pay for Jay's day care. "During that time, I was taking home three hundred dollars, you know, every paycheck, and we survived on six hundred dollars, the two of us, my little boy going to day care." Amy started working as an accounting clerk, received a promotion every year, and worked as a controller at the time of the interview.

At the beginning of the relationship, Amy's mother was not happy with John and tore up the pictures of Amy and John that Amy sent to the Philippines. John said, "I think she was disappointed in Amy having gone through marriage and getting divorced. I mean, Catholics, Filipinos, they do not get divorced. And she probably looked at me as, like, who is this stranger? It took a long time for me to get in her good favor. And I was telling her, whenever she would leave, or when we were leaving the hotel. . . . I hugged her and said, 'Don't worry about Amy, I will take care of Amy. You can always trust me.' She looked at me and she said, 'I know.'" Amy's mother was looking forward to more grandchildren, but she passed away soon after the first granddaughter, Amanda, was born, without getting a chance to see her.

All of Amy's Filipino friends immediately liked John and even expressed surprising attitudes about him. Amy remembered some whispering to her, "I've never seen a white person who's just so nice and good. . . . You found the white person who is actually going to be nice to an Asian. You are so lucky that John is so good and nice to you." Ironically, these women complimenting Amy's husband were also married to white American men. Amy viewed their comments as a reflection of how these Filipina women were treated unequally in everyday life: "I think that most of my Filipino friends have been exposed to insults by Americans. That's why they're saying it's very rare that we actually see a white person who's really nice." Amy's reference to white people encompassed both white men who were married to Filipina women and other white men and women who interacted with Filipina women on a daily basis.

Amy herself was treated badly as a result of her race, not only by her ex-husband but also by her coworkers. Amy remembered that, when she started working, her coworkers constantly either ignored or belittled her.

> These white people just like totally used me as a doormat, you know, they just totally ignored me or were being rude to me all the time. I was keeping it calm, not saying anything, because, well, yeah, I have the accent. I couldn't really speak the language really good. . . . I've been always yelled at or been ignored or been made fun of by these people. . . . Then, one lady I work with . . . she invited everybody else but there's one from Ethiopia, one from the Middle East, and me, and then one from Mexico, everybody else who's white and black were invited but us. This is my boss's birthday party. They're talking about it in front of us like we didn't exist. . . .
>
> "So is this like, are you just being a racist?" That's what I said in front of them. They're so shocked.

Amy's story illuminates the racial line that exists, not between white and colored, but between "Americans" and "foreigners." She expressed her resentment about xenophobia and about stereotypes of Asians as perpetual foreigners by telling coworkers to stop ignoring her. "I think that's the only way I actually gain respect. When they saw that from me, everybody changed ninety degrees." When Amy and one white neighbor argued about her son, Amy's race and nationality were targeted for insult. "She's like, 'You are so low, you are lower than the dirt, why don't you go back to the Philippines where you belong,' that's what she told me." Amy attributed the neighbor's verbal violence to her lack of education and her class standing, saying "'Oh, yeah, I can go back to the Philippines, but you know what, that doesn't change the fact that you are white trash.' That's what I told her. I'm always up-front like that." Amy, in this case, used her social class and educational privileges to place herself, in a sort of reactive intolerance, "above" her white neighbor. It is worth noting that, though Amy encountered numerous instances of racism, in varied settings, she did not encounter such mistreatment when with John.

Amy and John said it was not rare to see an unequal marital pattern between Asian American wives and white husbands. John perceived that Amy's Filipina friends who were married to white Americans were dissatisfied with their husbands' unequal treatment and disinterest in their cultures. John liked to go to Filipino parties with Amy, but he did not see many white husbands there. "When we go to the Filipino Association parties, when we go to a Filipino house, there's a lot of Filipino women who are married to Anglo men, who come alone because the husbands don't come." John said those white men were probably not interested in their wives' culture. He added that he thought these white men liked the stereotypical "submissiveness" of an Asian wife and rarely engaged with other aspects of their wives' lives and personalities.

Regarding parenting, John, who shared half the cooking and childcare, said, "It's like a partnership as far as it goes, and the only way to raise these kids without us both going crazy is doing it together." John was raised by his mother, who worked as a nurse. His father left the family when John was young, and John had seen him only a few times throughout his life. John's mother emigrated from Germany when young and had a lot of "Old World" mentality, according to John. John had kept up a very close relationship with her. He said that, before his marriage, he dated women from many ethnic and racial groups, including "plenty of Caucasian women," black women, and Hispanics. His mother was always open-minded about the women he dated. John also identified with his mother as a caretaker, having perceived her as "the strong leader of the house."

For John, understanding Amy's family, culture, and country was an important part of building their relationship. Amy joked, "He is pretty much like a Filipino now." "Yeah, as far as diet," responded John. Amy insisted, "He probably knows more about the Philippines than I do." John saw learning about Filipino history and culture as substantial factors not only in understanding Amy, but also in raising her son Jay. Amy always told her son how hard her own parents had to work to send five children through college, and how her siblings supported each other in the Philippines. John said Amy's parents' hardships would become meaningful to their son when he had to face survival in American culture.

John, who differentiated himself from the white husbands who belittled their wives' culture and family, reacted strongly to the stereotype of the typical white husband with an Asian wife. He remembered what the pastor asked him and Amy at their wedding: He wanted to know if John was a fifty-year-old, because he saw their marriage as another "typical white-Asian marriage." Amy said, laughing, "He was just assuming that the older white American is now getting a young girl from the Philippines to marry." John said, "I laughed about it because he's stereotyping. . . . People are going to think that I'm some loser guy who can't get an American woman. . . . It's funny. It's hilarious. If you meet Amy, she is not that way." John referred to a magazine, *Global Starlight*, that advertised Asian women from Asian countries as good wives for American men.

It would be something for an American to bring over like this Filipino wife who doesn't speak like two words of English. He's just going to let her cook and clean all day. I think that's the kind of guy I'm talking about. That's not a relationship. He just went and got a maid. . . . It's like, to me, it's just a step above slavery almost. . . . Paying money to have a person come over here. . . . I think that kind of shifts the relationship to a different dynamic. Because he could always hold that over her. Well, I got you out of there and paid for you to come over here. Now, wash my car, what do you know, be subservient to me.

John distanced himself from white males who desire this kind of marital dynamic, calling them "losers." He also distanced himself from stereotypes of Asian women as submissive. "I don't think that's a fair stereotype," he said, adding that such stereotypes derive in part from language barriers.

In the couple interview, Amy and John displayed two-way communication and offered each other confirmation. For instance, they frequently used phrases like, "What do you think?" There was no doubt that Amy's professional career and life experiences in the United States made their marital dynamic more equal, and John's respect for her role as the breadwinner for the previous two years contributed to their perception of each other as partners rather than as traditional wife and husband. It is also interesting that John was raised only by his mother and that he respected and identified with, rather than idealized, her.

Although I did not interview any professional foreign-born Asian American women other than Amy for this study, such a woman, who has her own profession, an equal or higher education to the man, and little or no language barriers in the country of residence, could have more leverage over the marital dynamics and more bargaining power with her husband than could a woman who lacks these advantages. Thus, education, occupation, and language skills allow women to maneuver and resist the gender and racial codes of American culture, and to defy or assail stereotypes.

BETWEEN FREEDOM AND PROTECTION

In this chapter, I discussed six foreign-born Asian American women's marriages with white men. In light of the economic and cultural differences between the United States and Japan in the 1950s, the United States and South Korea in the 1970s, and the United States and the Philippines currently, marriage for some Asian American women was a strategy for survival in the United States. The traditional feminine role was not something the women chose, but rather something they grew up with as part of the cultural disciplines and codes embedded in ethnic patriarchy, the collective family system, and Confucianism and/or Catholicism. The United States' assimilation imperatives absorbed these women's strategies of survival through marriage, which served to valorize traditional American masculinity. Interracial marriage between foreign-born Asian American women and white men also served to achieve the pluralist ideal of the emergence of a multiracial so-called New American Family. However, achievement of these goals came at the expense of Asian American women's alienated relationships with their husbands, who overly essentialized and fixated on the women's feminine roles, with little attention to their cultural and historical complexities. I am not arguing that the husbands I discussed here mistreated their wives, but I observed that the factors that made these women more desirable partners were the stereotypes of Asian women, the women's limited knowledge and options in the United States, and the men's social and economic privileges over them—and Pyke and Johnson argue that the stereotypes of Asian women "make them especially vulnerable to mistreatment from men who view them as easy targets."[17] I would add that foreign-born Asian American women are under much greater risk of such treatment than second-generation Asian American women, given the former's lack of skill in maneuvering the racism and sexism embedded in the popular stereotypes that develop many American men's attraction to Asian American women.

As we saw most vividly in the cases of Angelina and Linda, it is ironic and paradoxical that the rebellious survival strategies of some Filipina American women become absorbed through, and restrained by, the U.S. hegemonic hierarchies of race and gender, which often perpetuated these women's social and economic marginality. Their choice of white American men derived from their strategic resistance to powerless positions, but such choices also inevitably increased the women's vulnerability to, and dependence on, their white husbands. For many non-European immigrants with few socioeconomic resources, intermarriage serves as one of the few means to gain enough upward mobility to survive and possibly become "honorary whites" in the United States. As seen in the story of Angelina, the foreign-born Asian immigrant woman's desire for a white man can easily correspond to her desire for status as an ideal white American citizen, who at least has access to social privileges, a difficult achievement in "a 'nation' with whiteness" where non-European immigrants "encounter the challenges of being treated as second-class citizens" and "can at best become 'honorary whites.'"[18]

The discourse of the *ideal interracial marriage* has been governed by the question of who can and cannot be an ideal citizen, and such a process of scrutiny is gendered. As Lauren Berlant points out, this discourse of intermarriage does not make fine distinctions among the terms *ethnic, immigrant, alien, minority,* and *illegal.*[19] Gayatri C. Spivak argues that it is the logic of imperialism and globalization that leads to a desire for "the establishment of the good society," which is "marked by the espousal of the woman as an object of protection from her own kind."[20] What lies underneath this "good society" is "the dissimulation of patriarchal strategy" that aims to rescue these immigrant women and grants them free choice as subjects.[21] Berlant similarly describes this narrative, which values immigrant women "for having the courage to grasp freedom," as "the utopian rhetoric of national love anon" that feeds America's national vanity and offers critical reassurance of America's moral practice of freedom and democracy.[22]

It is certainly the logic of protecting the *immigrant, minority,* and *illegal* women that has allowed the foreign-born Asian American women I interviewed to exercise sexual agency in crafting their desires, images, and survival strategies by marrying white men. However, it is also this guise of a democratic and paternal discourse that provides men with a justification for gaining from the current racial, gender, and national hierarchies. As a result, these women, while giving the impression of choosing "freedom" when coming over to the United States and wedding a white man, have little choice except to engage in the roles of good wife and mother. When a "good society" is founded on the logic of patriarchy, the material and psychological entrapment of some women becomes inevitable. The discourse of protection and the myth of the model minority wife often generate contradictory gaps between the positive receptions of Asian American women and their subjugation to, and complicity with, the nationalist and patriarchal logic of America.

During their joint interviews, the five couples discussed in this chapter did not report any blatant racism, but most Asian American women reported individual encounters with racism. In other words, the public presence of white husbands served as a symbolic shield from the suspicion that these women might generate as immigrants, foreigners, or racial minorities. Thus, the public discourse of intermarriage between Asian American women and white men is based on the logic of patriarchy and nationalism, and illusorily perpetuates racial and gender hierarchies in which immigrant and minority women are seen as the recipients of approval and protection from their white husbands. Asian American interracial marriages can be positively perceived precisely because of this long-standing popular cultural discourse, in which white men, as ideal subjects, authorities, and citizens of the United States, *legitimize* foreign-born Asian American women as wives.

In these six families that included Asian American wives and white husbands, race was rendered invisible because often translated into a matter of culture and ethnicity. This was especially true with regard to the couples' children (with the exception of the daughter of Sachiko and George, who

married a black man). The couples' biracial children, especially those from
the more recent marriages, often were depicted in the interviews as positively
received by white mainstream society. The children were seen as having "less
of a problem" because of their racial invisibility, or perceived as unusually
valuable because of their "exotic" or "ambiguous" appearances. The couples
I interviewed referred to these children as "white," "Amerasian," "Eurasian,"
or "Asian American." Although Sachiko and Soonja reported their children
had sometimes faced racism in school (being called "Chinese" or "Chink"),
the couples who married in the 1980s and 1990s mentioned no such negative
incidents. All five white male parents expressed no concern about the race of
their children leading to difficulties with regard to schooling or employment.
Four out of five of these white men saw racism as an exclusively white–black
problem. All mentioned that their children had mostly white friends. In other
words, these parents expected their children to maintain the whiteness. Biracial
children of Asian American–white marriages are expected to assimilate into
white mainstream society as "white" and to exercise their cultural "privilege"
to craft their own racial identities in a U.S. multicultural society.

The typical marriage and family generally called "interracial" or "multiracial" by the couples interviewed are imagined by these couples as solely the
"white middle-class" normative family, wherein foreign-born Asian American
women are, as a model minority, expected to successfully learn white norms of
household maintenance and white disciplining styles, to repress their ethnic and
cultural origins, and to strive for American individualism. Intermarriage automatically moves the white man to a position of authority in a white middle-class
household; he can claim himself as a forerunner of multiculturalism, one who
still follows the intact imperative of American masculinity. But for foreign-born
Asian American women, intermarriage often stimulates amnesiac subordination to the patriarchal and national authority, and to the white privileges that
promise a white middle-class life. The imperative of multiculturalism tactfully
conceals such racial and gender-related differences and the machinations of
white male privilege.

Chapter 3　　　　　　A Woman Ascending

IF THE INTERRACIAL RELATIONSHIPS of foreign-born Asian American women reflect postcolonial/neocolonial gender dynamics, and if these relationships have somewhat reinforced the dominant images of Asian American–white marriage, nevertheless second-generation Asian American women flout such stereotypes of subservient femininity. Distancing themselves from stereotyped images of Asian femininity (but still fashioning themselves as "exotic" model minorities), second-generation Asian American women view the interracial relationship as a place to negotiate the racist gaze upon them and claim themselves as equal to whites. Possessing a white man becomes the strategic testimony to being different from racially subordinate or colonial subjects, and to being a part of the hegemonic orders of gender, class, and nation in which they imagine themselves to be independent, egalitarian, and upwardly mobile American women. If second-generation Asian American women see interracial relationships as a means to attain a modern subjectivity, how are their psychological investments in relationships gendered? How do such racialized images shape the gender dynamics of the couples? How do white men engage with the race of their partners?

It is also important to examine how a woman's upward mobility affects a white man's view of their relationship. This chapter explores how "successfully assimilated" second-generation Asian American women and their white partners negotiate ideologies of race, gender, class, and nation in interracial relationships. The chapter focuses on Asian American women's selection of white men in terms of the paradoxical juxtaposition of their own exercise of agency with their simultaneous reappropriation of, and conformity to, hegemonic discourses of race and gender.

This chapter has three parts. In the first section, "The Exotic and Upwardly Mobile Asian Women," I discuss three such Chinese American women and their white partners. These couples challenge mainstream stereotypes of Asian

American women as subordinates of whites by displaying such qualities as egalitarianism and the woman's success, ambition, and aesthetic signs of femininity.
The Chinese American women in these couples have aspired to be the equals
of whites, and, to reach this goal, have tactfully maneuvered racial and gender
ideologies. In the second section, "Aversion to Ethnic Patriarchy," I discuss how
a Chinese American woman's idealization of white masculinity derives from
her aversion to Chinese ethnic patriarchy. Because she saw white men as the
opposite of Asian American men, she looked at white men as her means to
self-liberation and her opportunity to attain ideal modern American womanhood. Finally, in the third section, "Aversion to Stereotypes," I discuss Chinese
American and Korean American women's aversions to these stereotypes, and
strategies for combating them.

The Exotic and Upwardly Mobile Asian Woman

From the late 1980s, with the rise of Asian countries as global economic powers,
Asia and *Asians* have been incorporated into the American imagination as
terms that signify a minority ascending economically, culturally, and aesthetically. Asian American residents' higher average income and higher average
level of education have further stabilized the image of Asian Americans as a
model minority. In my interviews, three Asian American women and their
white boyfriends positively employed such images and discourses and presented
the Asian American women as a successful and upwardly mobile subject. These
white men also perceived Asian women as possessors of ethnic moral values,
including a good work ethic and strong family values—values which they
perceived as lacking among white women of the same age.

DRIVEN BY ASCENDANCE, DEPLOYING
ASIAN AS CULTURAL CAPITAL

When I visited Victoria Chen and Paul Hoffman, they were just about to move
to a new home on the East Coast, where Victoria was attending medical school.
Paul recently bought their house in order to live with Victoria after a long-
distance relationship of nearly a year. Victoria described herself and Paul in
this way: "I'm very uptight. He's very relaxed." She talked in a fast high-pitched
voice, which contrasted with Paul's introverted quiet responses. Victoria,
a twenty-four-year-old Chinese American, said of their relationship, "It's so
common. All the Asian girls I know have gone out with white guys, basically."
She appeared to resent any suggestion that Asian American female–white male
couples might be perceived as unusual, emphasizing that these couples are now
not only common but even "normal."

Victoria met Paul, a twenty-four-year-old painter and entrepreneur, through a friend. When I met them, they had been dating for a few years. Paul had started his own business when he was twenty-one and now earned about $80,000 a year. Being self-employed allowed him free time to spend on such activities as backpacking and snowboarding in Colorado.

Raised by a homemaking mother and an engineer father, Paul praised Victoria's good family background as an important commonality between the two. As someone who valued family ties, he said he was willing to be a "stay-at-home father" in a projected future marriage with Victoria. Paul enjoyed playing golf with Victoria's father, and, for their next vacation, the couple planned to go to Hawaii with her parents.

During the interview, the couple also emphasized trust. "I trust Victoria more than anybody," said Paul. Victoria emphasized Paul's financial responsibility as a significant source of her own trust. "He can get basically whatever he wants," she said in an emphatic voice, referring to Paul's comfortable income. Paul had supported Victoria financially while she attended summer school. He had also flown her at least a couple of times each month from the East Coast to Texas when they were living apart.

Victoria was born in Hong Kong and moved to New York when she was a year old. Her father worked in a Chinese restaurant to support his family, and at the same time attended college as a full-time student. Victoria's mother worked as a hairdresser all her life, and now owns her own store. Victoria said: "I remember in New York, when we didn't have money, because we just arrived here from Hong Kong, we used to take people's furniture from outside thrown out to the street. We would bring it in. Because we had no money. We started from dirt poor. . . . Up until when I was ten, we were pretty poor. We didn't have a car for a long time. We just didn't have any money." After Victoria's father took a job as an engineer at one of the largest U.S. computer companies, in the mid-1980s, things changed dramatically. When she was about ten, "my dad started making more money. . . . We were middle class." Victoria spent most of her time as a teenager in a neighborhood with a white majority. Her friends were mostly white. Even though her family spoke both Cantonese and Mandarin, Victoria usually spoke English with her father (but Cantonese with her mother). She chose to speak English with her father "because [my] dad works for a big corporation and it's just easier for both of [us] to communicate in English."

In her individual interview, Victoria narrated her family's American-dream story, telling the events in precise chronological order as if she had repeated the story many times. Victoria talked passionately about how hard work eventually brought her family middle-class status, and referred to her father as her lifelong role model. "I knew how hard it was for my family to get here to the United States and to get to the point where they are now," said Victoria. When she was in junior high school, Victoria made the decision to go to medical school, and she said that she never let anything come before studying and the achievement of her goal. During the interview, she often raised her voice, tinged with a strong sense of pride, and made statements like "Anybody can do it." Victoria never complained that her parents enforced stricter discipline than the usual American family, including restrictions against having a boyfriend or spending too much time on the phone or in front of the television. "Career goals are very important. That has always been number one in my life." Victoria had no hesitation about expressing her ambitions.

Victoria emphasized her strong pride as a Chinese American, pride that flowed from the image of her father as hard-working and from her family's successful assimilation into the upper middle class.

> I'm proud of my culture. It's a lot about my culture and who I am because that Chinese determination got our family to the point it is now. I think Chinese people are very determined. The ones that make it to America are very hard-working. Chinese Americans are very hard-working. They study hard. They work hard. They deserve what they get. So I think that my culture has a lot to do with how successful I've been in school and attaining my goals. . . . So, me, I did really well in high school, graduated from college. I did really well in college, and now I'm in med school and I'm doing well.

Her presentation of herself as a successful and upwardly mobile Chinese American corresponds with the Asian model minority discourse. She strongly identified her success with her ethnicity.

However, Victoria also saw herself as equal to whites and never thought of herself as a minority. She said, "I never felt [like] an outsider before moving to Vermont." When Victoria moved to Vermont and attended a high school where "ninety-nine percent of students were whites," she first faced overt racial discrimination, in the form of name-calling and staring. Pawan H. Dhingra argues that second-generation Asian American professionals often see themselves as "'model Americans,' as opposed to 'model minorities,' since they had succeeded through playing by the rules established by the country."[1] Because of her educational attainment, work ethic, and middle-class values, as well as the neighborhood she grew up in, Victoria claimed, she should not have been treated as an outsider in a white-dominated school.

Victoria showed irritation about being seen as the same as the Asians she met in high school, since they had "just gotten there" from Asian countries.

"All people associated me with those Asians who have just gotten here. Those Asians weren't like me." Victoria emphasized her status as an "assimilated American," not an "Asian." "I think that Asians are seen as being shy and very quiet. I mean . . . I don't really fit that. I'm very loud and a lot more outgoing than most Asian people are . . . because I'm American."

Victoria's aversion to being seen as a foreign-born Asian derived from her aversion to whites' stereotypes of Asians as perpetual foreigners. Pyke and Johnson write, "As they [the second-generation Asian American women] are forced to work against racial stereotypes, they must exert extra effort at being outspoken and socially gregarious."[2] As a means of resisting popular negative stereotypes, Pyke and Johnson also found, second-generation Asian Americans believed that behaving like "white women"—exhibiting assertiveness, loudness, and independence, as opposed to behaving like "Asian women" (being submissive and quiet)—was empowering. In Pyke and Johnson's study, Asian American women strongly portrayed themselves as being authentic and true when they were with whites and acting like whites. In this process of identification with whites, second-generation Asian Americans commonly expressed their intolerance toward immigrant Asians and reinforced anti-immigrant sentiment, another author notes, because "immigrants are seen as fueling the stereotypes that have contributed to their conditional status as 'honorary' but 'not legitimate' Americans."[3] Thus, Victoria's disinterest in or disassociation from "other Asians," and her internalization of mainstream stereotypes of "incompetent" or "submissive" Asians, indicated a common "adaptive response" among second-generation Asian Americans.[4]

Victoria rejected the idea that race had had a negative impact on her interracial relationships. She mentioned that white men she had dated in the past, as well as their families, had had no problems with her race. Rather, she said, her being Asian was well regarded. "It's never been a problem for any guy that I'm Chinese. Their families are always very accepting. Because I think Asians in society are regarded as a good minority as far as we do well in school. Asians are just seen highly in the community. I think that it's actually a good thing [to be an Asian]." Victoria demonstrated what Palumbo-Liu calls the "New Orientalist discourse," in which Asians self-orientalize themselves to equate their "good" characteristics with modernity, and re-appropriate the model minority myth and Asian values selectively, consistent with the American Dream story.[5] In fashioning her self-image, Victoria emphasized her ambition and discipline but also presented herself as American so as to distance herself from negative Asian traits. Victoria spoke in a loud, defiant voice about how she was worthy of equal status in the eyes of whites.

Race and ethnicity mattered to Victoria as long as they meant traits considered positive within the mainstream culture. In the context of interracial relationships, Victoria saw her race as a form of social capital that attracted white men. Victoria talked about how Asian American women became desirable to white men. "It's almost popular for white guys to go out with Asian girls. I think it's very trendy. Because Asian culture has made a new revolution here. Like, a lot of dressing, the way people dress very Asian, like the dragons and red and silk. . . . I think it happened pretty recently." Victoria noted the image of Asian women as a "hypersexual minority," associating this image with the rise of the Asian economy, the appearance of the Asian aesthetic in popular culture and fashion, and the increase in exoticized images of Asian women in Asian film and other media—changes that, mostly, took place in the 1980s and 1990s. The incorporation of Asian values and Oriental fashions into mainstream American and Western consumer culture originated with the rise of Japan and other East Asian countries as economic powers in the late 1980s, and with the U.S. importation of large numbers of products from these countries. Kondo notes the subversive impact of Japanese fashion on American views of the Asian body in the early part of that decade: "Japanese clothing design enabled a valorization and eroticizing of Asian bodies as stylish in a contemporary way, rather than merely exotic or an inadequate imitation of Western bodies."[6] Victoria saw this "new revolution," the American fetishization of Asian-ness, as an opportunity for young Asian Americans to gain ascendancy in mainstream white culture. By self-orientalizing their appearance and values, and by imagining themselves as living the American Dream narrative, young Asian American women (like Victoria and the other women I interviewed) were able to present themselves as fashionable and exotic yet "real" and successful Americans.

Victoria's comments, however, reflected a largely white male–centered view of Asian American women. That is, she saw herself and other Asian Americans from a white male or hegemonic perspective, and implied that it was as "cool" for a white man to have an Asian girlfriend as for him to have a dragon-printed silk shirt. Just as the Asian "new revolution" was acceptable only within the model minority discourse, Asian American women were viewed as desirable and acceptable only as a reflection of the white male gaze.

Her parents had always told Victoria to marry either a Chinese man or a white man. Thus, Paul's race was acceptable to her parents, but she was surprised that they approved of his career as a painter. Victoria's mother used to tell her to "go out with a lawyer, doctor, or businessman" because "they can take care of you." Victoria rebelled against such a traditional idea of marriage.

"I don't need to go out with somebody like that, because I am already there," she said, emphasizing her professional career and expressing a view of herself as self-sufficient.

Regardless of her pride in being Chinese American, Victoria refused to date other Asians. "My preferences have been white guys," she asserted. Victoria's views of what constitutes Asian-ness reflected mainstream stereotypes. She possessed two ideas that she did not view as contradictory: first, Asian Americans like herself were a hard-working successful minority; second, Asian American men did not possess ideal masculinity. "I never dated an Asian guy. I think that Asian guys are not courteous to women. They are not as gentlemanly. . . . They don't know how to treat women nicely. I think that white men have more of an idea. . . . I'm also not very attracted to Asian men because Asian men are smaller. I don't want to go out with somebody that's smaller than me. Asian boys are just very small. I mean, not all—my brother is very tall. My brother is six-foot-two." My brother is very different. . . . My brother has gone out with white girls. He is very courteous to his girlfriend." In Victoria's mind, the Asian American man lacks physical and courtly masculinity; the white man possesses a more masculine build and more gallant manners. Victoria portrayed her brother as an exceptional Asian American, a man tall and courteous and who had a white girlfriend. In my interviews with Victoria and Paul, they each repeated that race did not matter; instead, they emphasized, the family one came from mattered most, in terms of one's ability to maintain their relationships successfully. Paul explained his white ex-girlfriend's unfaithfulness as the result of her coming from a broken family, with her mother having married five times. "A lot of white people are not from a good family. . . . If you are from a family that is really close to you, you usually have better morals and better self-esteem," said Paul. Victoria agreed, "It is not ethnicity, but it is the family that the person is coming from." She believed she had what many whites had not, a "good family" with Chinese values that taught her to treat others with respect, and said:

> I think that, with Asian culture, you are very appreciative of what others do for you. I always clean up after myself and I always offer to do dishes. . . . You should be very respectful and they don't have to have you over and they are not your servants to clean up after you. So if Paul's parents invite me over for dinner, then I would bring something over . . . just that they know that I'm thinking that, you know, thank you for letting me come over. But I don't think American kids do that. I don't think they think about anybody besides themselves.

Thus, Victoria and Paul agreed on the importance of coming from a so-called good family and possessing solid morals. Since she had such morals, Victoria said, she expected to be not only the equal of, but superior to, white women.

Victoria asserted her race not as a negative (a source of discrimination) but as a positive (a source of traits that made her an authentic American). She viewed whiteness not as an unapproachable ideal from which she should be excluded, but as a marker interchangeable with privilege in society, the privilege that she and her family deserved access to. To Victoria, her preference for white men was not unusual but was logically connected with her socioeconomic status, her high family values, her egalitarian expectations, and her desire for whiteness.

THE ASIAN AS AESTHETIC
AND UPWARDLY MOBILE SIGN OF FEMININITY

When I visited Peter's apartment, Vivian greeted me. She had long, blond-high-lighted black hair, and wore a small open-back draped tank top. She ushered me into the living room, where electronic sounds vibrated at fast speed. Peter, who had been recording new songs on several musical instruments in his room, came out to meet me. He was slim and stylish. In the couple interview that followed, Vivian was shy and quiet, while Peter talked and joked throughout. Vivian, like a little girl, leaned against Peter while he spoke, and would grab his arm, wanting to keep his attention on her.

Peter Davis, a twenty-seven-year-old multimedia designer and member of a jazz band, had met Vivian Kwan, a twenty-five-year-old Chinese American computer programmer, through a mutual friend a couple of years prior to the interview. His two older brothers were married to Asian American women. "There are four boys in my family. Strangely enough, one of them is gay, and the other three are with Asian women. But the other brother's husband is white. . . . It's just purely strange coincidence," laughed Peter. Asked about his first impression of Vivian, he said, "She was cute and intelligent." Peter grew up in a small town in the South, where "almost everybody is white." Over time, he developed a passion for rebelling against the white norm and a desire for difference.

Peter acknowledged that his desire to transgression the white homogeneity amid which he was raised contributed to his search for an ideal woman beyond white normative feminine figures. "We [Peter and his brothers] all tend to be more attracted to ideas and people who are more exotic," he said. "I think Asian features are prettier than white features. I tend to prefer darker-skinned women. The shapes of Asian eyes are I think really pretty, purely from an aesthetic point of view. I would notice Asian women a lot more than white women when they were around me." Peter made mostly techno and hip-hop music, but his tastes in social events ranged from black-tie parties to rave and underground hip-hop shows. His preference for Asian women related to his attraction to a range of hypermodern fashions and music, which he considered hard to share with white women. "That's what I'm into and I'm into more exotic underground type things, whereas that doesn't fit into the straight homogeneous white mainstream. . . . I need somebody who is a social chameleon. I think to a large degree Vivian is like that, more so than anybody else I have dated." By being "social chameleons," changing who they were through altering their appearance, Peter and Vivian enjoyed contesting white mainstream fashion, culture, and the normalcy of same-race couples. Peter viewed the Asian woman as an unsettled median between white and black, but in a positive way. "In the States, if you are dating Asian girls, probably it is cooler than if you are dating a black girl," he commented.

Peter was attracted to Asian women's hyperfeminine appearance, but, at a practical level, he did not equate Asian women with traditional femininity. He wanted to have a "relationship with somebody where you are equals," and he liked Vivian because "she is ambitious" (Vivian planned to go to medical school in a few years). He described his previous girlfriends who were white as "neurotic," "alcoholic," or "overly demanding," or as having "cheated" on him. Much as they were characterized by Victoria and Paul, white women were racialized negatively by Vivian and Peter as excessively dependent and lacking in self-discipline. Vivian, on the other hand, was "tenacious" and respected Peter's individual space and his life-style. Susan Koshy argues that white men choose "submissive" Asian American women as a "hyper-sexual model minority" because the men cannot deal with threats from white women. However, as seen in both Paul and Peter, white men racialize white femininity not as a marker of independence and egalitarianism but rather as a pathology of sexual promiscuity, lack of discipline, or poor family values.

Vivian Kwan came to the United States from Taiwan when she was two. She grew up in a traditional Chinese family in which both her mother and father worked, and, for thirteen years starting when she was five, went to a Chinese school every Saturday. Even though her parents wanted Vivian to date Chinese men, she had never done so. "I don't find very many Asian guys who I think are attractive," she said. According to Vivian, her mother did not have a problem as long as Vivian's boyfriend was either Chinese or white. "She says, oh, it's O.K. if you marry a foreigner. She called Peter a foreigner because he wasn't Chinese."

During the individual interview, Vivian, in addition to not revealing complicated feelings or describing personal problems, made it clear that she wanted to see her relationship with Peter as being between equals. She talked about Peter's intelligence, his good grades in college, and his upward economic mobility as important to her attraction to him. Avoiding any romantic language, Vivian said, in an aggressive tone, "We have a mental connection." She said, "When you think about it, would you date someone stupider than you? Most men can date dumb women, but most women can't date someone who's not smart." She emphasized her mental connection with Peter by saying, "I think we are equals." Equality for Vivian also meant being able to express her ideas and desires openly, a factor important for her because her parents' relationship "has always been restrained."

Although Peter and Vivian both enjoyed having "different" appearances and subversive public personas, they emphasized each other's professional ambitions, upward mobility, and work ethic as the main sources of their mutual attraction. Peter said, "I don't really think of this relationship as interracial. . . . In a lot of people's eyes, Asians are probably closer to being white than black." This fact arose, he felt, because of whites' and Asians' common socioeconomic status and a shared emphasis on education and upward mobility. Even "thousands of years of Asian culture that is so different from American culture" could not obscure these similarities. But, though Asian-white relationships were not a problem, according to Peter, black-white relations could be. For him, having grown up in a region where "there is a lot of racial tension between blacks and whites," racial difference meant negative and destructive opposition between racial groups. He remembered his uncle refusing to let his daughter and her black boyfriend into the house. Peter said his family would have a problem if he had a relationship with a black woman.

Peter sometimes noticed that he and Vivian received stares from Asian men; he interpreted this as Asian men's "territorial" hostility toward white men "who encroach on their women." Vivian also noticed this, but did not discuss its possible meanings. In the interviews, many respondents, both Asian American and white, reported such a "gaze" or "stare" from Asian American men. This certainly may reflect the "homosocial competition" in which men evaluate each other's manhood by assessing the women they possess.[7] Yet it may also indicate Asian American men's frustration with Asian American women's selection of white men, a choice that reflects a masculine social order that privileges white manhood over Asian American manhood. Erica Chito Childs discusses black women's resentment of black men who date or marry white women, arguing that it stems from society's devaluation of black womanhood and the black community's consequent belief in negative images of black women.[8] From this perspective, the Asian men's gaze at the couple might involve more than envy or jealousy; it might derive from these men's frustration with, and disempowerment as a result of, a racialized masculine hierarchy.

Vivian remembered hearing occasional negative racial slurs against her or her friends when she was growing up. "Somebody called me a 'chink' or called a friend of mine 'gook' or something rude like that," she said. Peter responded, "Usually comments like that come from either frat boys or rednecks. It's either people who are ignorant, from small towns, or people who choose to be ignorant." When Vivian cautiously continued by saying, "People may be just polite enough not to use a racial slur," Peter interrupted her and minimized her concerns about racism. Peter also looked down on the mainstream idea that an interracial relationship is not the norm: "I just don't understand why anybody wouldn't hang out with everybody. . . . Interracial children seem to be some of the most beautiful in the world. I think it's some kind of indication that people should probably not be so exclusive." This was an interesting exchange, because I found that white men I interviewed often did not understand Asian American women's personal experiences of racism, and subtly disassociated themselves from their partners' racist anecdotes. Even though Peter genuinely deplored the racism Vivian encountered, his view of racism as a problem only occurring among ignorant whites underlined his own white privilege and did not help to generate any effective strategies to address her concerns. Likewise, his optimistic reference to biracial children as a beautiful outcome of interracial marriage reiterated the hegemonic ideology of intermarriage as "the utopian rhetoric of national love anon."[9] Instead of facing racial problems as historical and structural issues, Berlent says, the utopian images of intermarriage minimize our concerns about racism and suggest, as a perfect solution, the culmination of interracial sexual desires in traditional heterosexual marriage.[10]

Although Peter pursued a nonconformist lifestyle and was attracted to the "exotic" look of Asian American women as a sign of difference from the mainstream, he seemed in many respects searching for someone like himself. Ultimately Vivian's race was immaterial because she possessed American values, such as upward mobility, that were similar to his. For many whites, model minority Asians are now welcome allies.

MARRYING A WHITE MAN, MARRYING DOWN

In Asian American–white intermarriage, Asian American women have been often seen as *marrying up*. This view assumes Asian American women's lower or inferior position with regard to race, class, and gender, in relation to white men. Such an assumption perpetuates the power difference between Asian American women and white men, and reinforces the subordinate status of

Asian Americans as "forever un-assimilable foreigners" lacking social status and power in American society.

In the case of a third-generation Chinese American woman, Rebecca, and her white fiancé, Matt, her family saw the marriage as problematic not so much because of his race but because of his low income and lesser education. Whites still maintain social and cultural privileges in their institutional opportunities, but when an Asian American woman with class status and a good education marries a white man who lacks equal status, the power dynamics shift. It can be the white man who is seen as subordinate, and who must struggle to attain approval from the upper-class (Asian) family.

Matt, a twenty-eight-year-old writer, became engaged to Rebecca, a twenty-one-year-old third-generation Chinese American student. At the time of the interview, they were living together and were planning to marry in a few months, upon her graduation. Matt, once an English and philosophy major in college, had dropped out a few years prior to the interview, and worked part-time at a local pizza store. He was working on a science fiction novel which he referred to as his "redemption project," a book about self-searching and personal growth.

Matt met Rebecca through a friend, a few years after his first marriage ended in divorce. He described his first impression of Rebecca in deracialized and degendered terms. "I thought she was a very smart and very happy person. Always smiling . . . which makes it harder for me not to be happy." But Rebecca's parents disapproved of the match. Matt acknowledged his lacking "successful" masculinity as a cause: "I am not what they wanted. Her parents wanted me to be a Chinese professional, preferably doctor, lawyer. They are very practical people, very concerned with having money to have family. . . . I am pretty far from that. I am white. I am not Christian. I am very nonmaterial, and I don't have a college degree. I deliver pizzas." However, he explained that his lack of successful traits was the result of his choices. Matt was averse to being driven by the idea of material success and competitive individualism, the core values of American culture.

Growing up in a traditional white lower-middle-class family, Matt had always been distant from his parents. He and his family had seen psycho-therapists since he was twelve, when his mother had tried to kill herself. Matt remembered his reluctance to talk to the therapists. Withdrawn from his family and revolting against American culture, Matt turned to Eastern religions such as Hinduism to search for meaning in life. "I don't really like American culture. People care too much how they look. By certain types of cars, houses, they try to impress other people to make themselves feel good. I think it is damaging to your development as a person."

Rebecca described herself as "unusually outspoken and opinionated for a female in Chinese culture." She described herself as having "no patience with nonintelligent people," talked vigorously and efficiently, and dominated the couple interview. She grew up in a very traditional Chinese family in which entrepreneurship was valued; her grandfather immigrated to the United States in the late 1940s, when Asian immigrants were restricted, and started a restaurant business. Her father worked as an engineer for a large computer company and also operated his own real-estate business. Since her brother, another computer engineer, did not want to take over these family businesses, Rebecca planned to.

Like Victoria, Rebecca grew up with the idea of strong ethnic pride and strict discipline. "If you didn't do whatever parents told you, you were bad kids. You got to be punished." Rebecca emphasized that the Chinese ideas of respect and discipline in parent-child relationships differed from those seen in the American family, which emphasizes "free individuals." (Her grandmother often spanked Rebecca by "using the end of the feather duster, the bamboo," until Rebecca cried.) Rebecca had much to say about how her family had "made it in America" through ethnic pride, familial ties, and the strength they gained from overcoming immigrant hardships. She emphasized her respect for her family as differing from what Americans feel for their families, a view that seemed to correspond to Matt's criticisms of the dominant American culture.

Rebecca described Matt as intelligent, and a nonconformist in that he differed from the mainstream culture, which valued appearances and material possessions most. Rebecca also said she could be expressive in her relationship with Matt *beyond* what was allowed by the traditional gender norms of "being a girl" that she grew up with. She said that, in Chinese and Asian culture, "as a girl, you are not supposed to say certain things and dance around." Regardless of her claims of being assertive and loud, she admitted to having such a girlhood side. She said her relationship with Matt changed her habit of silencing her views. "He said, it's not going to hurt my feelings, it's not going to make me want to break up."

Despite all the positives in their relationship, Rebecca's family had a hard time in accepting Matt as a suitable marital partner for Rebecca. "They [her parents] were disappointed because he is older. He is white. He had been married before and divorced. He is not Christian. He wants to be a writer. He is not working for the corporation. . . . All these things, you know. It was very odd. The only thing that really fit was he was very intelligent." In the beginning, no one in her family accepted the idea of Rebecca's marriage to Matt. "For three or four months, we couldn't talk about it without one of us either yelling at each other or crying," said Rebecca. Her sister-in-law called her "a bad daughter" for her "selfish" decision to marry someone her parents did not know, since "you are supposed to ask permission." Rebecca's mother, who married at the age of seventeen and remained a housewife, was concerned that Rebecca would miss out on career opportunities and higher education, as her marriage caused her to do.

Rebecca's mother did not understand why her daughter did not want to marry a Chinese man, but Rebecca had never dated Asian men. She viewed Asian men as too "feminine" to deal with her, and dated mostly whites and a couple of blacks. She said, "Asian guys like quiet girls. They are also kind of quiet. I think they get scared because I am so vocal, talkative, and opinionated." Rebecca did not hesitate to ask men out for a date. She in fact asked an Asian man out a couple of times. "I am really forward. I don't play the girl game. . . . They would get kind of taken aback and didn't know what to do with that."

Before Matt, Rebecca had dated a white man who "had a long history of rice chaser." In other words, he had only dated Asian girls, and, according to Rebecca, "I used to get some crap from dating him." Since then, she had followed her brother's advice: "You got to watch out for those white people who show up at the Chinese Bible studies." By that, he meant that white men who acted like they knew Chinese culture or showed great interest in Chinese culture were highly suspicious, as they might have a sexual fetish or other ulterior motive for dating, and perhaps mistreating, Asian women.

Such experiences indeed illustrate the difficulties Asian American women face in the mainstream dating scene as they have long been stereotyped as being hypersexual, submissive, or willing to please white men. Even highly educated and native-born Asian American women are warned to use extra caution so as not to encourage white men with such motives as possible dates.

Matt's lack of upward mobility and class status, and his not being Christian, were big hurdles to clear in winning over Rebecca's family. Thus, not only was his manhood marginal in American society; it was also disapproved of by her Chinese American family. Her parents also strongly opposed her sister's marriage with a Filipino American man, Rebecca noted, and they did not even attend the wedding. It was partly a religious difference between Protestantism and Catholicism, she added, but she viewed it also as deriving from hierarchies and animosities among different Asian American ethnic groups.

> There is a hierarchy in Asian ethnicities. Chinese regards themselves the best among all. Korean regards themselves the best. . . . Vietnamese, Laos, Cambodian are the bottom basement of Asian. . . . Also, Koreans have the reputations for being the wife-beaters, or very domineering.

Japanese have been very tight-fisted. And Vietnamese, Laos, Cambodians, they are really flashy with their money. . . . So they [her parents]
concluded you should marry Chinese because Chinese husbands are
good money managers but flexible enough. I imagine that lots of Korean
grandmothers saying the same things about Chinese people.

Although Rebecca did not identify herself with such stereotypes, she saw
animosities among Asian ethnicities as strong enough to cause difficulties in
achieving a pan-Asian coalition or in leading families of each ethnic group to
support intraethnic marriages.

Rebecca's parents eventually did come around to Matt and Rebecca's
union. "The fact that they ended up accepting the marriage is phenomenal,"
Rebecca said. Matt made an effort to fit in, describing himself as different
from "a lot of Westerners" who "disrespect Eastern cultures and philosophies
as 'cultures of the Third World countries.'" Matt talked about his struggle
to present himself correctly in front of Rebecca's family, saying, for example,
how embarrassing it was for him to forget the custom of taking off one's
shoes, at Rebecca's parents' house. "The worst thing in Chinese culture
is to be selfish and ungrateful," Matt said. "I am trying to be aware that
there are probably things that I'm doing that are rude to them. So I try
to be consciously polite whenever I speak with them." Rebecca said her
parents ended up liking Matt because "he is very honest and genuine. He
is intelligent and wise at the same time." But her parents wanted him to at
least convert to Christianity.

Rebecca possessed bargaining power over Matt, who saw himself, and who
was also seen by her family, as lacking power. His interest in Eastern knowledge
may have contributed to his lack of interest in dominating Rebecca or her
family. But the marginal masculinity resulting from his lack of upward mobility,
and his dissatisfaction with the hegemonic values of American culture, left him
with few options other than striving to respect and please her successful family.
In the household Rebecca and Matt had just started, Rebecca mostly managed
the cooking. But she expected her marriage to be egalitarian, as she was the
one in charge of the money.

In Rebecca and Matt's relationship, the racial issue became secondary
to the issue of social class. Yet, whiteness was also racialized. Whiteness is
a desirable object as long as it comes with normative socioeconomic status.
But when a white man lacks such a crucial dominant trait, his whiteness
has inadequate power to compensate for that lack of social standing. Race
may have the least impact on gender dynamics in a situation in which a
white man lacks upward mobility and his Asian American woman partner
has greater upward mobility. Another couple I interviewed, Jennifer Ryu, a

twenty-year-old Chinese American student, and Daniel Tyler, a twenty-two-year-old white factory worker, had encountered family opposition similar to that which Rebecca and Matt faced. Jennifer's parents strongly disagreed with her relationship with Daniel because he had no college education. Jennifer expressed her frustration not only with her parents' opposition but also with Daniel's denial of it. "I told him my parents don't like him because he hasn't gone to college. He said, no, maybe that's part of it, but I think because I am white." Daniel, she is saying, used racial difference as an excuse to deny the powerlessness deriving from his lack of education or high-income job, and blamed her family as the problem. Race can be used deliberately as a claimed source of "difference" when a racial minority's higher class status becomes threatening to whites.

While Rebecca and Matt criticized the emphasis on *appearance* in American culture, they praised the appearance of biracial children as the "best aspect of interracial marriage." Matt asserted that interracial couples have "cute babies. They look like anime [characters]." Rebecca joined in, saying, "Every single child I have met that's half-Chinese, half-white, they are pretty." She described her niece, the child of her sister and the sister's Filipino American husband, as beautiful because of the girl's "big eyes and caramel color." Lauren Barlant discusses a 1993 cover of *Time* magazine that portrayed "the future face of America" as a female cyborg symbolizing "mixed race but still 'white enough' children"; in this example, future racial mixing was imagined under the continual hegemony of whiteness.[11] So, despite Matt's lack of socioeconomic power, his whiteness certainly retained the power and the privilege, in this couple's imagination, to produce beautiful children who would succeed in a future multiracial America.

Aversion to Ethnic Patriarchy

Many second-generation Asian American women whom I interviewed commented negatively on their parents' marriages, when compared either to their own relationships or to mainstream white norms, as having lacked exchanges of affection, verbal communication, and gender equality. Just as mainstream culture has defined intimacy as a place to develop expressive individualism, the young second-generation Asian Americans I interviewed saw intimacy as romantic, egalitarian, emancipatory,[12] and indeed a source of expressive individualism.[13] They considered the traditions of ethnic patriarchy in which they grew up as deviant from those of mainstream romantic marriage, and equated dating white men with liberation from the constraints of such traditions.

White Man as Liberator

Grace Wong, a twenty-four-year-old computer engineer, welcomed me into her brand-new condo, which she had just purchased. She pushed her hair, cut into a stylish short bob, behind her ears with her fingers. In the corner of the living room, old furniture that she was fixing leaned against the pastel pink wall. At the time of the interview, she had been with Jacob, a twenty-six-year-old project manager in the computer industry, for a couple of years. Grace described Jacob as "affectionate and a gentleman" and "dependable." She enjoyed spending time doing outdoor activities, including cycling, with Jacob. He was also a hard worker, which was important to her. She had dated a few white men who had ambitions to be great, she said, yet turned out to be "really lazy."

Grace was born in Taiwan and came to the United States soon afterward. When her family first reached this country, they had a hard time economically. Her father helped out in his family's business for a while, but was also a day trader and "lived by stocks" for a long time. Grace's mother worked at a jewelry store full-time from the time they arrived. "When we were younger, our family was pretty poor. We were pretty frugal and we fixed things up. My parents always told us we have hands so we would be able to work, to fix things and create things." Grace pointed out the old furniture she was working on. "That's sort of, like, just from growing up and doing those things," she said.

Grace, after a moment's pause, started to talk about her father in a bitter tone. "I think the reason why my sisters and I, we date outside of our race, is because my mother herself is pretty unhappy with her marriage." (Her older sister dated a black man, and Grace and her younger sister had dated white men.) Grace's mother worked all her life and took care of the children. Her father "is very quiet and withdrawn. He thinks that our personal lives are my mom's responsibility." He "controls the money my mother makes," did not allow her to spend money, and "bullies her around." Grace resented the fact that her father neglected her mother and controlled all the family members. "He never gave her anything as a present, not for her birthday and not for Christmas, nothing. . . . I hate my dad." Grace's father went out with his friends, often until past midnight. Even though these seemed the standard cultural privileges of Chinese men, Grace can't forgive the fact that her mother "is alone" all the time.

Grace's mother usually suppressed her anger about her husband, but she did sometimes complain about him to her daughters. "I feel very, very sad when she tells me things like that. . . . I don't want to end up like her. I don't want that to happen to me. . . . I don't feel like I can do anything about it. Sometimes she gets really sad, I can tell."

When Grace listened to her mother, she adopted her mother's unhappiness, sadness, and powerless anger as her own, and directed these feelings against the Asian masculine norm by which her father maintained authority. "My father is the opposite of what I want. Just because I can see the pain that my mother goes through." Grace expressed great aversion to her parents' unequal gender pattern. She transferred her negative image of her father, along with her mother's anger, onto the Asian American males around her. Grace remembered what her mother used to tell her: "Once in a while, she would say American guys are just a lot more polite, and they are so much nicer. They treat women so much more fairly." Her mother's unhappiness provided Grace with emotional and psychological validation of her employment of the hegemonic view that white men are better than Asian men.

Her selection of white males also provided her with a psychological outlet for her vengeance against ethnic patriarchy. She defied Asian masculinity, arming herself with the racial and gender power of white masculinity. By connecting with white male privilege, she was seeking a form of empowerment through which she could testify to the injustice of Chinese male oppression. Grace's aversion to Asian ethnic patriarchy colluded with negative stereotypes to bolster the hegemonic view of white male privilege, thus making it difficult for her to criticize white male sexism.

Through her aversion to ethnic patriarchy, Grace also identified with stereotypes of Asians as feminine. Although Grace masculinized Asian American men as domineering like her father, she at the same time emasculated them as incapable of dealing with "independent women" like herself. "I am not attracted to Asian guys. . . . They are not gentlemen. . . . They are not affectionate. At least the ones I've met. I think my personality clashes with a lot of them, because I think I'm too independent. I'm too outgoing. I'm just too myself kind of a person. A lot of Asian guys like Asian women. . . . Either they are dainty or they are pretty or they are very almost like submissive in a way." This is the most common view of Asian American men that I observed among second- or later-generation Asian American women. Like Rebecca, Grace perceived Asian American men as incapable of dealing with the so-called masculine characteristics she embodied, such as independence and assertiveness. Grace said, "I feel Asian guys are intimidated by me. So they would never approach me." Asian American men were presented as dating only quiet and submissive Asian American women. Grace effeminized both Asian American men and Asian American women stereotypically as quiet and submissive, while depicting herself as clearly different. Although her aversion to gender inequality in her family was one reason she embraced white masculinity over Asian masculinity, her aversion to Asian men also evidently derived from negative stereotypes.

As Pyke and Johnson observed, many second-generation Asian American women identify with mainstream white womanhood, express an aversion to Asians, and describe themselves as more white than Asian: "The glorification of white femininity and controlling images of Asian women can lead Asian American women to believe that freedom and equity can be acquired only in the white-dominated world. . . . The perception that whites are more egalitarian than Asian-origin individuals and thus preferred partners in social interaction further reinforces anti-Asian racism and white superiority."[14] Rather than criticize negative stereotypes of Asian women, Grace distanced herself from these negative stereotypes by claims of her own uniqueness. Second- or later-generation Asian American women often emphasize their differences from stereotypical Asian women; many cite white men's comments about them as evidence of their uniqueness, just as Grace did. "All the white guys loved me because I am not submissive. This guy thought I was really cool, and he was like, 'I'm glad you are not submissive because I wouldn't be able to have this conversation with you, and have arguments.'"

Grace's mother looked favorably on her relationship with Jacob, and often made comments to Grace about Jacob's physical features. "My mom is like, oh, he has such pretty eyes!" Grace also believed that white men's appearance was more attractive than that of Asian American men. "If the guy is good looking, he is lot more self-confident. . . . I think a lot of Asian guys, they feel inferior to Caucasian guys. I think they feel like they try hard to make up for their looks. So instead of being super nice to the girl, they act bitter and so they are all like, trying to act macho." Several of Grace's Asian female friends mostly dated white men, some dated Hispanics, and one dated an Asian man "that was tall." Grace, that is, expressed aversion to Asian American men's masculine presentation as compensatory masculinity, and she rejected this gender strategy as rude and domineering.

The racialized image of white men provided Grace with imaginative empowerment. By obtaining recognition from her white boyfriend, Grace said, she gained strength and confidence in relation to Asian authority in general and to her father in particular. Having never seen her mother disagree with or express disapproval to her father, Grace, while growing up, never raised her voice to him, either, and learned not to express her point of view to him. Grace talked about Jacob as thus a source of personal change for her, as he helped her become more willing to vocally express her opinions. "Ever since I was young, you know, you don't talk back to your elders. You don't say in front of their face, like, or you don't disagree with them. . . . I would keep it to myself. But with Jacob, though, he would tell me, 'Why don't you tell him no?' In their culture, it's OK to speak up and disagree with, or even yell. . . . Back then I would keep it to myself. I wouldn't say anything to my father. But now, I would tell him 'No' or . . . 'What are you talking about?' It's a big change."

Grace described Jacob as a rational thinker, a patient listener, and a dependable partner. She felt that, with his support, her confidence in her ability to express herself and in her right to do so have grown dramatically. This was a confidence and assurance that Grace's mother never knew in her relationship with her husband. Grace not only intentionally embraced white masculinity and identified with hegemonic individuality, but even saw Jacob as a liberator who freed her from ethnic constraints and patriarchal dominance. Yet such so-called dependence on, or expectations for, a white man as a source of her personal growth could also feed white men's view of Asian American women as obedient and passive.

Grace's rejection of Asian American men represented both her aversion to repeating her parents' unequal relationship and her desire to identify with the image of independent womanhood, an image that she felt Asian American men could not accept. Inevitably, Grace also saw her mother as a powerless feminine figure, and avoided identifying with her powerlessness, through rejecting Asian American women as "quiet" and "submissive." Her aversion to Asian American men, even though it originated in a resistance to Chinese patriarchy, was in keeping with hegemonic stereotypes of these men. Grace's contemptuous view not only of Asian American men but also of Asian American women as submissive and dainty reinforced mainstream negative views of Asians and Asian Americans in general.

Aversion to Stereotypes

Although the controlling images of Asian women as hypersexual and submissive have been criticized, how such images operate in actual relationships and how they influence Asian American women's perceptions of themselves have not been explored. Like Victoria and Grace, some women I interviewed adopted only the positive images of Asians, distancing themselves from the negative ones as inapplicable to themselves. It is often difficult for an individual woman to consciously observe a man's motives, his imposition of stereotypes, and her willingness to conform to such images, but the following stories illustrate Asian American women who expressed an aversion to white men who fetishized and commodified Asians. Although frustrated with her boyfriend's apparent "Asian fetish," Irene did not express this view to him; Lisa, resenting her former boyfriend and the stereotypes he believed about Asian American women, tried to find a partner among Asian American men.

WHITE MAN WITH AN ASIAN FETISH

Irene Huan, a twenty-five-year-old Chinese American and a film major, was born and grew up in the United States. When I met her, she had her hair cut very short and wore cat-eye glasses. Irene told me she was busy working part-time as a waitress at a topless bar (waiting tables, but not dancing). Due to time constraints, I was able to interview her and her boyfriend Brian only individually, not as a couple.

Among all the second- or later-generation Asian American women I met with, Irene was the only one whose parents had divorced, and whose father encouraged her to date only white men. After the divorce, which took place when she was sixteen, Irene's mother went back to Taiwan. She blamed herself for being a bad wife and, as a divorced woman, was isolated from the Chinese community. Irene used to go to Taiwan to see her mother once a year, but at the time of our interview, she communicated with her mother only by telephone. "I'm not very close to my family," she said. Irene's father was an engineer in the computer industry. She described him as "very unconventional and very liberal," a man who took political stands against mainland China. He had lived with a white woman for several years, at the time that I met Irene. He once told Irene not to date or marry Asian men, and he himself only dated white women. "I remember him telling me, 'I never want you to ever marry an Asian guy.' And I was like, 'Why?' He goes, 'Well, I know how they are, and I don't want you to marry an Asian.'"

Unlike her father, Irene was interested in Chinese culture, especially in terms of finding her cultural origins, and this desire became stronger after her mother left for Taiwan. Although born in the United States, Irene told me, she had always felt "foreign" and lacked a sense of belonging. She had traveled to fifteen countries—including France, where she had lived for a year. "When I go back to Taiwan, I don't really feel like I fit in there. But when I'm here, I don't feel like I'm fitting in here. . . . I'm not 100 percent. . . . I'm American. . . . I was born here, but I'm still a minority." Irene felt that she would never be the same as white people in this country. She remembered how her past boyfriends' families would react to her; her comments, which follow, demonstrate how the stereotypes of Asians as perpetual foreigner influenced her view of herself.

> They always treat you the same way. They treat you as someone Asian first before they treat you as American. I remember so many times going to my boyfriends' houses for Thanksgiving. You know, my ex-boyfriend's mother has a place setting for everyone; in my place, there were chopsticks. I felt uncomfortable with that. Of course they always

ask you questions like—you know, my name is Irene—how do you get that name? It's just unusual for a Chinese girl to have that name, you know. How long have you been in the States? Stuff like that. You have to react politely.

Although she expressed strong resentment of white families' views of her as a foreigner, she had to suppress such negative emotions, around them, to be polite. Irene said she had tried to find the most comfortable place and person with whom to be; even though she had usually dated whites, she did not view race as a priority in choosing her dates. She had not taken her father's advice not to date Asian men; one ex-boyfriend was a twenty-three-year-old Vietnamese student.

> There was a while when I wanted to marry someone Asian if I was going to get married. I think, growing up in America as an Asian person, every Asian kind of goes through that phase. Especially if you grow up around a lot of white people, you never dated anyone of the same race. And you finally do that. It's kind of weird. Of course you can talk of the same kind of background. You can relate in certain ways about the cultures. But again it also just depends on the background. . . . Those guys I dated, regardless of our cultural similarities, you know, we still have a lot of differences.

Irene found that this ex-boyfriend was too much of a "traditional Asian guy" for her. He segregated himself, having relationships only with Asian people, and he became hostile to Irene's non-Asian friends. "I grew up around a lot of white people. Most of my friends are white. I have a lot of Asian friends, too. He was the kind of person, he is like, I just don't like white people. He didn't like to talk to white people. He's kind of very close-minded about that. So he knew he wanted to date, he wanted to marry, an Asian woman."

It is clear that Irene expressed her aversion to racial animosity against whites among young Asian American men but, instead of exploring the reasons for this hostility toward white people, viewed it as Asian close-mindedness. Despite the fact that she dated this man for a year, Irene was hesitant to call him a boyfriend. "I never considered him really as my boyfriend. I knew that he wasn't the one for me."

Irene met her current boyfriend, Brian Thompson, a twenty-six-year-old law student, at a club. "I remember the first thing he said was, he asked about my tattoo and he thought it was Kanji. It's just insects. But, from far away, it looks like a Chinese character." Brian told her that he was thinking about getting a tattoo on his back saying "Shiao-Guei," little ghost. "In Chinese, we call white people ghosts because they are white," Irene explained to me. But when she found out that his Chinese ex-girlfriend had given him the nickname, she reacted strongly, and turned him down at first when he asked for her phone number. She thought, "Oh no, he likes Asian girls. I didn't like dating guys like that. No, not at all." Irene explained that she always tried to avoid white men who came to Asian women with a set of stereotypical beliefs. From a very young age, she had been aware that certain white men exoticized and sexualized Asian women because they are Asian, and she had avoided going out with these men. "Growing up Asian, you inevitably meet guys like, oh, I love Asian culture. . . . I hate that." Irene raised her voice when she added, "I had made this conscious decision not to date a guy that was interested in Asian women."

However, she eventually changed her mind and called Brian, and, at the time of this interview, they had been in a relationship for three months. "He is very smart. I like intelligent people," said Irene. On the other hand, she still struggled with the fact that Brian had only dated Asian girls and was, in fact, particularly attracted to Asians. Irene tried not to think too much about whether his liking for Asian women could be called a fetish. "That's what his idea of beauty is, so that's acceptable. . . . He finds a certain type of person attractive. . . . There's nothing you can do about it logically," she said. But she suspected that Brian liked all girls who were Asian. "That's another one of the weird suspicions when you date a guy that likes Asian girls a lot, because you think he is indiscriminant about it. And he's always making these comments. There would be some girls at a club. He would be like, 'Oh, she is really cute,' some Asian girl. She is totally not attractive. I would be like, 'OK, you know . . . she is cute because she is Asian?'" Brian had almost too many female Asian friends, she thought, and knew so much about Chinese, Korean, and Japanese cultures in part because those were the cultures of his former girlfriends.

Every time Brian mentioned his knowledge of Asian cultures, Irene felt ambivalent about his attraction to her. "Sometimes I ask myself if it is because I'm Asian that he's attracted to me. Because I know that, initially, of course, that's what it was. But sometimes I kind of ask myself if that is the only reason why. I know it is not. But in the back of your head . . ." Irene also expressed resentment about how white men seemed to "lump" all Asian cultures and people together and were sometimes oblivious to her specifically Chinese origins. When Brian pointed out certain Asian characters in a movie or talked excitedly about a Japanese film he saw, Irene remembered Seth, the man she had dated several years before. Seth often told Irene how fascinated he was by Japanese culture and girls. Irene compared this to talking about Mexican culture to a Colombian, "because Chinese culture and Japanese culture are different." Irene continued, "People basically think all the groups are similar, and they all think the same way." Irene questioned whether Brian cared about what she thought, when he said, "We should really go and see this Japanese film." She sighed. "I was sort of like, OK, but not because it's my culture and I need to see it. Because it's not my culture."

Such an imposition of stereotypes, coupled with Brian's lack of awareness that he was imposing them, was problematic. Irene felt she was racialized or excessively exoticized as an Asian American woman in her relationship with Brian. Her sense of herself as a "perpetual foreigner" was reinforced by the otherness and foreignness she felt in her relationship with Brian. Responding to my questions about difficulties in the relationship, Irene spoke of "being made to feel that you are different." She sensed that she served as a pleasurable and exotic sign or object, similar to the characters in Asian stories and films, for Brian and other men who, she sensed, exoticized Asian media and culture. In her interactions with Brian, she was annoyed to be expected to live up to his exotic ideal. She said that men like Brian wanted a girlfriend who was "different" rather than "just a white girl," while she preferred to simply be a person in a human relationship. Yet, she did not express her annoyance to Brian.

Irene was highly aware of, and even cautious about, the fact that Asian American women as well as Asian culture could be commodified and stereo-typed as *exotic* by white men, and that white men could act on such stereotypes. She felt she was alienated in her relationship with Brian not because of a different mode of beliefs or thinking, but because of white men's fascination with "different" appearances and exotic manners. She wanted relationships based more on sameness, but knew that it was her racial difference in large part that fascinated Brian. Nevertheless, she thought she would go to Los Angeles with him when he started working as a lawyer there in a couple of months.

During my interview with Brian, he was friendly and talkative, but he responded to my questions carefully. He was eager to talk about how he had always felt excluded from the Asian families of the women he had dated. Brian liked the fact that Irene only spoke English with her father, since he did not feel left out. He described his first impression of Irene: "She is very pretty." Brian said she was "very different" from any other Asian women he had dated. Besides mentioning her having tattoos and a job at a topless bar, Brian spoke of her father's dissimilarity from the fathers of his previous girlfriends: "Her dad has long hair . . . the appearance of an outdoor type. He wears like an Alaska T-shirt or something. . . . Traditional Chinese parents that I've met were more standoffish. At least, they tended to be more reserved."

In contrast with Irene, Brian's ex-girlfriend, a Korean American woman, had lived in a segregated community in which he had always felt "excluded on purpose." Brian was not allowed to see this woman's parents; "I mean, they are Korean American. She was born here and raised here. They are American. But . . . they always speak Korean to each other. . . . It was very inaccessible. . . . She never told her parents she was dating me. We dated a year." By saying that they were American, Brian was making the point that they could have communicated with him in English and welcomed him into their community with more civility. He said this bitter experience had made him not want to date another Korean woman. "I kind of said to myself that I'm not going to date Korean girls anymore. It's like dating a black girl." He did not understand why he was excluded from the community, and the couple perhaps did not communicate about such racial tensions in depth. Instead of coming to understand that their views of him might result the history of the United States and Korea, or the history of sexual exploitation by American GIs of Korean sex workers,[15] Brian interpreted his girlfriend's family's and friends' reaction as close-mindedness and indicative of Korean Americans' feelings of racial superiority toward whites. He explained: "Because there's sort of a racial superiority that Koreans felt they were the best in the world. Marrying a white person is like marrying a second class. Her parents always said that they would be so embarrassed if she married a white person, because it would just make them look bad in front of their friends, all of their Korean friends, Korean community . . . it sucks. These people never met me before. I'm a good person . . . I'm successful. I am making a lot of money."

Brian was frustrated because his genuine attempt to approach the Korean American community and his ex-girlfriend's family, and his hope of developing empathic understanding between him and the Korean Americans, were rejected. Race easily fuels the tension between whites and racial minorities when each holds onto the *difference* discourse of race and whiteness. This is strongly expressed in Brian's resentment. Even though Brian's victimization by the narrowmindedness of his ex-girlfriend's family might have been the major cause of racial tension, his reluctance to see his own race from other racialized positions and his reliance on color-blindness also worked to give this tension no solution. The discourse of color-blindness prevented him from further reflecting upon the Korean American community's negativity toward him.

Charles Gallagher argues that whites often define race only as a cultural symbol, since it "allows whites to experience and view race as nothing more than a benign cultural marker that has been stripped of all forms of institutional, discriminatory or coercive power,"[16] and this "color-blindness allows whites to believe that segregation and discrimination are no longer an issue because it is illegal for individuals to be denied access to housing, public accommodations, or jobs because of their race."[17] In Brian's color-blind view of himself as a "successful, good person," the violent history between the United States

and Asian countries has been erased, and this view has created, in him, anger
toward Korean Americans for practicing reverse racism.

Brian showed his inability to understand the racial and ethnic differences
of his ex-girlfriends. When they told him about their experiences of racism,
Brian "felt bad." He added, "That's the barrier between the two of us. I couldn't
say 'I know how you feel.' There's always something that I could never understand." He viewed racism as having nothing to do with him individually, and
thus found it difficult to develop full empathy with the women about it. Brian
was frustrated by his lack of knowledge; he also did not see himself as sharing
in white people's collective responsibility.

Instead, he resented the negative prejudice against white men who only
date Asian women. "I think there's a certain stereotype you fall into when
you're dating an Asian girl. I think other Asians think you have some strange
sexual preference or something like that. . . . My friends have always teased me
about it. . . . I get the feeling that they feel like it's sort of indiscriminant, like I
just date any girls who are Asian." Brian denied that he would date any Asian
women indiscriminently. He said his first Filipino girlfriend's physical appearance shaped his preference for Asian women. "I think dark hair is beautiful, or
brown eyes are beautiful. . . . I fell in love with her." Brian said physical attraction to Asian female features was the main reason why he only dated Asian
women. Like many other young white men who date Asian American women,
he viewed Asian women as representative of attractive femininity, but was not
interested in the racial history of, or tensions between, Asian Americans and
whites in which white privileges were questioned.

BETWEEN AN ASIAN MAN AND A WHITE MAN

Lisa Kim, a twenty-one-year-old Korean American student, was born in Los
Angeles, where her father had arrived as an immigrant and started a motel
business. Her family went through a stressful period as she was growing up.
Later, Lisa attended college, majoring in architecture, in a large city in the
South, and then worked as an intern for a large company in New York. At the
time of the interview, Lisa had dated only white men, never Asian men, but was
in search of a Korean man who, preferably, was into the arts and who had "good
taste in music."

Lisa decided to choose an Asian American man because of her aversion
to many white men's Asian fetish. She strongly criticized mainstream culture's
sexualization of Asian women. "Being Asian there [in New York] is very hot
right now. Guys really like it. There's a porn industry for that, too. Like escort
services and stuff like that. So you get a lot of whistling and catcalls. . . . People
like Asians. I don't want to say it's trendy. But it's kind of like that. A lot of

guys right now like Asian women. . . . In New York, there's beautiful Asian girls and these really weird-looking white guys. They don't even look like they belong together."

Lisa noted that the sex industry and advertisements emphasize Asian women as submissive and demure, making them more attractive to white men. She remarked on the influences of these images on her relationships. "Sometimes I feel that, well, does he like me because I'm Korean? Is that part of it?" Lisa thought some white men came on to her only because she was Asian. "He is a white guy. He's gone out with Filipino girls. . . . He's really into Asian girls. I know he's just friends with me because I'm Asian. That's like the only reason why he started talking to me. . . . And if I go to the shows, I know guys are looking at me because I'm Asian. That's how I feel."

After a year in a relationship with a white boyfriend, whom she described as "so white" and a "typical suburban kid," Lisa decided to find an Asian American man to avoid feeling commodified and inferior. She said that, while in the relationship with her white boyfriend, she felt inferior to him and his friends, who reminded her of "all the popular white kids from high school." Her ambivalence toward whites arose from a mixture of a poor sense of self and a degree of envy toward white mainstream culture. She admitted that her lack of confidence in herself drove her to seek whiteness by suppressing her Korean identity. "I was just an immigrant's kid, you know. I didn't really know that much until I came to college."

So now Lisa had shifted her attention to Asian American men. "I don't really like seeing Asian girls with weird white guys. It really annoys me. But I think two Asian people, that's pretty solid," she said.

Lisa had previously avoided dating Korean men, having been affected by the stereotypes associated with them. "I hear that Korean boys are really nice to you at the beginning. But if you marry them, they totally change. They are very chauvinistic. I can see that, though. They grew up under that." She added, "Asian guys here are kind of nerdy. They all want to be doctor, lawyer, pharmacists." Nevertheless, she was excited about the "many good-looking Asian men" she had met when spending time in New York. Lisa planned to move to New York soon and hoped to find a "stylish" Korean boyfriend.

Asian American Women and Color-Blindness

In contrast with the first-generation Asian American women, many of the second- or later-generation Asian American women I interviewed presented themselves as ideal egalitarian and success-driven partners of white men. These highly assimilated Asian American women's relationships with white men demonstrated that they differed greatly from early stereotypes of Asian women as foreign, demure, and dainty ("the Lotus Blossom Baby, China Doll, or War Bride").[18] Yet this did not mean that Asian American women were finally free from submissive stereotypes—nor did the women I spoke with engage in particularly egalitarian partnerships with white men. Given that only one of the second-generation Asian American women was married. It is difficult to know if the couples' claim of being egalitarian is more than their ideal image of themselves. As feminist scholars point out, gender dynamics emerge distinctively in marriage. Asian American women were actually valued by white men for possessing rather traditional feminine traits that not only included small physiques and long dark hair, but also their loyalty and quietness (a few men said things like "they don't complain as much as white women"). Collins argues that skin color does not hold as much significance as it did before race-blind beauty norms, yet women are still judged for feminine physiques and submissive demeanor.[19] Collins writes, "The women need not have submissive personalities; they only need to recognize the boundaries of White male authority."[20] Asian Americans were highly valued precisely because of such feminine characteristics; Asian American women's claim to being upwardly mobile and egalitarian, while debunking some old stereotypes, does not necessarily subvert stereotypes of them as subservient.

Second- or later-generation Asian American women's selection of white men as mates represents resistance to negative racial stereotypes, aversion to Asian ethnic patriarchy, and desire for an independent modern subjectivity. Many of the stories discussed here illustrate how Asian American women's preference for white men, while often derived from the women's aversion to racist stereotypes of Asians as perpetual foreigners and as subservient, and to the ethnic patriarchy within which they grew up, ironically reinforces negative images of Asian Americans. A few young Asian American women I interviewed viewed their identification with white masculinity as the point at which they could overturn their racial marginality and gendered constraints, constraints or marginality sometimes acquired through transgenerational transference, and transform themselves into modern egalitarian subjects. These women's emulation of the dominant racism against Asian American men, seen in their resistance to dating such men, needs further examination. Also, despite couples' color-blind views of themselves, and despite white men's positive views of Asian American women as upwardly mobile and successful Americans, such color-blindness still protects the logic of white patriarchy and promotes stereotypes of Asian Americans.

Pyke and Dang, citing Russell, Wilson, and Hall, point out that the process of racial minorities' internalized racism has rarely been addressed in scholarly literature as a result of the embarrassment and discomfort associated with the topic as an "intellectual taboo."[21] They discuss the internal racism among second-generation Korean and Vietnamese Americans who, with their higher, "whitewashed" status, look down on co-ethnic Asians by mocking their English accents, fashions, styles, and friendship choices, and refer to them as "FOBs" (Fresh off the Boat). [22] Pyke and Dang's study illustrates Asian Americans' "compliance that replicates inequality"; though they themselves do not want to be stereotyped as Asians, these Asian Americans emulate mainstream racism in deriding co-ethnic Asian groups. According to Pyke and Dang, "A major concern is that because internalized racism reveals dynamics by which oppression is reproduced, it will lead to blaming the victims and move attention away from the racist institutions and practices that privilege whites at the expense of people of color. Internalized racism also causes discomfort because it suggests that the effects of racism are deeper and broader than many would like to admit."[23] Such an aversion to revealing internal racism may also help to explain why so little research has been done on Asian Americans' interracial relationships. As I discussed in this chapter, Asian American women's views of interracial relationships demonstrated their own replication of sexism and racism against Asian American men, and in some cases against other immigrant Asians. Among eight second-generation Asian American women I interviewed, six never dated Asian American men and four expressed an explicit aversion to, or a sense of the deficiency of, Asian American manhood by comparing it to "normal" white manhood. Asian American men's negative characteristics were usually mentioned in connection with comments about their physical size. The white male body symbolized physical strength, prowess, confident individuality, and Western civility, which these women claimed were lacking in Asian American men.

These Asian American women's desire for the white man, as a possessor of a larger body, capability to deal with nonsubmissive women without being threatened, and an egalitarian sensitivity, also signified emulation of white femininity. Asian American women's choice of white men represented their exercise of agency in rebelling against white racism and sexism through approximating to white hegemonic femininity. In their study of second-generation Asian Americans, Pyke and Johnson found that second-generation Asian Americans repeated the "white is right" mantra in their view of "white femininity as the right way of doing gender."[24] The Asian American women discussed in this chapter also viewed dating white man and acting "non-Asian" as the right thing to do to present themselves as American. At the same time, however, the second-generation Asian American women critically looked at white women of their age as lacking loyalty and discipline, and as being too individualistic, and viewed their ethnic upbringing as critically different from that of white American women. The Asian American women's agency lies in this contradictory and conflicting view of themselves: they are torn between their desire for white privilege and their strong familial bonds formed through a history of immigration and racial or ethnic survival.

Susan Koshy argues that liberal pluralism and the neoconservative politics of the 1980s and 1990s transformed the ideology of race by morphing the concept of race with the idea of ethnicity. This change has enabled racial minorities, except blacks, to have wider access to upward mobility, and an affiliation with whiteness.[25] Dhingra's study also shows that second-generation Asian American professionals do not see themselves as true minorities but claim they are "real Americans" because of their work ethic, their acculturation, and their educational drive, in contrast with African Americans whom they view as "true minorities" because lacking in these traits.[26] Among the couples discussed in this chapter, race often emerged as a positive theme, particularly with regard to Asian American women's physical appearance and ethnic pride, the source of cultural and social capital. Victoria had Asian values overlapped with the American Dream story, and Peter saw Asian women as a trendy cultural sign even while acknowledging few racial differences between himself and Vivian. The couples discussed in this chapter saw dating African American women as a "problem" and thus viewed these relationships as more "interracial" than their own. Asian American women seemed to view white men as the only racial group they would date or marry. Only one among all the Asian American women interviewed had dated an African American man, and one other had dated Indians and Hispanics.

In the context of Asian American women's interracial marriages with white men, Koshy argues that Asian American women's embrace of and collusion with white male patriarchy disables the political critique of white patriarchy.[27] Pyke and Johnson argue that Asian American women's idealization of dating white men as a way to attain gender equality, combined with white men's expectation of Asian women as submissive, sustain Asian American women's availability to white men and enhance the women's vulnerability to mistreatment.[28] Likewise, although the women discussed here claimed to possess hegemonic white femininity, characterized by assertiveness, independence, a professional orientation, and egalitarianism, their idealization of, and general portrayal of, white men showed their gender beliefs to be highly traditional. That is, their upward mobility—evidence of egalitarianism in their eyes—did not make these women free from collusion with the logic of white patriarchy. The white men whom I interviewed expressed their attraction to the "exotic" and "feminine" appearance of these women, and also appeared drawn to other important factors such as the women's "not complaining too much" or, as a result of the cultural inhibitions they grew up in, expressing little about themselves. As long as white men expect such racialized femininity from Asian American women, and Asian American women pursue white men as ideal possessors of masculinity, their interracial relationships will continue to operate within the logic of white patriarchy.

The women I interviewed were not particularly interested in engaging critically with mainstream sexism and racism. Perhaps, even though they knew popular racist and sexist images of Asian/Asian Americans, they did not want to see that their relationships were in any way affected by them. Irene and Lisa expressed an aversion to white men who approached them on a basis of racist and sexist images of Asian women, yet Irene was hesitant to express such concerns to her boyfriend, and weighed her attraction to his potential successful career as more important than her aversion to his insensitivity. Such silence can perpetuate the stereotype of Asian women as subservient or passive and may further promote mainstream stereotype's exploitation of Asian American women.

Most of the white men I interviewed did not see race as an issue in their relationships. They enjoyed getting to know their Asian American partners' ethnic customs and familial traditions. Compared to the men discussed in chapter 1, those studied in this chapter showed more interest in Asian cultures and enjoyed their interactions with Asian American families. This may be explained by generational differences. Also, the fact that the women's families had higher or equal social class status than these white men might have had a strong influence on the dynamics. That the Asian American women and their families were upper-middle-class "Americans" seemed to encourage the white men to communicate willingly with them. There was little racial tension between the Asian American families and the white men as the families often approved of whites, not necessarily as the best match for, but as at least the second best match for, their daughters. Asian American families saw a white man's lack of upward mobility and lack of higher education as more problematic than his race.

When a few second-generation Asian American women reported episodes of racism that they individually encountered, and shared these reports with white men, the men did not usually show particular interest in or concern about them. It was often the white men who presented an optimistic color-blind view as the couple's view, which the Asian American women abided by. Just as Paul minimized Vivian's experience by describing racism as a problem of ignorant whites, no white man mentioned racism against Asians as a serious social problem. The young white men I interviewed perceived *Asian* as merely signifying cultural and ethnic differences; some men, like Brian, saw reverse racism in their interactions with a girlfriend's family. For a young white man who grew up with a belief in multiculturalism and liberal pluralism, Asian American experiences do not seem associated with white racism. From such a white male perspective, Asian American communities' negative responses to white men may be seen as "their problem" or even viewed as reverse racism against white people. Such deracialization or color-blind views toward Asian Americans, combined with the strong stereotypes that remain regarding Asian Americans, further promote white men's blindness to public and individual racism against Asian American women. In other words, interracial relationships between young Asian Americans and white Americans do not appear to serve as opportunities for critically engaging or combating racism and sexism in mainstream society.

Part II

Asian American Men
with White Women

Chapter 4   A Man's Place

To DATE, NO STUDY has empirically examined Asian American manhood with a particular focus on heterosexual relationships, much less in an interracial context. Perhaps because of "the larger society's taboos against Asian male–white female sexual union[s],"[1] the social environment surrounding Asian American men's relationships with white women, through which some Asian American men negotiate their manhood, has remained unexplored. Although much of the existing research addresses the inequalities in interracial relationships between Asian or Asian American women and white men, especially in the context of transnational marriage,[2] little work has been done on relationships between Asian American men and white women.

With contemporary color-blind views of race, racialized masculinity and femininity are not bound by legal codes, yet they still take on ideological meanings. Among these are the fact that men of color have been excluded, historically, from access to white women, and the notion that white women are viewed as the possessors of ideal femininity. Historically, white femininity has been characterized as encompassing the most beautiful traits of womanhood; that is, white femininity as a normalized type of beauty "operates as a tool of white supremacy and a tool of patriarchy by elevating men and whites in importance and status."[3] In the cultural imagination, white women have long been perceived as morally superior, pure, and true, "the guardians of European civility, moral managers who . . . protect child and husband in the homes."[4] The media have bombarded society with images in which white female beauty has been associated with symbolic capital as a source of power and status. "The pervasiveness of racist ideologies that value whiteness and [the] emulation of it"[5] have also reinforced the symbolic image of the white woman as a trophy or currency prohibited to men of color. Collins argues that for an African American man to marry a white woman is a status-enhancing act, and such marriage can be an essential component in a racial minority man's achievement of "honorary" membership within hegemonic masculinity.[6]

However, the reality of minority men's wedding white women is far more complicated than mere status enhancement, in large part because race and gender continue to shape multiple aspects of these marriages. Intermarriage and the interracial family emulate the logic of patriarchy, the imperative of color-blindness, and the assimilation discourse. Thus, minority men's marriages with white women consist of not only their negotiation with racial stereotypes but also their subjection to the principles of the "American" family, character- ized by white middle-class manhood with breadwinner traits, multicultural or color-blind discourses, and assimilationist disciplines.

This chapter examines three cases of middle-age Asian or Asian American male professionals' marriages with white women. In considering these cases, I discuss professional Asian American men's images of white women, and inter- marriage as a critical marker of social acceptance, assimilation, and evasion of racism. The chapter also highlights negative receptions of Asian American men paired with white women, as well as white women's gendered positions and negotiations with race, including their use of color-blindness, color-cognizance, and essentialism as strategies for maintaining their marriages. Looking at these three marriages, I observe social processes by which the logic of patriarchy, imperatives of color-blindness and assimilation, and racism shape the couples' lives. I also argue that professional, middle-class Asian American men's socio- economic status has appeared to make white middle-class masculinity a more attainable goal than it would be for lower-class immigrant men of color.

This chapter consists of three parts. In the first, I examine a third- generation Filipino American man's desire to marry a white woman and his longing to attain normative white middle-class manhood. I contrast this color- blind marriage with race-conscious marriage, described in the second section. To examine gender dynamics in professional Asian and Asian American men's intermarriages, I discuss, in the third section, a white woman's racialized views of her upper-middle-class Chinese American husband.

Blond Fetish and Color-Blind Marriage

When I met them, Keith Banzon, a fifty-two-year-old, third-generation Filipino American engineer, had been married to Debra, a fifty-year-old white woman who worked for a publishing company, for eighteen years. Keith, balding and sporting a goatee, welcomed me at the door and introduced me to Debra. She was sitting on a sofa in a large living room, where several portraits of Native Americans by Edward Curtis hung on the wall. She had a slight smile but talked very openly with a deep strong voice. She usually expressed her view first, and the relaxed, soft-spoken Keith added to her comments. In the couple interview, the two spoke emphatically about their many multicultural projects, such as trips to Native American reservations, weekends spent meditating at Buddhist temples, Keith's life-long vegetarian diet, and the Kwanzaa holiday celebration they were about to undertake.

Keith was born in California. His father was a Filipino American who was in the U.S. army, and his mother, a Filipina American, was a music teacher. Due to his father's service, his family left their relatives and cousins in California, and Keith spent most of his childhood and adolescence on the East Coast and in the South. Keith remembered vaguely that his father had many friends in the Filipino American community in California, but Keith said that he himself "wasn't much with Asian cultural stuff."

Only in his individual interview did he talk about his experiences with racism. Growing up with racial slurs and stereotypes of Asians as "perpetual foreigners," he said in that interview, he often felt "uncomfortable" and "alienated" and that he "didn't belong anywhere." He was often mistaken for Chinese and encountered racial slurs such as "Chink." "All kids who saw an Asian automatically thought that [he or she was] Chinese. They didn't even think of anything other than Chinese." His race continued to make him the target of distrust even before his first marriage, he said, when his fiancee's father conducted an entire background search on him. "Asians . . . are not trusted. . . . The only thing they can base it on is how you look," Keith added.

Being a third-generation Filipino American, and growing up mostly with whites, Keith had disassociated himself from his Asian ethnic identity but expressed an interest in Asian culture as a therapeutic tool for dealing with his American identity. Keith said he had never been attracted to Asian women, and thus had never considered them as potential marital partners. Throughout his adult life, Keith had dated mostly white women. Both Debra and his first wife were white with, to one degree or another, blonde hair. (He emphasized their hair color when describing them.) Earning a white woman's desire also became part of Keith's masculine strategy; as he put it, "a lot of Caucasian women were interested in me because I was different" and "I kind of played on that interest." Keith remembered that many white women would describe him as mysterious. As Debra joked that Keith liked to tell how he was popular among white women, it became apparent that the attention from white women bolstered his confidence.

Keith described white women as the most beautiful in any race. "In my eyes, Caucasians, especially blondes, were more attractive. When I was an adolescent and in college, that was to me the image of beauty." According to Keith, all of his cousins were attracted to blondes, and all married white women. "My ex-wife is blonde," said Keith. Whenever his Asian coworkers asked him why he did not marry an Asian, he would answer, "I wasn't attracted." But he also acknowledged the following: "I think part of that has to do with acceptance. You know, being different, you can latch onto, you know, be part of the mainstream by marrying Caucasians." Asked if Debra is blonde, Keith answered, "Well, kind of. She was kind of reddish brown, but she streaked her hair, making it light. So, kind of blonde." He smiled. Keith's desire for white women emulates a mainstream desire for the white normative masculinity with its many privileges, including possessing white blonde women. If a white woman symbolizes a white man's property, then possessing her would elevate Keith's status to a white man's. To Keith, dating white women may have served as vital evidence of approximating to the white man and freeing himself from the stereotypical portrayals of Asian Americans as perpetual or unassimilated foreigners. It may have seemed to reduce distrust and the frequency of a suspicious racist gaze being directed at him.

Having protested the Vietnam War and resisted the draft for that war, Keith had been a part of the counterculture and had always been interested in soul-searching. In the early 1980s, working as a financial analyst for an oil company, Keith became more interested in "self-discovery" and joined a self-help training program, where he met Debra, who would become his second wife. At that time, she had just left an eleven-year marriage. In talking about his first impressions of Debra, Keith focused on her appearance. "I thought she was good-looking. We had the same philosophy and ideas about things. So I felt lucky to have met someone that is good-looking." A few years after Keith and Debra dropped out of the self-help training program, they decided to marry. At their request, a friend of Keith's, an astrologer, did a natal chart for each, read their signs, and set the date and time for the marriage ceremony based on their conclusions about what would be most advantageous. Keith and Debra wrote their own vows, employed a female preacher, and married each other at the top of the highest mountain in the town. Both described this ceremony as "very nontraditional" and "very progressive."

In our interview, Debra, as a self-claimed liberal and a "progressive" white female, consistently employed the discourse of color-blindness and a multiculturalist view of her marriage with Keith. Although Keith talked in his individual interview about encounters with racism, in the couple interview he presented himself as an ally of whites and as a multicultural ambassador of local Asian communities. "Politically, we are progressive. And I think we really believe in cultural diversity," said Debra. "Americans are sort of a melting pot. . . . It's kind of like Asians mix into the American mix . . . pulling the Asian race into this way that is American." Keith nodded and added, "Now Asian is becoming part of the mix that loses its identity because it's part of America."

Debra, although able to talk passionately about "Asian" food or Zen meditation and Buddhism, did not show the same eagerness to talk about racism as a social institution. She said her parents were surprised to see Keith "because he was different," but she quickly added she "didn't even worry about it." Debra explained that her marriage with Keith was her second marriage and her family was more concerned about money than race, so even though she knew that Keith's being Asian raised anxiety in her parents, she could quickly put that concern aside. Keith mentioned that, although Debra's parents "didn't express it toward me overtly," he had noticed "that both of them had a lot of racial biases," especially when "they would talk about blacks and Mexicans," and "some of the language that they used offended me." Debra didn't address this, focusing instead on herself, the "I" who relies on a liberal humanist discourse as well as a multicultural acceptance of diversity. She tried to separate her ideal self, who did not worry about race, from what she characterized as the racist views of whites in general. "My feeling was, you know, I am with this person because of who this person is, not because of any external stuff. . . . I mean, all those horrible things you go through in life have absolutely nothing to do with what your nationality is, what your ethnicity is, any of that stuff. We all go through life in the same way. We all have the same tragedy and the same joys to share. Those are the things that transcend other things."

Debra's emphasis on common humanity was what Frankenberg sees as a discourse of "color and power evasion," typical among white women. Frankenberg writes about how this use of the concept *common humanity* as a way of erasing *whiteness* emerges innocently in white women's discourse of race.[7] Debra's avoidance of the "difference of race or color" exemplifies "an attempt [by whites] to distance themselves from essentialist racism."[8] Debra emphasized basic human life experiences as the most important determinants of "who this person is." She saw "race and nationality" as "external stuff," separate from, though attached to, true human essence. This is a strategy employed by many of us human beings to find out the similarities and commonalities beyond race. At the same time, this view obliterates the notion that a person's joys and especially her or his tragedies are extremely racialized and nationalized, and that these tragedies frequently are a result of a white-dominated political and economic system, both within and outside the United States.

Debra's belief in herself as a liberal multiculturalist and humanist was undercut by her actual interactions with Asian people in the community. She expressed a degree of discomfort about communicating with Asians due to her fears of being blamed, as a white person, for racism. Although she claimed to want "to learn about Filipino culture," she said that "Sometimes I am uncomfortable, I think because I'm white. I feel left out or worry that, because I am white, it's just a stigma on the white race." Keith affirmed, "I know she is uncomfortable, especially if they don't speak English."

Debra was reluctant to see whites as a collective agent of racism, or to acknowledge structural racism. She talked about her concerns regarding white supremacy and how "fear" among those white supremacists drove them to engage in hate crimes. But adding that "it was not just whites," Debra said, "Every race has this sort of wanting to be pure, not mixing things up."Her view, Debra quickly added, is that fear of racial mixing is a problem not only among whites but also among racial minorities.

This view, that whites' fear of racial mixing and racial minorities' fears of such mixing are similar, is a problem: such a view obliterates or effaces the fact that the whites' fear of racial mixing has occurred primarily as a result of their discrimination and prejudices against racial minorities, while racial minorities' fear has reflected their distrust of whites resulting from the historical and structural racism against themselves (as noted in Childs' book *Navigating Interracial Borders*). Claiming that the racial motives of white supremacy are the same as racial minorities' clinging to their own race makes it difficult to criticize structural and institutional racism and white privilege.

In the couple interview, as Debra consistently resorted to the color-blind discourse, Keith portrayed himself as an active agent of multiculturalism and a loyal ally of whites. He talked about how he had recently become eager to learn about Asian culture. In contrast with having grown up with a sense of racial alienation at being Asian, he even claimed it was a tragedy not to have an authentic knowledge of Filipino culture. He explained he was now exploring Asian cultures so that he could "continue to understand my roots." Keith started teaching martial arts in the late 1980s, a skill that attracted many Americans: "All my students are Caucasians." Keith also talked about his responsibility to "represent Asians to the entire city" or to organizations, work he started doing in the mid-1990s. This political activism and interest in multiculturalism dated to the period in the late 1980s and early 1990s when, with the rise of the Asian economy, positive images of Asian Americans as a model minority became prevalent in the United States. Accordingly, Keith's attitude toward his own race then changed; rather than feeling racial alienation, he began to see the advantages of embracing Asian cultural and physical differences. Keith's strategic engagement in Asian cultures and willingness to represent "Asians" in the community illustrated his privileges: he entered the space of the Asian as an "Americanized" Asian or a "white" Asian, with more social resources than other Asians.

Even Keith's blond fetish has subsided recently, coinciding with the rise of positive images of Asians. Keith said, "In the last five years or so, I have started finding Asian women to be attractive." His interest in Asian culture even seems to have been tied to the market's discovery of Asian culture as a self-healing and self-creating commodity. Once rebellious markers of the New Age dissent in which Keith participated have become popular American remedies for identity crises and stress.[9] The voice of dissent has been appropriated by corporate capitalism[10] and market-oriented multiculturalism, and has become fashionable. Thus, Keith's cultural engagement and political activism as an Asian American exactly reflected his participation in the hegemonic inscription of Asian culture and the depoliticization of Asian Americans into a "good" model minority.

In his employment of the hegemonic discourse of race and culture, Keith's blonde fetish and celebration of biracial appearance did not contradict his activism and multiculturalism as an Asian. Keith proudly commented on his biracial children as being attractive "Amerasians." "All my children were half-Filipino and half-Caucasian. But I think that their features were very, very good-looking." Speaking of his daughter Julia, Keith said: "Julia has a strong tie to the fact that her grandmother is French. So she likes using her French middle name. So she thought she is half-French ancestry and Filipino. She doesn't say she is Filipino." However, Keith described his feelings about his granddaughter who was half-black very differently: "I do continue to carry some stereotypes of African Americans—I myself have [some]. You know, the thing is my daughter has mostly in her adult life dated blacks. My granddaughter is half-black. So, that's the only thing I am a little bit uncomfortable with. I think it is the way that Americans just see them differently. And now that's changing, and hopefully it's changing for me as well. But I've got to accept it." Facing the introduction of African American blood into his familial line, Keith's view of multiracial children as a solution to racial problems was replaced by a feeling of discomfort. His concerns about his granddaughter, and his acknowledgment of his own racial prejudice, showed that the celebratory discourse of multiracialization neither changed the hierarchical markers nor replaced the current structure of race.

Keith saw his exotic-looking biracial son as a possessor of social capital. But he also acknowledged his son's reluctance to "act like an Asian." He said, "I see a lot of myself in my younger son, in that he tries not to act like he is Asian. He tries to fit into the Caucasian culture and tries to move away from doing things that are Asian. At the same time, he likes being different and he likes being unique. And that's something that I didn't recognize in myself until I was in college." Keith believed his son's negative feelings toward being Asian were compensated by his pride in his exotic appearance, as Keith's own appearance eventually gave him the confidence to develop an Asian American masculinity that would be acceptable in white society.

Another important factor in Keith and Debra's marriage was class difference. After growing up in a small town in a working-class family, Debra first married at the age of eighteen. Eleven years later, she divorced her first husband, Nick, and started her college degree. After Debra's divorce, her mother would say, "What would Nick think if you married someone that has a lot of money?" Debra's marriage to Keith, someone she met in a self-help group, marked her flight from the lower class to the upper middle class and the attainment of independence. Just as it was, above all, the whiteness of Debra that Keith desired, it was probably Keith's social class that mattered to Debra. She frequently used the term "a meeting of the minds" to refer to their mutual recognition and respect, a marker of egalitarian marriage. She confidently presented her life-style, marriage, and project of self-discovery as evidence of being progressive and independent. Again, if Keith's alignment with whiteness represented a reconciliation with his past racial alienation, Debra's passionate resort to nonwhite culture as a source of self-discovery, though limited and contradictory, also provided a way to expand her consciousness of race and of her own femininity.

Keith's marriages to white women represented a strategic bid to attain social recognition from white society. By aligning with whiteness in his marriages, and by his "discovery" of Asian culture, he tried to establish himself as a multicultural Asian American masculine subject. Keith imaginatively approximated the middle-class white husband with a liberal, multicultural, and independent white wife who praised his capacity to listen and share in their relationship. (However, although they shared most life events, it was still Debra who did a larger share of the cooking and housework. And Keith's masculinity was also based on his strategic utilization of his "exotic" appearance and on an Asian-white fluidity that safely adhered to the hegemonic discourse of American multiracialization.)

Racism, Loss, and Refugee Masculinity

As discussed in previous chapters, the negative effects of racism on Asian Americans and their white spouses were rarely reported by Asian American women paired with white men. But a few of the Asian American men paired with white women that I interviewed did report occasional negative social receptions. The following discussion of Sothy and Emily demonstrates the public's reluctance to accept a marriage between an Asian American man and a white woman. Like Keith and Debra, Sothy and Emily strove for a traditional middle-class marriage, with Emily assisting Sothy according to the norms for the white wife of a professional American. However, in contrast to Keith and Debra, Sothy and Emily encountered negative receptions of Asian American men, making the couple unable to employ the color-blind discourse.

War immigrants and refugees from Indochina have endured a much more difficult resettlement in the United States, socially and economically, than did Asian Americans who were assimilated earlier or who entered the U.S. as middle-class professionals relatively soon after 1965.[11] Polumbo-Liu notes that, though the first wave of Indochinese refugees, in 1975, tended to be relatively well educated, proficient in English, and experienced in urban living, the second wave of refugees—those who arrived as "boat people"—were poorer, less educated, typically did not possess the skills needed for employment in a technologically complex society, and were in greater need of federal assistance.[12] Despite these differences among refugees, as well as between refugees and other immigrants, both groups were monolithically categorized as Asian within a generalized narrative of immigration and assimilation.[13] The narrative of the model minority was thus also employed to manage this flood of refugees from Southeast Asia.[14] Sothy's life history illustrates the employment of the assimilation discourse by a male refugee. Intermarriage and racism played critical roles in his self-making as an "American."

When I first met this couple, at a local restaurant, Emily, a thirty-eight-year-old schoolteacher, caught my eye from a distance because of her height and slim figure. Sothy, a forty-five-year-old Cambodian American electrical engineer, appeared her opposite, with a very strong voice, dark skin, and muscular physique. When I visited their house in a new suburban area, their two children, a seven-year-old boy and an eleven-year-old girl, both of whom Emily referred to as "Asian Americans," politely welcome me in, for Sothy was on the phone talking with his long-time Indian friend. During the couple interview, Sothy did most of the speaking, and Emily primarily affirmed his comments. She never expressed disagreement with him, except when discussing cooking or the discipline of the children. In their individual interviews, each talked about the racism that they had encountered either as a couple or as individuals. Sothy spoke passionately about his resettlement in the United States, and his active role in a local organization to combat racism against Asian Americans. Emily talked about how her loss of family and Sothy's loss of country had become the emotional cornerstones of their bond.

Sothy told me about his early years. His mother had passed away soon after he was born, and he was raised by his grandmother. His father served in the military and owned a large piece of land with many large banana trees as well as rubber plants, cows, and buffaloes; Sothy remembered these well. Sothy was drafted into the navy at fifteen, fought in twenty-four battles, and suffered several injuries. He did not contact his father after he entered the military. When he turned twenty, Sothy left both his family and his country, and started a new life in the United States at a refugee camp in Pennsylvania. The year was 1975, the year the Vietnam War ended and the communist dictatorial regime, the Khmer Rouge, seized power in Cambodia. For Cambodia, it was the beginning of a period of terror in which two million people were murdered. Far away in the United States, Sothy remained cut off from his family. He received one letter from Cambodia fifteen years ago; it was from his sister, and it informed him briefly that his father had passed away.

Sothy had little time to reflect on the sequence of tragic events in the country of his birth. To leave the refugee camp in Pennsylvania, he had to find a sponsor, so he wrote to a friend he had known in the navy in Cambodia. Once away from the camp, he found a job washing dishes and cleaning shrimp at a Chinese restaurant in Rhode Island. "War made me a much tougher individual. War made me work harder, much harder," he said. Later, he worked at a factory, making coffee machines, and he also worked at a fast-food restaurant for $2.75 an hour. "My supervisor was some kid in high school. I felt humiliated, but you just have to do what you got to do." He worked three years in the United States before he was able to study engineering at college. In his individual interview, he talked about how his strength and sprit enabled him to attain his current professional status.

Emily, an elementary school teacher, grew up in a traditional family with a homemaking mother and an authoritarian father, who was a lawyer but who had served in the military when Emily was young. Emily met Sothy while they were students in college. She said of Sothy that, in contrast to the stereotypical image of Asian men, "he has a loud voice. You can hear him before you can see him. That strikes me as ironic, because Orientals usually seem very soft-spoken." Growing up in a military family overseas, she said, she used to be attracted to "people with dark hair and dark eyes," often Hispanic men, but she only dated whites because of her father's strong opposition to her dating nonwhites. One time, Emily said, she was dating a "half-Hispanic" man and brought him home, but this time her father did not comment on the man's racial background, because he "was a part of the oil business." Emily added, "So that was money. And that's okay."

As for Sothy, before he married Emily, he had dated women of almost all races, including white woman, black women, and Asian women. Although he jokingly suggested he would have dated a Cambodian girl if one were available, he also spoke negatively of marriage with Cambodians and denied his interest in such a marriage.

When Emily finally told her parents that she and Sothy were engaged, her father stopped talking to her. Then Emily received a letter from her father, which simply said that her family would disown her. She said, "They gave me an ultimatum. 'You either drop him and you can be our child still, or you go with him and you don't ever come back to this house again.' That's exactly what they said." Emily's father also forbade her to talk to her sisters and relatives. Emily had not forgotten what her older sister told her: "If he'd been another person, if he hadn't been an Asian, he wouldn't have been so unaccepted." Emily sent wedding invitations to her family and sisters in California and offered to fly them out. About two hundred people came to the wedding, but, as Emily expected, none of her family's seats was filled. Seven years after her family disowned her, her mother finally started speaking to Emily again. Her father, however, never talked to Emily and Sothy, and her mother's and sisters' attitude toward Sothy had not changed, even up to the day I met them. "Her family by and large discriminates against me. Her father has never spoken to me. We have never met. Her mother basically looks down on me," Sothy said in a distant tone. Even though Emily's mother visited sometimes, "she spends only two hours here."

On occasion, Emily and Sothy had also encountered racism outside her family. Emily invited her white friends to dinner many times, but whenever they came to Emily and Sothy's house, they seemed to have "an air of uncomfortableness." One of Emily's good friends, a half-Japanese and half-white woman whom she met at work, explicitly expressed negative attitudes toward her and Sothy. Emily saw her friend's mixed-race heritage as a potential marker of openness to racial minorities, but she found this was not the case. She tried to find explanations other than race for her friend's reaction. "When she saw him, she just kind of backed away from me. I noticed that she was very disapproving of me going out with him. He has a very strong personality. So it might be a combination of his personality and the fact that he is Asian. I don't know what her suspicions or reservations really were. I just know that we weren't friends after that, very much. That happened several times."

In contrast to Emily, who had to deal with racism only after the couple's marriage, Sothy talked emphatically about how he had dealt with a series of discriminatory incidents and prejudices from the time he started his life in the United States. Frequently his appearance and strong accent seemed to make him a target of suspicion. For example, his company's clients sometimes asked for a white representative instead of him. He and his boss would respond by informing the other company that Sothy was the person in charge of communications. Sothy ended up receiving the same response from one company four times. "They wanted a white guy from our company . . . instead of me." Sothy emphasized that he had learned to live with such distrust, but he said he felt bad about Emily's racialized loss of family and friends.

> It hurts me when I see my wife crying. She is unable to separate herself from herself as a woman of white family, of these people, and also as the faithful, loyal wife of mine. You couldn't separate at all. She had to take one goal or the other. This is tough for her. I feel bad. It hurts me. . . . I've gone through the war. My mother passed away when I was six months old. I lost my country. I became a refugee. I relearned how to speak all over again, because nobody can understand me anymore here. You know, I've gone through a lot in my lifetime. . . . I learned how to cope with loss very well, you know. . . . I never met these people. They don't want to be with me. They don't want to know me. They don't want anything to do with me. To me, that's not a loss. That's their loss.

Sothy rejected the idea that racism was his loss, claiming, instead, his own country, language, and parents as his authentic losses. Sothy's refusal to be the victim of racism deprived the racists of power, overturned the paradigm of the racist and the victim, and redefined racism as "their loss." Given that Keith also mentioned early life experiences of racism, it is wrong to think of Sothy's experiences of racism as something unique to *refugee* Asian American man. Three professional Asian American men whom I interviewed, regardless of the generation to which each belonged, or his professional status, reported having encountered explicit racism. For example, Kenneth Miyake, a fifty-year-old divorced Japanese American engineer, mentioned that, since he was used to "overt hostility to him and his family" (to the extent even of his parents' internment during World War II), the negative receptions he received when he was with his white wife seemed minor to him.

Regardless of the discrimination and prejudice he experienced in the United States, Sothy's goals remained: striving for professional success, and being a good father to his two children. Sothy repeated that he was "an American," as if trying to displace his memories from Cambodia and become assimilated into American society.

> I despise Cambodians. I am proud of the country that gave me birth. But the system is of savages. The communist regime is one thing . . . two million people died because of the war. . . . I will never go back to Cambodia. The power struggle between the U.S., China, and the Soviet Union created the wedge in our country. One group wanted to follow the Russians, one followed the Americans, one followed China. That wedge got bigger and bigger and bigger and finally broke into

pieces . . . small pieces after a while; it's shattered. It's just like tearing
a pillow bag. That's Cambodia. That's what it is today. It's a country
without hopes. I am an American, get it? I don't have any place to go
back to, you know.

Sothy's evocative description of Cambodia was filled with resentment. He
tried to resolve his loss by claiming that he was an American and had no
place to which to return. His mourning took the shape of destruction of the
memories of his homeland.

For a refugee, the development of identity is a process of loss and assimilation. Cuban-American performer Carmelita Tropicana's depiction of an exile's
assimilation locates the formation of Cuban refugee identity at the intersection
of amnesia and the memories of homeland. The Cuban refugee's assimilation has
been defined as the process of "corrosive forgetting" and the "nostalgic reconstruction" of homeland.[15] But Sothy's remembrance of his homeland included
both resentment and love, and did not allow him the "corrosive forgetting"
of what he and his country went through three decades before. Thus, Sothy
intentionally displaced his loss with his new identity as an American. Freud, in
his discussion of mourning and melancholia,[16] suggested that a subject suffering
from loss sometimes "demonstrates his liberation from the object which was
the cause of his suffering, by seeking like a ravenously hungry man for a new
object—cathexis."[17] Sothy passionately talked about being an American—the
only option, he felt, available to him, and the only strategy for surviving his
loss of family and country.

By shaping his sense of loss and memories of homeland into the hegemonic
discourse of assimilation, Sothy strove to attain the status of a successful
American. He wanted his children, he said, to grow up as Americans who
would embrace the American life-style. He said, "Anything that's outside of
it . . . my Cambodian things, that's mine." He viewed his marriage with Emily,
a white woman, as an important element of his becoming an American and
building a normative white middle-class family. "She helped me to assimilate
better. I got a lot out of it . . . the culture white people come from, the way
the white people think, what white people say, the way the white people look,
the way white people do, the way white people behave, the way white people
believe, she helped me out a lot." Emily worked full time as a teacher, but it was
her work at home, such as decorating the house for family events and cooking
traditional food, that was most important to her. She often accompanied Sothy
on company outings and get-togethers outside of work, and would join him at
community functions. "I really try to be involved whenever they have a function. I try to participate," she said. Emily's desire to create her own family, and
Sothy's desire to be assimilated into American life, created a gender dynamic

similar to that found in the white middle class. Emily supported Sothy both in private, by maintaining the traditional white middle-class home, and in public, by attending the meetings of organizations to which he belonged.

White Women with Upper-Middle-Class Asian Professionals

I have discussed two cases in which white women portrayed Asian American husbands as good partners with traditional masculine traits such as a being good breadwinners and attaining professional status. However, two white women I interviewed individually reported racialized views of their Asian American partners with far more negative overtones. They associated their spouses' ethnic patriarchy with conflict in their relationships, and dealt with ethnic patriarchy by making concessions and giving in to their partners' socioeconomic power.

Marie was a forty-five-year-old white woman and mother of two children, ages five and eight, whom she called Chinese or Chinese American. She explained that her husband, a forty-five-year-old Chinese American computer engineer, would not be available for an interview due to his busy schedule, and that he would not have spoken about himself anyway. Thus I was able to interview only her.

The couple had been married for seventeen years. Their large house was located on a small hill near a quiet lake. I passed through the front gate security system and saw a well-cared-for English garden decorated with colorful lights. Marie appeared at the door in a white cotton shirt and blue jeans. Inside, there was a Latina maid. Marie said she could not take care of the large house well enough to meet her husband's expectations, so they decided to hire a couple of cleaning women. Marie's schedule in the afternoon was, as usual, tight, so I accompanied her to her older son's school to buy books recommended for his classes. Back at the house, Marie often had to leave the room during our interview to help with the children's homework.

According to Marie, her husband James came to the United States from Taiwan with his family when he was twelve. Now he and his family lived in the same town. Marie met James when she was working on her master's degree; he was living in the same apartment complex and was also working on a graduate degree. Marie remembered James as "good looking; he had a good ability to listen. He had a real tender side in him." Three years after they met, they married. Marie stopped working as a teacher and decided to focus on taking care of the home.

Marie's marriage with James was affected by her feelings of enormous pressure and fear. A couple of years ago, she started to go to a therapist. No longer the "good listener" and "tender" man whom Marie had dated, James had turned out extremely dominant and controlling of her. He had "impossible standards" not only in his own work, but also in his expectations of her as a caretaker. He criticized her constantly. Marie said:

> He's got this feeling and mind-set about things. Everything is in its place. He wants to see everything wonderful and clean . . . . He says how I could have done better, and how he would have done that. He's like, "Why are you doing it this way, that way. . . . Why didn't you do it this way?" He even orders how to cut vegetables. . . . He used to compare me a lot. Why, the other person over here, they can do it, why can't you do it? That kind of thing. Other wives can do all these things and raise kids, and why can't you do it? It is a compulsive thing. How dinner could have been better. What was good and what wasn't good. Too much salt and . . . he just can't relax and let me do [it] my way. He likes to control. . . . He gets to use "always" or "never." "You always blah-blah-blah . . ." He uses that expression, which really, really irritates me. I say, "James, would you just rephrase that? It just annoys me when you say always." Because always is illogical. So when he starts arguing, I just ignore a lot of it.

Marie related that James usually yelled at her when they argued. "He gets louder and takes over with his voice. . . . Sometimes I have to hang up the phone." It was not unusual for him to yell at her in front of their children. She lamented the fact that, even though James "is real huggy and loving" toward the children, "he is not equal when he treats me. He treats me so differently, so harshly and coldly."

Marie explained James's dominant traits by relating them to the pressure he went through being raised as a "number one son" in his traditional Chinese family. James "needed to be always really perfect. . . . James has been criticized all his life by his family. You are not doing right. You are not doing good enough." Marie spoke emphatically of how, in his relationship with her, James repeated and reinforced what he learned as a child. "Maybe it's an Asian thing . . . kind of raising your voice when you are angry." Marie reported that James's family members "are cold to each other and just argue all the time." James was often furious at his mother, Marie commented, and she herself was in a similar position to that mother, who was constantly bullied and yelled at by her own husband and by the son to whom she was devoted.

To Marie, James's practice of his ethnic masculinity seemed to contradict his constantly expressed aversion to Chinese culture. She thought that he avoided being viewed as Chinese, and tried to escape from the cultural responsibilities and obligations imposed on him. He often mentioned to her his sense of relief that marrying outside of his race freed him from having to fulfill certain obligations, for example "Chinese protocols, like a lot of gift giving. Those are built into the system. He's just relieved about not having to worry about [that] materialism . . . because Americans don't do that."

Marie also said that James tried to show his more Americanized side by going out mainly with whites and not joining Chinese groups. She said, "He doesn't feel like he's part of that group." She said James looked down somewhat on the Chinese and distanced himself from them, saying, "Chinese men, they are kind of goofy." His Chinese friends joked, "James wants to be an American guy, not a Chinese guy." James would also compare Marie with Chinese women and express his racialized preference for white women over Chinese women. "He says I have a sweet personality. He likes that. He says that a lot of Chinese women are not that sweet. They are rude, they are yelling, antsy, and nervous."

Although it made her miserable, Marie liked James's masculine drive, she said, to "push himself and be ambitious" and to strive for an "impossible standard." But what was hardest for her was the fact that, within their marriage, her husband was not so romantic as she had expected him to be. "Chinese people don't say I love you. They don't do that verbal affection." Although "white guys sometimes just do too much flattering," she said, she missed affection, because even a "physical hug is not available" in Chinese culture. She felt there was a lack of romantic "knighthood," an essential part of white masculinity, in James.[18]

James's marriage to Marie sounded like a demonstration of his achievement of white middle-class masculinity. His resistance to Chinese norms was not resistance against male dominance, but complicity with it. Male dominance and privilege in American patriarchy and Chinese patriarchy enabled James to retain his control as an odd cultural hybrid, realized in his interracial marriage. As a result of his embrace of ethnic patriarchal privilege and American patriarchal logic, James was not forced to recognize that his power was founded on the devastation and devaluation of Marie's life and on the repudiation and devaluation of women in general.

Marie, rather than work outside the home, engaged solely in the traditional roles of wife and mother, though unhappy with the situation. The problem for her was not only the difficulties associated with playing these traditional gender roles, but also her lack of control over the private domain, the domain that traditionally the woman has controlled. She saw James's dominance over her more as a result of cultural influences than of gender inequality. Because Marie blamed Chinese culture and James's family, the gender inequality that exists in white middle-class families and among professional men within white

American culture had become invisible to her; James's "problem" became solely a problem of Chinese ethnic patriarchy. Marie often described James's Chinese family as "harsh" and "cold," contrasting it with the "warm" white family she grew up with. Her depiction of this Chinese American man as a possessor of deviant masculinity, and her emphasis on cultural differences, served to perpetuate hegemonic views of the white family and white culture as superior to those of this racial minority, and to reinforce negative stereotypes of Asian American men.

However, some white women were willing to look hard at noncultural or nonracial aspects of Asian American man with whom they were partnered. Laura Martin, a thirty-year-old physical therapist whom I interviewed without her Chinese boyfriend (who declined to be interviewed) reported problems similar to Marie's. Her boyfriend, Andrew, a physician, often yelled at her when they argued. She said, "He's more emotional and gets escalated a lot quicker." Laura, however, said that she and Andrew always found a solution by talking about the problem. Andrew often blamed his upbringing as a Chinese man for his not communicating openly or expressing feelings, but Laura was reluctant to view his behavior as a "cultural" difference. She argued that there are "varieties of differences even among white families." Throughout the interview, Laura emphasized not Andrew's ethnicity, but his upper-class upbringing (his father was a high-ranking government official, and his family was wealthy enough to employ maids) as having made Andrew "unique." As in the case of Marie and James, this Asian American man's class status could create room for his maintenance of gendered power and privilege over white women.

Logic of Marriage

Professional Asian American men perceive intermarriage as a critical marker of their assimilation, and of attainment of social recognition. Intermarriage, or having a white wife, plays a symbolic as well as a practical role in their perception of approximation to white norms of manhood. Professional Asian American men racialize their white wives, either as objects of ideal femininity or as supportive domestic aids, as a marker of privilege, privilege that they could not attain with Asian American wives. These marital dynamics emulate traditional gender dynamics in that the men earn higher incomes than the women.

In the case of Keith and Debra, the couple saw interracial marriage as a site to practice color-blind love and to raise a multicultural family. With Keith's desire for whiteness and his adroit performance of mainstream views of the Asian, the couple viewed the ideal marriage and family as color-blind and emulated the hegemony of the middle-class American family. In the case of

Sothy and Emily, the discourse of assimilation through economic achievement emerged as a goal to enable Sothy to attain middle-class American status. Sothy emphasized his assimilated status and his "American" children, who would be free from the racism that he and his wife had endured. Marie was engaged in creating the "perfect" upper-middle-class household by criticizing, and distancing herself from, her husband's ethnic upbringing.

In all three cases, regardless of the individual partners' racialized images of their spouses, the formation of the ideal family was imagined as color-blind. The American family and marriage were imagined as sites for individual happiness and love, where race should not interfere with normative relationships.

The gender and racial imperatives of white middle-class family formation were seen in these couples' views of their children. They saw biracial children as possessors of cultural capital, as well as inheritors of white privilege, though each referred to the children differently. Marie and Emily called their children Chinese or Asian American, while Sothy described his and Emily's as American and Keith emphasized his and Debra's children's "white enough" appearances in a positive way. Another interviewee, a divorced second-generation Japanese American man named Kenneth, called his eighteen-year-old half-Japanese daughter Asian American but added that she felt "more Caucasian than Japanese." No couple mentioned the race of their children as a potential problem.

Patriarchy/gender governs the logic of intimacy and family. Whether marriage is authorized by a white man or an Asian American man, the logic of patriarchy shapes the power dynamics of interracial marriage and the multiracial family. One example, as discussed in this chapter, is the depression experienced by two white women, Marie and Emily, which was gendered. Marie struggled with her husband's expectations; Emily was punished for not having subscribed to her father's view of the ideal marital partner.

Class status is critical for Asian American men in demonstrating their authority as ideal middle-class husbands and fathers, and also for repudiating the emasculated stereotypes of Asian American men. Yet, even with their class status, it seems much more difficult for professional Asian American men with white women to gain public approval than it is for white men with Asian American wives. The normative marriage and family are still those imagined under white male authority. And a white woman who pairs off with an Asian American man can be seen as deviant and suspicious, as she is, however tacitly, supposed to be subject to white male authority.

Chapter 5   Playing the Man

LIKE THE PROFESSIONAL ASIAN AMERICAN MEN already discussed, who symbolically viewed intermarriage as a validation of their middle-class manhood and as a critical component of assimilation, young unmarried and nonprofessional Asian American men in my study viewed white women's approval and recognition in interracial intimacy as critical to consolidating their own Asian American manhood and to refashioning their racial identities. This chapter focuses on Asian or Asian American men in their twenties, and on their white partners, and discusses Asian American men's strategies for competing within, and ascending, the hierarchy of masculinity. The chapter illuminates how these men's strategies have been interrupted, undermined, or recast in the presence of white women. It further details how these men's social class and generational status made differences in their strategies.

In the system of American manhood, men of color "jockey for position within this hierarchy of masculinities" to "enter the inner circle, often as 'honorary' elite White men."[1] Studies of masculinity, as well as feminist studies, have addressed the idea that masculinity is a product of male competition with other males; such studies have also addressed the notion that masculinity enhancement derives from men's desire for women who possess symbolic capital in the form of an attractive physical appearance. However, the psychological or emotional processes through which men of color must compete or jockey for their hegemonic positions in relation to white women have rarely been examined.[2] By looking at interracial intimacy as a process of negotiation with normalized white manhood, this chapter questions how Asian American men in their twenties deploy strategies of manhood and how white women's presence influences these strategies. It details how men's relationships with white women provide them with not only racialized recognition, but also with the means to distance themselves from race- or state-bound identity.

In the first section, I examine how a Chinese American man resented and resisted the mainstream "racial castration" of Asian men and the misogynistic white masculinity of U.S. university culture. In the second section, I discuss a Japanese man who, due to his lack of class status, to language barriers, and to his inability to perform gender sensibility, failed to maneuver and construct a competitive masculinity. In the final section, I discuss a Korean American man's resistance to the traumatic ethnic masculinity formed in his transnational upbringing between South Korea and the United States; I also discuss his view of himself as "white," a view deriving from his class status, marriage with a white woman, and immersion in white culture.

Stylish, Romantic, and Successful Knighthood

Anthony S. Chen discusses Chinese American men's "hegemonic bargaining," observed in nine Chinese American men's "gender strategies."[3] In his study, four professional heterosexual Chinese American men "struck bargains" with hegemonic white manhood, compensating, deflecting, denying, or repudiating their marginal masculinities by trading their own social and economic privileges such as athleticism, frat-boy-like behaviors, gender-egalitarian behaviors, or aggressiveness. This section shows how a Chinese American man similarly competed with white hegemonic masculinity, and bolstered his masculinity, by using his class status, cosmopolitan upbringing, and a white girlfriend's validation.

When I first visited the apartment of Kevin Cheung, a twenty-year-old Chinese American computer science major, he came to the door wearing a tight long-sleeved shirt and large baggy pants too big for his slim body. A little later, Karen, a twenty-year-old English major, arrived at the apartment for a study session, wearing a long tight blue skirt and black cat-eye glasses.

Kevin spent his early childhood in England, Norway, and Hong Kong, before he moved to the United States at the age of seven. His father had long worked for a major oil company and, at the time of the interview, worked for a computer company. Kevin was raised in a very traditional environment; though his mother also worked, at a Chinese restaurant, she was the family caretaker. Kevin did not speak Chinese fluently, so he communicated with his parents mainly in English. He emphasized his cosmopolitan upbringing: "I grew up in an international environment. I always had all kinds of friends, not just of a different ethnicity. I've got friends with different sexual orientations as well." His past girlfriends included a few women who were white and a few who were biracial. He described himself as "a bit shy," but confidently added that he "never got rejected by girls."

Kevin grew up with expectations that he would be ambitious and successful, and he always "tried [his] hardest" to make good grades in school. He was only in the fifth grade when he was given an SAT study book by his parents. Like other second-generation Asian Americans, Kevin employed, during his interview, the model minority discourse or ascribed to himself what he called "pan-Asian values" (values making Asian people ambitious and successful, different from other minorities). "I guess all Asian people are ambitious. You have to make money. You have to choose a viable career." Kevin planned to work at a computer company, as did his father and two brothers, after graduation.

Kevin had met Karen at a rave party. Both had been regular rave party-goers since they were in high school. Karen had never dated outside of her race before, but she said this was not a matter of choice but a reality dictated by her white-dominated small-town upbringing; "I lived in a town that was predominantly white. So I just ended up dating white." Kevin and Karen had been together over six months when I met them. Karen said of Kevin, "He's really cute and he's a really fun person. I like that. We have similar goals. He studies hard. That kind of compulsion. . . he's got the same values as I do."

Although Kevin's two brothers were both married to Chinese women who spoke fluent Cantonese, and his parents preferred Kevin to date a Chinese woman, they had not discouraged his relationship with Karen. "I've dated all kinds of women," said Kevin. His parents liked Karen when he brought her to his home for the first time. "Karen was very nervous when she met my family," Kevin said. "She didn't want to go to my home." Karen noted that she had fear and anxiety about being the only white among Asians, and that she tended to see Asians staring at her as a sign of hostility. "He took me to have dim sum for the first time. Everybody there was Asian. They spoke Chinese. . . . I was really worried. I thought that I'm extremely white," said Karen. Her own parents viewed her relationship with Kevin favorably, although one time they told her that any children the two might have would have a hard time. Karen described this as a "derogatory comment," and said, "I didn't like it."

In my individual interview with Kevin, white men often emerged as objects of rivalry. Kevin explicitly expressed his disgust with, and resistance to, popular white manhood. Not only Kevin, but also Karen racialized popular white manhood as sexist and racist. In a tone of derision, Kevin spoke of the white hegemonic masculinity that was popular on college campuses as "one-dimensional" and "ignorant," criticizing it as a lifestyle characterized by sex, alcohol, and sports. "White guys . . . they are just so the same . . . beer, girls, and football . . . that's all they think of." Kevin admitted that his perception of white men mainly derived from the marginality and subordination he encountered as a Chinese American man every day. He saw white men's expression of masculinity as a reflection of their desire for aggression and toughness, of their wish to conquer "the other." He described his apartment complex as "the middle of frat country," and detailed a code based on white supremacy, misogyny, and the quest to conquer in sports; these elements apparently united and solidified groups of white men in college by excluding and devaluing "the other" (racial minorities and women). Whenever Karen saw their white neighbors having a party in their courtyard and screaming loudly, she said she felt uneasy about their racial animosity toward Kevin: "I'm kind of concerned they are going to pick on him one day or try to start something with him because he's not white. It bothers me anybody can still think like that."

As a testimony to his attractive manhood, Kevin repeatedly quoted Karen's praise of him. "She thought I was different. She feels that I treat her better than other white guys . . . I listen to her, I cheer her, I treat her as a person, I respect her, I like her family. I treat her so well. . . . She tells me that no one has ever been nice to her, like ever. She said she wouldn't date another white guy again." Both in their individual and their couple interviews, Karen agreed on this, ardently praising Kevin's non-hegemonic traits: "He always wants to listen to me, listen to my side of the story. He is not self-righteous. . . . He tries to give to me, or tries to comfort me or consult me. . . . He's also very honest with me." Karen often contrasted Kevin with white men she had dated in the past and praised his ability to listen to her. The couple had celebrated their "six-month anniversary" a few weeks before, and Karen said, with a smile, "Kevin bought me flowers and perfume. . . . I didn't want him to spoil me." Kevin emphasized how Karen's affirmation enhanced his perception of his manhood, or helped him gain confidence in himself. "Karen means a lot to me. . . . She feels that I treat her better than white guys have. White guys, she said that they are only interested in sex. . . . I was different."

Both agreed it was usually Kevin who initiated communication to resolve their conflicts. Kevin said, "If I know something's wrong, I keep asking and asking until she tells me. Because I want her to talk about it no matter how bad it is." Karen said that this had never happened in her past relationships, in which her boyfriends usually controlled situations of conflict by "ignoring [her]" or "not talking to [her]."

Kevin and Karen criticized not only white men's homosocial culture, but also such white hegemonic masculine characteristics as "self-righteousness" and "belligerence." Karen explicitly contrasted her Asian American boyfriend with white men, asserting, "Actually, all of the white guys I dated were not sensitive." She attributed Kevin's different approach to masculinity to his racial difference: "Most of the Asian guys I meet seem to be more respectful toward women. . . .

[Here] there are lots of frat boys and they are all white. . . . I've seen so many drunk white guys yelling at girls and using girls. . . . I've had white guys yelling at me . . . never Asian people." Karen emphasized Kevin's nondomineering traits, that is, by inadvertently essentializing Asian men. "I don't even pay attention to white guys. . . . I've really started liking Asian guys as opposed to white guys," she said. She characterized Kevin as sensitive and caring; these features were confirmed as positive traits of his Asian American masculinity. Karen's portrayal of Kevin seemed to derive in part from her stereotyping of Asians as a model minority, characterized by not drinking too much, being polite, and studying hard.

Because the popular myth of Asian and Asian American manhood as asexual and emasculated remains pervasive, Karen's confirmation of Kevin's attractive manhood seemed important. Kevin believed that the racist and sexist portrayal of Asian American men made it difficult for them to receive attention from middle-class white women, who represent "hegemonic femininity":[4] "In Hollywood . . . we are kind of desexed because the role we've always played is always a demeaning or a domestic kind of role. You can look at a Latin guy, very sexy. Black guy, very sexy. White guy, sexy. White girls don't really see Asian men as sexy. . . . It's just obnoxious. . . . I think that's why white girls don't think, 'Oh, I like Asian males.'" As Kevin pointed out, since Hollywood films reinforce Anglo-American, bourgeois, male hegemony,[5] the absence of and disregard for Asian American men has not been an unfamiliar theme for these men in real life. "Some white girls don't even look at me," Kevin said. Further, the hegemonic portrayal of white women as the property of, or as partnered with, white men proclaims their inaccessibility to most Asian or Asian American men. "I think a lot of Asian men don't really hit on white girls. They are interested in white girls, yet they don't bother because, I think, they think they don't have a chance, or something. None of my Asian friends date white women." Kevin felt humiliation and frustration about the fact that Asian men receive so little attention as masculine figures. Karen commented: "But Asian guys never look at or check me out either. I don't think Asian guys ever look at me like I'm attractive. They only look at other Asians. I think they only want Asian women." The two agreed that there was a strong racial and gender wall between Asian men and white women; however, Kevin quickly distanced himself from those Asian American men who would "only want to date Asian girls. I'm different in that respect. I'm proud of [dating Karen]. . . . I know I'm different."

In college culture, where traditional white upper-middle-class gender norms are dominant, an Asian American man dating a white woman is an anomaly. Kevin and Karen received unwelcome stares from Karen's white female friends.

Karen described her dormitory as "all-white . . . where rich, spoiled, sorority, upper-class girls live." She claimed these women stared at Kevin. Kevin responded that this was due to "the way I dress, then I'm Asian, and I'm with a white girl." Karen said that her friends had not welcomed her Asian American boyfriend; she said, "They all like frat boys. They only date white guys. Very rarely do they date outside their race." When Karen had told her close friends about Kevin, she had not received a good response. One friend had a habit of making fun of Asian people and other racial minorities, using racial slurs. Another friend "just said, 'OK.' She didn't say, 'Oh, that's great.'" Yet another said nothing, but asked Karen how her parents felt about it.

That is, when Karen deviated from the norm of dating a white man, one friend implicitly expressed her perceptions of Karen's deviance, and demonstrated anxiety, by asking about Karen's parents' reaction. The strangers' staring at the couple was an indication that Karen and Kevin's union was a disruption of the normative racially segregated romantic relationship. Karen's choice of Kevin, an Asian American man, rather than a typical white fraternity man, threatened that norm of young white upper-middle-class womanhood in which women uphold upper-middle-class white men. Her choice disturbed the racial and gender hierarchy, implicitly sending a message to these white women that their white partners might not be adequate.

During the couple's interview, Karen, on the large couch, put her legs on Kevin's knees and rested her arms on his shoulder. She was very affectionate toward him throughout the interview. Karen was speaking more passionately and vibrantly than in her individual interview, taking the dominant speaking role, while Kevin was less vocal, expressing viewpoints supportive of hers. He said, "I like women who speak their mind." Karen held Kevin with both arms and said: "I dated a lot of white guys. None of them are really, like, great. The first Asian guy I meet, dating is just wonderful! I think Asian guys are sexy. He has a good family. They care about each other. They taught him well. He's supported by his family. He dresses good. He can dance good. He's good-looking. He is very romantic." Kevin blushed and responded briefly in a very shy tone, saying, "I care about you" as he put his hand over her legs.

"Yeah, he cares about me a lot. He always does," said Karen, hugging him again tightly. Even if these behaviors could be dismissed as "impression management," or as constituting the couple's performative strategy against stereotypes, the couple's affection also gave me a glimpse of how "the couple of [the] future" (Kevin's words) might interact once society has critically engaged the hegemony of gender and race.

As seen in the gender dynamics in this particular relationship, Kevin's nonhegemonic engagement in the relationship challenged the traditional presumption of feminine submission and masculine control. Feminist psychoanalytical theory has critically viewed masculinity in terms of "the male refusal to recognize the other" and "the woman's own acceptance of her lack of subjectivity."[6] In intimate relationships, "one person ('the woman') is not allowed to play the subject; one person ('the man') arrogates subjectivity only to himself."[7] In sexual relationships characterized by a traditional gender division, the woman is expected to act as an externalized ego-ideal, and the man is expected to possess the ability to define the position and value of the love-object.[8] Karen's relationship with Kevin appeared to let her be the desiring subject and him the desired. By being the desired subject of a white woman, Kevin gained the masculine recognition that is not accessible to most Asian American men in mainstream representations of manhood and sexuality.

One may argue that Karen's seemingly dominant role and Kevin's more submissive role reflected women's greater tendency in our society toward self-disclosure, and men's resistance to it because it signifies a loss of power. As feminist scholars have argued, one critical component of interpersonal power lies in "active forms of loving," or the "ability to define the position and value of the love-object" in an intimate relationship.[9] Karen exercised this power during the interview. (Of course, while this is a plausible interpretation of her behavior, it may be gjven different explanations.)

Further, Kevin was valorized for, in addition to his nonhegemonic traits, more traditional masculine traits, many of which often overlap with model minority stereotypes of Asian and Asian American men. His class status and ambition, characteristics associated with the traditional masculine provider role, were significant components of the masculinity that he had constructed and to which Karen responded. Karen repeatedly mentioned that Kevin was "from a good family." She described him as having a compulsion to work hard, another traditional provider trait and/or model minority stereotype. Karen also offered, with evident pleasure, examples of Kevin spending money on her as an indication of his chivalrous sensitivity and romantic masculinity. However, Kevin and Karen were neither married nor living together at the time of the interview, and it is important to note that gender roles do not fully emerge until couples engage in marriage and parenting.[10]

Failing in the Attempt to Maneuver White Masculinities

Kevin consolidated his masculinity by fashioning an image of himself as someone with class privileges, a cosmopolitan upbringing, tactful and sensitive com-munication skills, and a romantic and chivalrous nature, but other men whom I interviewed were less able to perform such a gender display in their relationships. One such individual was Kenji Tanaka, hampered by language barriers, an inability to maneuver American gender codes, and a lack of class privileges. Kenji could not critically engage in mainstream masculinity, much less gain a white woman's recognition. Instead of viewing the couple's marital problems as deriving from differing life-styles or from Kenji's lack of class privileges, his white wife blamed his ethnic upbringing for his lack of egalitarian sensibility or the sort of communication skills idealized in white manhood.

Tracy Tanaka, a twenty-six-year-old waitress, had been married to Kenji, a twenty-nine-year-old Japanese musician, for a year when we met. Kenji had grown up in Japan; when he finished college, he left Japan to study music in the United States. "I never wanted to be a typical salary man in Tokyo," he said. He worked two jobs to make ends meet, while playing guitar for several bands. One of his jobs was working as a waiter in a restaurant; there, he had met Tracy, who was waiting tables.

Tracy reported negative judgments from her friends and neighbors on her choice of husband. Her close friends asked her several unexpected questions, such as whether he "had a bad temper" or "drank too much," implying that they had stereotypical views of Asian American men. Tracy and Kenji also had a white neighbor who, according to Tracy, "wouldn't speak to us because we [were] an interracial couple. He wouldn't even say 'Hi.'" The owner of Tracy's apartment complex "rented it to [her] and Kenji because [she] was white," but "he wouldn't rent to two Asian men" who worked at the same restaurant in which she worked. Tracy worked briefly at a Japanese restaurant, where she was the only white waitress and where "white men come to pick up Asian women"; Asian American women who worked there, Tracy explained, tended to "only see the bad side of white people"—that is, their tendency to sexualize and commodify Asian American women—and, as a result, associated Tracy with such white men. One Korean American waitress even sarcastically commented on Tracy's marriage as "some kind of Asian fetish," asking her "what her problem [was]."

Kenji only dated white women, simply because "[he] did not want to date Asian women in America." He equated white women with the highest standards of beauty and power. He had had two white girlfriends before he met Tracy, but the relationships ended when these women left him because "[he] was not romantic." The language barrier was also a problem. Tracy said of Kenj, in an irritated tone, "he doesn't talk . . . because he gets very frustrated if he doesn't understand people's English." Soon after their marriage, Kenji and Tracy began to fight frequently over household responsibilities and over their communication difficulties. While Tracy had expected more egalitarian attitudes and behavior from her husband, Kenji said that he "had a hard time understanding the concept of equality" because he believed that he was "doing [the] right amount of work and she [was] still not happy." Tracy was frustrated with what she perceived as Kenji's expectation that she would be responsible for the upkeep of the household: "It wasn't natural for him to help me very much. I am the one responsible for the bills. I am responsible for the house. I am responsible for making sure the car gets taken care of. . . . It's been really hard. . . . I'm an artist. I haven't picked up my pen in a year and half now."

Just as Marie associated her Chinese husband's dominant traits with his Asian background and his having been raised as "a number one son" in his family, Tracy believed that Kenji's lack of willingness to help take care of the household derived from his Japanese upbringing, in which "his mom, [who] never had worked outside the house . . . took care of everything for him." But even more than cultural differences, Tracy and Kenji's different life-styles, and their lack of time spent together, increased the tension between them. When Tracy met Kenji, he was drinking and partying all the time, yet she believed he would change these habits. In our interview, she talked about how she wanted him to quit smoking and drinking. Tracy, as a strict vegetarian, also wanted him to stop eating fish. Kenji responded, "Eating fish is a part of how I grew up. I am not sure if I can stop." Tracy also expressed her frustrations about working two jobs as a waitress, not having traveled much, and not having spent time on her creative work.

And, just as Marie blamed her Chinese husband for lacking communication skills and sensitivity, Tracy pointed out Kenji's lack of interest in communicating with her as a source of marital problems. She said that she missed the "deep talk" that she was used to from her past relationships. "I think [white] American guys talk [a] little more," she said. "They talk to their girlfriends." Tracy wanted to go to couples counseling, but Kenji resisted, causing her to once again compare him unfavorably to white men. "I know a lot of [white] guys who went to counseling," she claimed. Tracy also complained about Kenji's lack of romantic traits. "It's really hard to understand. I'm not 100 percent sure that I can live without that. Because I like the idea of always trying to keep things new. . . . I like to stay interested in the relationship—like, bring me flowers or I bring you flowers or something like that." Kenji admitted that he was not good at expressing affection easily. But, he attributed that to his aversion to an "American" norm of gender display in which, as he indifferently described it, the "man always [has] to say to [the] woman, "You are pretty, you are beautiful, . . . I love you."

Although complaints about a male partner's inability to communicate and unwillingness to share housework are commonly reported among white couples,[11] white women often viewed these qualities in their Asian American partners as the result of an ethnic patriarchy that was less egalitarian and more male-dominated than white culture.

For Kenji's part, he felt blamed for his inability to meet his white wife's expectation that he be romantic, communicative, egalitarian, and more like the white boyfriends she had known in the past. In the face of expectations about romantic chivalry and egalitarian sensitivity, critical elements of the new gender display of class-privileged white men,[12] Kenji felt marginal and constrained. He said that he did not know how to improve the relationship with Tracy except by "apologiz[ing] whenever she [got] mad" and "punch[ing] the wall" silently.

Besides language barriers and cultural unfamiliarity, class status plays a role in how much room Asian American men have in which to negotiate masculinity in relationships with white women. Tracy eventually left Kenji. But Marie, the woman with the domineering foreign-born Chinese American husband, felt powerless to leave her marriage, despite her hopelessness about the gender inequality she suffered, because her husband had sole financial control over her and her children. Marie's situation demonstrates that, although a white female partner may judge Asian American masculinity as lacking in important modern masculine qualities, the judgment has little or no power when the woman has little power in the relationship.

White Americans, Class Status, and Cultural Identity

Intermarriage may serve as a cultural tool for destabilizing and resignifying one's racial identity and for providing wider racial and ethnic options. I will now discuss a case in which a Korean American man, Tony Rhee, laid claim to a white identity on the basis of his social class and intermarriage. The case illustrates how racial and ethnic categories become options not only for white Americans,[13] but also for Asian Americans with transnational backgrounds and class status, and also how intermarriage with whites can further widen such optional categories for Asian Americans. Tony's emphasis on his class background and his identification with whites illustrated his desire to approximate to hegemonic masculinity. Large numbers of Korean immigrants entered the United States as military brides, adoptees, labor migrants, political exiles, and international students under the militarization of the Korean peninsula in the post-1945 period;[14] Tony's transnational experiences exemplified this diversity among Korean immigrants, and demonstrated the difficulty of labeling individuals who would not neatly fit into the general categories of Korean or Korean American.

A twenty-six-year-old when we met, Tony Rhee worked part-time at a computer company. He had also returned to school recently to finish his undergraduate degree. Michelle Rhee, twenty-three, worked as an immigration advisor at a local college. The two had been married for about a year and a half. Tony and Michelle lived in a large new house, where Tony's mother had previously lived.

Tony was born in South Korea in the mid-1970s, when the country's dictatorial regime had just begun radical Westernization and modernization. When Tony was four, his father moved from South Korea to America with his wife and son to attend graduate school. Tony proudly described his father as being "the best. He went to the best school from middle school all the way to graduate school, in Korea." After his family came to the United States, Tony's mother became a breadwinner, taking a job as a nurse to support her husband. His parents communicated with each other in Korean, but Tony always spoke English with them.

When Tony was eleven, his father took a job at a state university in South Korea, so they moved back to that country. In the 1980s, South Korea was still governed by a military regime, which harshly controlled student movements. Military coups, civil unrest, and protests calling for democracy were part of the daily scene. Tony remembered people's fear and concerns regarding the actions that the government was taking in the name of national security. Many South Koreans were arrested for participating in the pro-democracy movement.

When his family had moved back to South Korea, Tony's life had changed abruptly. "I was never accepted," he said. In middle school, he became the target of other students' bullying because of his faltering Korean and fluent English. He was excluded as an "American." To be like the other students, he studied harder than he ever had before; he attended school from eight in the morning until eleven at night, then had to spend a few more hours finishing his homework before he went to bed. His grades were within the top 15th percentile, but did not reach the top 5th percentile; this was shameful for his father. Day after day, his father yelled at him and physically beat him. "Instead of support, I got abuse. That was really bad." Tony's father started drinking, around this time and became abusive toward Tony's mother, too. During our interview, Tony was able to look back and explain his father's change in behavior as result of the extreme social pressure arising from the political turbulence and rigid social hierarchy in South Korea.

Because of his inability to achieve the necessary grades in Korea, Tony felt he had failed to survive that society's competitive system and to achieve ideal Korean manhood, something he had strived to do for his father. After five years, Tony convinced his father to let him return to the United States. His father agreed with Tony's choice to attend one of the best American private high schools, which cost more than $20,000 for room and board alone at that time.

Michelle and Tony met at that private high school, when he was eighteen and she was sixteen. Tony said his friends were mostly from that "upper-class, mostly white" private school. "I never had any Korean friends. . . . It's hard to find the hippie Koreans. . . . A lot of my friends are freaks and geeks. They are not mainstream. They are not popular. Like Gothic kids and drug rats . . . who always wear chains and black." Many of his friends were kicked out of school for smoking cigarettes and skipping class. Michelle said, with a laugh, "I thought he was a bad boy. Because he always wore black. The bottom of his head was shaved."

Throughout the interview, Tony emphasized his upbringing in white upper-middle-class surroundings as a critical source of his identity as a white man. Tony passionately talked about how white protest masculinity became his cultural vehicle—the armor through which he recovered from his failed Korean masculinity and became a possessor of white masculinity. Tony had always searched for a social outlet to express his resentment and his struggle with authority figures in family and school, and he found this in rebellious white youth culture, which rejected hegemony and positively asserted marginality through fashion and life-style.

Tony fell in love with Michelle because she was "really smart, pretty, and very thoughtful." He asked her to marry him a year after they met, when they were still in high school. After Michelle graduated college, they finally married. According to Tony, his long relationship with Michelle "changed the relationship between me and the world, and made it more stable." Tony eventually gave up the drinking habit that he had picked up from high school friends, but he kept failing in college and eventually dropped out. Every time he failed, he said, he blamed himself, as if such self-debasement could help him regain his father's love.

Tony said he renounced his identity as a Korean a long time before, "because I couldn't fit in there," even though "I understand what it means to be Korean and I am Korean." Tony also rejected the label "Korean American." He said, "I would consider myself to be very American, but not Korean American. Because that's another culture, too. They are very fashion-oriented. Guys are sort of macho, certain cars. . . . It's like that in Korea. But it is different. . . . There are lots of ethnicities in the whites. . . . They are all different. They don't share the same culture. Asian Americans don't, either." Tony rejected identification as a Korean or a Korean American, that is, because both categories were built on common national and cultural beliefs and a common transnational history that he claimed not to share.

Identification as a "white American" provides cultural leeway for people like Tony, who refuse to have essentialized categories imposed upon them on a basis of their transnational backgrounds and social class. Tony argued that the ethnic category of *Korean American* referred to very specific historic American-born Korean experiences and did not include "other kinds" of Korean transnational experiences such as his; other Asian American men made similar comments about not belonging to particular Asian American communities because of their distinct cultural and historical differences. Kevin, for example, criticized Asian Americans as "self-segregating," and did not view himself as a part of their communities; he said, "They are very fashionable, very upscale. . . . Even if you go to the parties, you see huge groups of Asian people only hang out with Asian people." Such comments by Tony and Kevin marked their racial marginiality, not only in having white spouses but also in not having any sense of belonging to Asian American youth culture.

It is also interesting that both Kevin and Tony reacted strongly to applying the racial category of *Asian American* to themselves. Such ethnic categories can be seen as providing entitlement to U.S.-born Asians, proclaiming them more authentically "American" than other groups of Asians, and it inevitably causes tension, not coalition, among the diverse Asian American identities in the United States. Calling Asian Americans' cultural nationalism "the desire to banish *Asian(-)American*," Eng critically discusses the risk of Asian American studies focusing exclusively on American-born Asians, saying, "Any serious understanding of Asian American racial formation must be considered in relation to a comparative and internationalist model of subject formation and subjection beyond the real and imaginary borders of the U.S. nation-state."[15] When Tony claimed a multiplicity within Asian Americans, he was being critical of the dominance and exclusivity of groups of American-born Asians and the consequential lack of representation of diverse foreign-born Asian Americans, who came to the United States as a result of relatively recent shifts in global capital and labor.

Tony avoided not only the essentialist labels of *Korean* and *Korean American*, but also the essentialist categories of race and ethnicity. Instead, he presented himself as white in social class. In the couple interview, Michelle agreed, saying, "We are pretty much white American. He is very much more like me and our culture." Tony echoed, "We are pretty much white American as a social class." He regarded class status, which he became very aware of while attending an upper-class private school, as more powerful than race in terms of divisive power. Tony confidently said, "I think that money can buy the differences. In fact, actually, I think that racial differences are predominantly class differences, predominantly socioeconomic differences. The degree of whiteness is based on economic class." Michelle agreed, saying, "It is becoming like Mexico. As long as you are wealthy, you are white. You could be black, but they call you white, and you register as white."

Tony's masculinity, albeit rebellious, arose from white-dominated class and cultural beliefs acquired in an upper-class private school. His marriage to Michelle and her affirmation of his ability to "be like me and our culture" further stabilized his possession of *whiteness* as cultural capital and as social class. Because he possessed these resources, he avoided subjecting himself to a racialized Asian American or Korean American masculinity, and he obtained access to different kinds of white masculinity.

In the individual interview, Michelle described Tony's interest in feminism. "He is more interested in gender issues and feminism than I am. It's just because [he] went through the fear. Also [he] saw what [his] mother went through with [his] father." However, Michelle saw a wide gap between Tony's ideals and his practice, and this disparity was one of her frustrations in the relationship. In Tony and Michelle's house, Michelle was the one who ended up doing second shift; she did the grocery shopping, cleaning, and cooking. Before they married, Michelle remembered Tony saying that he wanted to stay at home as the "house husband," but it was difficult for him to practice this feminist ideal. "He comes home from work, and says 'I'm so tired' and watches TV, or 'I am going to eat dinner because I'm hungry,'" Michelle sighed.

Masculinity, Race, and Class

As we saw in considering Kevin and Kenji, looking at Asian American men's interracial relationships in terms of the men's cross-racial competition enables us to see that interracial relationships have served as a vehicle for these men to challenge of or ascend within the masculine hierarchy. With his command of good fashion and a combination of cosmopolitan upbringing, class status, and drive for success, Kevin displayed a confident brand of masculinity, positioning himself outside both white hegemonic masculinity and stereotypical Asian American masculinity. However, his display of seeming softness, sensitivity, and egalitarianism needs a cautious analysis; some men use these qualities, within the guise of the "New Man," as signs of class privilege and from this position project aggression, domination, and misogyny onto subordinate groups.[16] Thus Kevin's "New Man" behavior, treating Karen nicely, is not necessarily a departure from a position of hegemony.

Also, Kevin and Karen were neither married nor living together, and the operation of the external dimension of hegemonic masculinity would be less visible without the necessity of dividing housework or parenting tasks. Further, given that Karen drew on the model minority myth by lumping Asian men together as nondomineering, her testimony about Kevin subverting traditional traits of hegemonic masculinity ironically coincides with or even reinforces the stereotypes of Asian and Asian American men. Kevin and Karen's testimony regarding Kevin's nonhegemonic manhood is insufficient to allow us to reach a conclusion that the couple is engaging in profeminist gender work. Finally, since previous studies have demonstrated that men act differently depending on social settings,[17] it is not clear that, if a man relates to his intimate partner in a manner that runs contrary to hegemonic imperatives of masculinity, he will relate to all other women in the same manner. (Obviously, although I have offered plausible interpretations of Kevin and Karen here, different interpretations are possible.)

In contrast with Kevin, Kenji's failure to attain a white woman's validation of his manhood illustrated his failure to compete with white normative masculinity. Whereas much of Kenji's life was about working low-paying jobs, paying bills, and learning different cultural norms, he aimed to become a successful musician in America. But when he immigrated with the goal of becoming a musician, his social status descended from that of a college student with the potential for a successful future in Japan, to that of a blue-collar worker barely making ends meet in the United States. Even though he dated white women and even married one, he could not ascend the hierarchy of American manhood, nor did he have any adroit strategies for transforming or benefiting from hegemonic masculinity.

Tony's story did not address his explicit rivalry with white normative masculinity but instead focused on his aversion to manhood bound by race (Asian American) and nation (Korean). This does not mean that Tony was indifferent to the hierarchy of racialized manhood. In his emphasis on class status, and the intentional marking of himself as "white," a designation approved by his white wife, he demonstrated his potential to approximate to white hegemonic manhood. Tony maneuvered white protest masculinity and his upper-middle-class upbringing, portraying himself as an ally to, or even a part of, white society.

These three men had quite different immigration backgrounds and transnational experiences. Although all three desired white women's validation of their manhood as a source of empowerment, their differences in class status and ability to maneuver white norms of gender sensitivity made a difference in their maintenance of relationships. Kevin would have faced more difficulties in acquiring white women's affirmation of his nonhegemonic masculinities without his class privilege—which is, of course, also a critical component of hegemonic white masculinity. Similarly, Tony's interracial relationships and identification with his white friends might not have occurred had he gone to public school.

As seen in the contrasting stories of Kevin and Kenji, differences in generation or in childhood socialization in the United States can be a distinct marker of status that affects Asian American men's positioning of themselves. In addition to their ability to speak English without accents and to maneuver gender displays with a knowledge of fashion and chivalry, American-born or American-raised Asian Americans are more likely to understand the demands and desires of white women. Foreign-born Asian American men lack these cultural resources, and often find themselves further toward the bottom of marginalized masculinity. In Kevin and Karen's case, Karen spoke highly of Asian men by essentializing them as having qualities that Kevin manifested. However, her "racial lumping," common among white Americans (though positive and well-intended, in her case), obliterates the socioeconomic and cultural inequalities among Asian American men. It is very possible that Karen might never be attracted to foreign-born Asian American men. Karen and Tracy's different perceptions regarding their partners' abilities to communicate seem to relate to each man's generational status.

Public disapproval of Asian American men with white women remains strong even in the younger generation. This is in distinct contrast to the reception of Asian American women being paired with white men, which seems to engender little negative public response. Further, white woman's stereotypes of "Asian" masculinity, as seen through the filters of the model-minority myth, hypermasculinity, and the notion of "perpetual foreigners," remain strong. The essentialization of Asian American manhood through comparison of Asian Americans to white norms of masculinity seems to heighten the barriers between white women and Asian American men. But white women use essentialism both positively and negatively: where Karen negatively racialized white masculinity when she praised Asian American masculinity, the same tactics were employed by Tracy in negatively viewing Asian American masculinity by comparing Kenji with her past white boyfriends.

As seen in the cases of Kevin and Tony, many young successful Asian American men might deploy a "New Man"-complicit masculinity, which also reifies the model minority myth, to challenge traditional images of white masculinity. In a much broader context in which increasing interracial marriage (with whites) promotes Asian Americans to the status of honorary whites, Asian Americans' ascension to and claim of a hegemonic position, through complicity with hegemony (or "racial crossover,")[18] might become an even more prevalent phenomenon in the future. However, this strategy will not be effective in helping those Asian American men who lack class privilege, such as Kenji, to overcome the threats or insecurities they experience in relation to white women. Further, many factors—the importance of class status, the view of white women as symbolic capital, the pervasive stereotypes of Asian American men (including the images of the model minority and the perpetual foreigner), and the reification of one hegemony over another—appear huge obstacles to the future possibility of a cross-racial and cross-gender alliance between Asian Americans and white Americans. Even white women's affirmation of upper-middle-class Asian American men as subversive "feminine" men may feed the model minority stereotype and maintain racial divisions between Asian Americans and white Americans.

Chapter 6   Men Alone

THIS CHAPTER DISCUSSES WHY SOME Asian American men, regardless of their past histories of dating white women, ultimately prefer dating a woman of their own ethnicity. In the previous two chapters, I discussed Asian American men's competition with ideologies of normalized white masculinity; in this chapter, however, I discuss two Asian American men who expressed a desire *not* to follow the path of approximating to white masculinity. Although both had dated white women in the past, they were single at the time of the interviews. I discuss how awareness of mainstream racism and sexism in America and a desire to belong to an ethnic community led these men to set themselves the goal of marrying within their own race.

The chapter consists of two parts. The first section discusses a second-generation Chinese American man's failed attempts to attain hegemonic masculinity, his previous marriage with an Hispanic woman, and his current reluctance to date American women and preference for dating overseas Chinese women. The second section discusses a second-generation Vietnamese American man who, growing up, intentionally resisted Asian model minority stereotypes by trying to attain a white-like ideal manhood and a white girlfriend; I examine his race consciousness and his desire to identify with the label *Asian American*, which led him to want to marry a woman of his own ethnic group.

Eschewing White Masculinities, Utilizing Capital as an "American"

William Lin, a thirty-five-year-old, tall, friendly, Chinese American graphic designer, was born on the East Coast of the United States. His father and mother, born in China, left for Taiwan in the late 1940s to flee political turmoil, and in the 1960s immigrated to the United States to attend college. William's father worked as a librarian at a local university, and his mother was a homemaker.

William described his personality, during his childhood, as shy and quiet. Due to his father's work, William's family moved to the northern United States when he was in grade school, and he was the only Chinese student in his new school. He was often teased for his mispronunciation of certain English words that he had learned from his mother. He went through several years of grade school before people stopped pointing out his accent. Even though William "never associated [this harassment] with being Chinese," he had always felt different from others; displacing his racial difference, he viewed his treatment as the result of a difference in personality. "I was different because I was really shy," he said. But then he added, "Although, thinking back . . . if you are shy and Chinese, those two things maybe separate you from the rest of kids."

As an adolescent, gaining masculine acceptance by being seen as "social, popular, and cool" had been his goal, but he never attained it. "A lot of Chinese people run into that," he added. William instead became an overachiever; as his parents expected him to, he did well in school. For William, "not to shame [his] parents" was always the most apparent motivation for his deeds. But the real reason he worked so hard, he said, was not his parents' influence so much as his own desire to compensate for not being cool. "I think one of the reasons I wanted to do well in things, music or school, was that was my way of trying to become accepted. That was the only thing I knew how to do. To be accepted [and to] stand out . . . but I was never good with the whole popularity thing."

When William joined the track team, his parents did not let him attend early morning training or stay late at school; they discouraged him and his younger sister from many activities they did not value. As a result, William felt, he lost many opportunities to prove his masculinity to his peers in school, and he still resented this at the time of the interview. "They [his parents] didn't realize that it was really important for a guy, or boy, who is trying to prove himself or trying to get in with the crowd." His sister Brigitte, who was good at dancing, had to quit because her mother "was afraid she would grow up to be an exotic dancer." Brigitte became the opposite of their mother, William said; "She is spunky and tough." As a college student, Brigitte minored in women's studies and was very involved in feminism. William's parents told him to study to be an engineer but had few expectations for Brigitte, "because I'm the boy" and "it doesn't matter what kind of career she has. They wanted her to marry a nice guy."

William's was a traditional Chinese family: he had never seen his father treat his mother as an equal in their relationship. "He looked at her almost like a child and he never trusted my mom to do stuff, really," William said. But instead of expressing sympathy toward his mother for the ways she was belittled by his father, William expressed resentment about her "emotional abusiveness" toward her children, and her strict discipline. He complained that his mother always tried to shame him and his sister, saying such things as, "Look at those other kids, they are doing this. What are you doing here? You are making me look bad." He went on: "She spanked us a lot. She yelled at us a whole lot. So little things would annoy her, just any little thing." William described his mother's "meanness" as "common" among older women in Chinese culture. In his own relationships, William came to desire "someone who was equal, who I can trust, so I can depend on them"—someone, in other words, the opposite of what he saw his mother to be.

William had dated several white women and Hispanic women, but only one Chinese woman, whom he met while working at a Chinese restaurant. He denied that race mattered in his forming and maintaining relationships with white and Hispanic women. "Race did not affect my relationships with white women at all because I was born in America and raised in America. We are pretty much the same." He continued, "I am American. . . because I know everything that they know. Because I was born here and lived here as long as they have. In that regard, there's no problem with Caucasians." William, without referring to racism, emphasized "his sameness [to whites] as an American." Just as in his struggle to attain popularity in school, he denied any racial difference between whites and himself.

William met his ex-wife, Martha, an American-born Hispanic woman, at work. She was several years older than he and had a one-year-old boy from a previous marriage. William said, "I thought she was very street-smart. She grew up kind of poor, so she knows a lot about how to deal with things in life." For William, whose life had been very sheltered, Martha's outgoing personality and sociability were immediately attractive. Her strength and independence were also appealing to him.

Even though his parents granted William certain freedoms as a male, they disagreed with his marriage to Martha because she was Hispanic, divorced, and a single mother. William said: "I think they would've been very happy with a Chinese person or Caucasian. Chinese people have this image that, you know, white people are better than other minorities except Chinese people." After six years, his marriage to Martha ended in divorce, and his family members "were relieved" by the marriage's failure. Even though everybody in his family got along with Martha and "they really liked her," they felt that "she wasn't right" for him.

William's parents disagreed even more strongly with Brigitte's marriage to an African American man. "My whole family had a hard time about it. . . . My dad argued with her for a long time, and he was really mad. He felt it is just not right. Plus the babies, half-Chinese and half-black. They couldn't get around that, you know. . . . I don't think they can come up with any really good reasons for it other than prejudice, you know." His parents even refused to attend the marriage ceremony and disapproved of Brigitte's marriage until it ended.

William observed that racial minorities tend to see the racial hierarchy in a way that always puts whites at the top, their own group next, and others after that. When William and Martha went to a party together, attended by many of her Hispanic friends, one of them came up to Martha and said to her, "Oh, your husband, he's Chinese. You are pretty enough for a white boy." William said: "She didn't say she is pretty enough for a Mexican or Hispanic guy. She said she is pretty enough for a white boy. That's a funny comment, to me. So, white was the standard and was the highest. Chinese, I guess, is maybe a little bit below Hispanic but is still above black. That's a terrible thing." William came to the conclusion that "Americans, Caucasians, are least concerned about interracial relationships, compared to other races." William said that Chinese and Hispanics "have the most things to say about race" and that "white people are the least concerned about ethnicity, compared to other ethnicities. . . . White people are used to seeing differences." He blamed minorities for not having acted on politically correct or color-blind attitudes, as many whites have.

There are two possible reasons why William perceived white people to be the group least concerned about race. First, white people see their white privilege as the norm and are therefore not aware of race as the visible and critical essence of their power over racial minorities; as a result, they may regard other types of power differences, such as class and gender, as more important. Second, the white mainstream discourse of race intentionally avoids seeing power in race; Frankenberg, in her study (1993) of whiteness, claims that white women consciously and unconsciously engage in a "color-evasive and power-evasive" racial discourse; such discourse, she states, emphasizes essential human sameness rather than racial differences, and tends to overlook the sociopolitical inequalities with which race has been historically constructed.

Although the white mainstream culture may engage in this color-blind or power-evasive discourse, racial minority groups may possess a much more acute awareness of racial disadvantages and racism in their everyday lives. They recognize that whiteness constitutes privilege and access to social and cultural capital; consequently, they tend to put whites at the top of the hierarchy of desired objects, however ambivalently. What William was emphasizing was in fact that some racial minorities adopt the dominant group's gaze when they judge those whom they view as lower than their own race in the hierarchy.

It did not take William long in his marriage to Martha to find himself repeating to his stepson what his own mother used to say to him; he had to notice that he was engaging in the same pattern of emotional punishment as his mother had. His attempts at fatherhood, like his attempts at adolescent masculinity, did not succeed despite his efforts, and he said, "The best thing I could do in the situation was to remove myself . . . as much as possible." Brigitte's marriage also ended in failure, partly because her husband wanted to have children, yet they never had any. Still, William said quietly, "I hate to blame my mom for this, because everyone is responsible for what they do."

William's failed masculinity—his sense of his inadequacies as a man and as a father, as well as his strong sense of powerlessness—might be recovered by his new strategy of shifting his attention to Chinese women. At the time of his interview, William was dating Chinese women whenever he visited his family in China. There, he felt he had more power and money because he was American. "Here in America, women are independent," he went on. "They have more power. It is hard to ask [them out]. Women feel honored [to be asked out] in China. . . . In the U.S., women don't need men. . . . You have to be good looking. You have to be really rich. . . . They can choose what they want and make the guy less powerful."

Although his new strategy contradicted his stated preference for "someone who is equal," William was still trying to realize idealized masculinity; going out with women in China, he could compete without the pressure of white American masculine norms. He enjoyed his popularity there. When he asked women out in China, "they [felt] honored" by his offer. "Women in other countries are happier, even though they don't have much freedom," he noted. "American women are not happy." In William's eyes, "happy" women seemed women satisfied with men like him.

William's preference for Chinese women over American women appeared to derive from his desire to avoid the feeling of powerlessness that he experienced within the system of American manhood. His attraction to the happiness of women in other countries, who remained content in spite of their economic, political, and social deprivation, seemed related to a desire to enhance his own manhood by exercising his material and social privileges as an American. Although he claimed he wanted an "equal" partner, William wanted these women from China over whom he could exert his material and social advantages.

William frames American women as independent and assertive subjects who may emasculate and threaten his marginal manhood.[1] He referred to the difficulty of attracting "American" women, rather than that of attracting "white" women. By using this language, he may have avoided making references to his racialized manhood, instead presenting his powerlessness as part of American men's common experience with American women. Or possibly he was implying that hegemonic masculinity is transracial rather than solely white, and thus attainable without possessing a white woman. Certainly, his powerlessness may have been caused not so much by American women as by the white normative masculinity from which he was excluded. His transnational family ties and the global capital of America also allowed him to choose a woman in China; thus, by eschewing American women and avoiding competition with hegemonic masculinity in the United States, William could deny his marginality in the hierarchy of hegemonic masculinity.

Searching for Interethnic Marriage, Reconciling Ethnic Masculinity

The fashionable bright blue sports car in the driveway was not at all in keeping with my first impression of Leslie Duong, a twenty-six-year-old Vietnamese American man. Leslie, with cheekbone-length straight hair which frequently fell forward over his eyes when he spoke, came across as very shy and reserved. But he also had a strong and vigorous speaking voice, and a frequent, friendly laugh. Leslie worked at a large advertising company, but at the time of the interview planned to go to the West Coast to become a professional filmmaker.

Leslie was born in the United States in the same year that the Vietnam War ended. His father was an officer in the navy in South Vietnam, but as soon as the war was over, his parents and older brother and sisters flew to the United States. The process of leaving Vietnam was, Leslie emphasized, far easier for his family than for most Vietnamese refugees at the time, whose desperation was often extreme. "It was a little bit easier for our family. Because [my father] was in the South Vietnamese military . . . U.S. government supported him. Basically we just went from there through the military to come over here. But, say, my brother-in-law, my sister's husband, whom I live with, his family came to the United States in 1980. They just had to go out to the ocean and claim a siren and then a boat came and picks them up." Leslie spoke about the details of how his close family members managed to escape the oppression and poverty of postwar Vietnam, lived in refugee camps in the Philippines and Hong Kong, and sought after the boats that eventually would take them to the United States. Nothing about coming to the United States as a war refugee could have been "easy" for Leslie's family either, but he meant that his family was exceptionally privileged, hardly typical of the many Vietnamese people who risked their lives to reach the United States with little or no support. Leslie's parents had never told their children about living through national turmoil and how their lives had since changed; "I guess we just never really talked about it," he said. "I haven't really asked a lot, either."

Leslie was the youngest of four children. His father had worked as an engineer in the United States after obtaining a graduate degree. Achievement and success were mandatory for Leslie and his three siblings: "My father, he always expects us to win and be number one in everything, whatever it is sports, or art, or anything. . . . My father, he taught us, when we were very young, try to be leaders among our friends, to lead people. That, I think, influenced all of us. Achievement is very, very important. . . . We accepted challenges." Leslie and his brother learned at an early age not to fear competition. Leslie did well in classes, played French horn in the school band, and worked as the main producer of a series of shows in high school. And he accepted challenges not only in academics and the arts, but also in sports. "We had a lot of competition, like running, track and field, jumping, and things like that. We had to compete at a young age. He wanted us to be the best. We didn't think it was unfair or anything, because that's the way we grew up." His father would reward all four children when one of them won first place in a school competition.

Nevertheless, Leslie was reluctant to push himself to compete and achieve in math and science, precisely because of the racial stereotype of Asian Americans as being good at these subjects. "There is this whole idea about how every Asian is good at math and science. Asians are very technical." Although he knew he could do well in these subjects, he avoided studying them and intentionally received some bad grades to avoid being stereotyped. "I knew I was stereotyped. So, as a kid, I made myself not be good at math and science, just to prove people were wrong. I grew and say, hey, look at me, I'm not good at math or science. I am really bad at it. But I can write a story. I can write English very well. So can you have any stereotype about me? Now I hate that I did that—because I am not good at math and science. I should have been, because I was when I was little."

"I knew that people always thought that I was a smart guy because I am Asian," Leslie said. He remembered that his "conscious" rebellion started when he was in about sixth grade, and lasted at least until the end of junior high school. He had attempted to subvert the model minority discourse; every time he saw an expression of ambiguity in people's faces as they regarded this "deviant" Asian boy, he felt a sense of relief. "They would say, man, that's weird. Weird kid." Eng and Han write that the model minority discourse "delineates Asian American students as academically successful but rarely 'well-rounded'—'well-rounded' in tacit comparison to the unmarked (white) student body."[2] Leslie had sensed this negative side of the model minority myth and, by taking on the role of "the leader" and mastering the arts, sports, and language, tried to create a transgressive image of himself.

Since Leslie's parents both worked outside the home, his two sisters always took care of the house and their two younger brothers. "My older sister, she took the role of raising us. She would teach me how to read [a] whole book," said Leslie. Leslie's house was different from those of his friends, whose mothers always took care of the house and children. Leslie remembered this difference in his family as a "shame" and an "embarrassment." He said: "I have always felt difference. But I never thought I was different because of race. I did not grow up where there was a mother cooking dinner every night at seven o'clock. Where the whole family gets together and eats dinner at table, like a lot of American families. . . . Also . . . my parents, chores and stuff, my parents have always worked, so we were kind of a dirty household. I didn't want people coming over to my house." Leslie said race was not the cause of his feeling of difference, and it may be true that he always knew that he would attain success by working to "be the best," as his father taught him, and could therefore subvert his race through his own efforts. But race cannot be entirely separated from history, class differences, and cultural practices. The "difference" of which Leslie spoke carried with it a sense of alienation, resulting as it did from a lack of economic resources (this was brought up in the interviews, though not discussed in this chapter in detail). Leslie wanted to play baseball just as much as many of his friends did, but he sensed the economic constraints that this would impose on his family and knew he could not ask them to pay for baseball supplies. If the embarrassment Leslie felt, and the lack of familial economic resources, reflect common experiences among Southeast Asian refugees, then they need to be understood as part of the racial dilemma.

Leslie started dating Kelly, a white woman, when they were in high school. His relationship with her lasted about three years. As Leslie recalled, "I think my girlfriend liked me . . . because I did different [things]. I liked different things." Leslie referred to Kelly's ability not to be afraid of doing "different" things herself, and to the fact that she chose an Asian American boyfriend rather than a white one. Leslie also presumed that Kelly liked his achievements in unusual fields, and his strategic deviance from the traits of the stereotypical Asian man.

Leslie, while not having thought of his relationship as interracial, was often aware of people, especially Asian people, staring at Kelly when she was with him. "We were bowling one time. There was an Asian group over there. So there's a lot of staring. Actually one of the guys called me something like 'white boy.' They didn't like it. Making fun of me. . . . I'm white; I'm not Asian." With reference to this, Leslie said that there was "a lot of racism within the race. It is not necessarily white vs. Asian, or white vs. black, but within the race itself." Leslie emphatically noted racial hostility that was directed not at whites but at people of the same race who were with whites. This claim of internalized racism corresponds to Pyke and Dang's findings in their study on second-generation Asian Americans who employ mainstream society's stereotypes to define themselves and other, co-ethnic Asian Americans.[3] In the study, the authors note that second-generation Asian Americans often have to strive for acceptance by whites by "expending much energy in the display of an assimilated status via language usage (e.g., speaking without an accent), clothing, attitudes, and behavior."[4] Asian Americans engaged in this process by labeling co-ethnic Asians either as "too ethnic-identified" and thus a target of derision, or as "whitewashed," i.e., "forgetting their roots and being under the illusion that they can actually join the white race."[5] Asians whom Leslie and his white girlfriend encountered might have seen Leslie as making this sort of display of emulating whiteness, and thus have expressed their deep racialized resentment toward him. Cheng calls this reaction a "suppressed racialized resentment," a racial melancholia that comes from the yet ungrieved loss of whiteness. She argues that it has been deeply embedded in the racial structure of the United States.[6]

Leslie had made a couple of films, and when he was eighteen he submitted his first film, "Haircut," to a local film festival. He explained that this film is about reverse racism: "A Mexican guy, he gets a haircut, and he thinks the white guy didn't like him because he was Mexican. He thinks this guy giving the haircut is going to kill him, hurt him. . . . I got the idea from getting a haircut from a guy I'm scared of, and I wrote it for myself and then had my Mexican friend acting in it instead of an Asian." In the film, Leslie portrays the anxiety and fear that a racial minority, who has less power in society and is a vulnerable customer, might experience in sitting and letting a barber work on him with scissors and a razor. Leslie said, "The white guy didn't like him because he was Mexican," but this view is only in the main character's mind; there is no way to know the extent to which this discomfort between the white barber and the main character is racially motivated.

This film can be seen as a testament to Leslie's unspoken racialized fear of white men. It also illustrates an Asian American man's perception of the racial dilemma that exists between whites and racial minorities. The main character is obsessed with the idea that the white man will kill him because he is Mexican. Leslie expressed his paranoia ambivalently by referring to the film as an example of reverse racism, in which excess paranoia ended up producing the minority's delusional self-injury and justifying his psychological revenge on whites. But his sense of being injured did not change the power dynamics between whites and Asians; it is the main character, the Mexican (or Asian), who is torn between his repressed resentment and his guilt regarding his own hostility toward the white man.

This racial paranoia sheds light on the crucial structure of the racial hierarchy in the United States. Ann Cheng, referring to Ralph Ellison's *Invisible Man*—in which a black man accidentally bumps into a white man and, resenting the white man's failure to see him, yells "Apologize! Apologize!"—discusses the racial dynamic that emerges as a "mutual projection" based on everyday social scripts deeply embedded in the social structure of race.[7] Cheng calls this socially embedded script, in which the black man perceives an injury in having been ignored, a racial melancholia. This is racial melancholia for the racial subject: the internalization of discipline and rejection—*and* the installation of a scripted context of perception. The invisible man's racial radar, at once indicative of both perspicacity and paranoia, is justified. For the invisible man is both a melancholic object and a melancholic subject, both the one lost and the one losing.[8]

In racist society, the racial minority, consciously and unconsciously, already has a psychic script about being rejected and dismissed for his or her race, and is tempted to validate this script in daily encounters with whites. This psychic pattern of projection is part of racial relations; as Cheng argues, the lack of public and social language for describing the minority's psychic injury makes it difficult for the minority to grieve the racialized loss and injury. Leslie's *reverse racism* could be seen as the minority man's psychological negotiation between his fear of being invisible to the white man, and his resentment at losing his racial subjectivity in front of the white man.

At the time of my interview with him, Leslie had only dated white women, but he wanted, he said, to begin dating Asian women; "A while ago, I told myself I probably wanted to marry an Asian girl." Recently he met a Vietnamese girl, but "she didn't like me back." He speculated that "she wanted to have a white boyfriend."

His decision seemed strongly affected by his parents' preference. His parents wanted him to marry a Vietnamese woman, and, he said with a laugh, his mother "sometimes goes out and looks for the girls" for him.

Leslie's decision to marry a Vietnamese woman also related to his "social reception" as a filmmaker, he said:

> I want to be a filmmaker, making American films. But I guess, maybe part of it is, I don't want to be like, I'm just an Asian guy trying to be an American. I want people to know that I still stick to my culture and that I am not leaving my culture behind me. . . . Whoever I marry, it doesn't matter, obviously. But I think people seeing me with an Asian wife, just

by seeing that, understand that I'm not just trying to be another white person. I'm trying to be ethnic. I'm trying to belong to an ethnic group while I am still doing American things. . . . And that's just an image obviously. Inside, too, I want to make sure I stay ethnic as well. It's not just because of how people see me.

Leslie referred to Connie Chung, the first Asian American anchor on a major network evening news program, as an example of an Asian American "just wants to be white" and continued, "She gets that all the time. She married a white person. They say, oh, she doesn't care about her community." Thus, Leslie viewed marriage with an Asian woman as critical evidence of his belonging to Asian America and as part of being responsible toward the Asian American community.

Leslie recalled being called "white boy" by a group of Asians and viewed this as an example of "racism within." But his view of Connie Chung as one who "just wants to be white" showed the same negativity toward interracial couples displayed by that group of Asians. Although he was aware of a deep ambivalence among Asian Americans toward Asian–white interracial couples, and knew that Asians with white partners are often seen as using their relationships to be accepted as white and to acquire the privileges of whiteness, he seemed to be exhibiting this ambivalence himself.

Leslie, who had mainly white friends and who had dated white women, intentionally proclaimed himself an Asian American. His expressed preference for Asian women was also a strategy to mark himself as an authentic Asian American, not one who wants to be white. Behind this decision was resentment regarding the model minority myth and mainstream America's racism toward Asian Americans: "Americans think that Asians are the best because it seems like they play the game the same way the Americans do. They just do it without making any noise about it. They don't make a mess. . . . They do not knock anything down. . . . I feel that's how people feel." Leslie resented the fact that Asians are assigned seemingly positive attributes by the dominant whites to contain them and depict them as safe and subservient *others*.

Leslie said his ambition to make films was partly a desire to help solve the problem of the poor representation of Asian American actors, directors, and producers in the U.S. film industry. "There are not many Asian film makers. . . . There are not a lot of Asian stars, either." Every day Asian Americans become even more invisible in films, he noted, because of the prevalence of colorful "oriental" characters and the popularity of foreign Asian films—exotic enough not to evoke much racial anxiety about Asian Americans.

Leslie searched for the racial and ethnic space in which he could assert his public identity and resolve his melancholic agency. As for his parents' silence about the past, he said, "One day, we will talk about it." He was trying to find the racial location from which he could regenerate his racial identity as an Asian American and vocalize his family's past and, more than anything else, reconcile his ambition "to be the best" (i.e., approximate to white normalcy) with his fear of being "killed because [he is] Asian."

Masculinity and Socialization

These two second-generation Asian American men, William and Leslie, each viewed his wish to marry a woman of his own ethnicity as a critical component of ethnic manhood, distancing him from the norms of white masculinity. Even though William blamed his family's strict socialization, especially the actions of his mother, and his own personality for his inability to acquire the traits of ideal manhood and establish a successful marriage, his sense of marginality was also shaped by the structure of gender and race in American culture. The difficulty that Asian American men find in attaining popularity in dating or the marriage market can hardly be ignored as a cause of William's frustration, and his lack of class power must have made his search for a white American woman even more difficult. Racialization, and the gender dynamics involved in socialization in schools, families, and the dating market, are critical to fully understanding Asian American man's development of self-esteem and self-confidence.

Leslie's decision to marry a Vietnamese woman derived from his aversion to the pervasive racism he had experienced, and from negative images associated with intermarriage, such as the idea that it indicates a "lack of ethnic commitment." Leslie expressed considerable ambivalence about race and ethnicity, as seen in his desire to avoid coming across as too Asian, his efforts to display normative manhood, and his choice of a white girlfriend—indicators of his conformity to white supremacy and of his implication in the perpetuation of racism against Asian Americans; for him, the eventual decision to marry within his own ethnicity meant he was consciously resisting mainstream racism and striving to empower his ethnic manhood without employing the guise of, or relying on the symbolic power of, whiteness. This way, Leslie hoped to display his racial and ethnic responsibility and commitment.

This view of interracial marriage as a marker of "abandonment of racial and ethnic commitment" brings to mind Childs's findings regarding black women's views of intermarriage; Childs showed that black women believed black men's marriage with white women showed a lack of commitment to African American communities.[9] Although those who intermarry do not, in fact, necessarily lack ethnic commitment or responsibility toward their communities, such couples almost certainly find it more challenging to negotiate ethnic practices and share experiences of racism and marginality.

One important factor in deciding whom to marry is parental preference,[10] and both Leslie and William described the strength of their parents' wish for them to marry within their own ethnicities, which had to have an impact on their eventual decision.

These two second-generation Asian American men's views of intermarriage revealed a clear link to the difficult socialization process they endured, a process shaped by racism and sexism, in the United States. They had been constantly forced to emulate white manhood and to scrutinize their own racial and ethnic practices, including their speech, their parents' discipline styles, their socio-economic status, and their co-ethnic members' evaluation of themselves and their dating habits. For Asian American men who experience a childhood and adolescence full of such racialized and gendered scrutiny, an interracial relationship may become an unappealing, even extremely political, choice as it relates to deep racialized resentment and denial regarding their marginalized ethnic masculinity. Compared to first-generation Asian Americans who lack such a negative socialization in the United States, these second-generation Asian Americans may view interracial relationships as unpleasant reminders that their manhood has always been evaluated as deviant, foreign, and marginal.

Conclusion

Matters of Race and Gender

THIS BOOK HAS ILLUSTRATED DETAILS of various Asian American–white relationships. Asian American–white intimacy shares more commonalities than differences with same-race relationships. It is similar to same-race intimacy in that is shaped by ideologies of gender, marriage, and family more than by race. But it is also different, and not because of essential racial and ethnic differences but because of the continuing impact of historically produced discourses and images of race, compounded by discourses of nation, citizenship, and immigration.

Structural inequalities have emerged distinctively through the surroundings of, and gendered patterns within, Asian American–white American intimacy. As the central force behind love, marriage, family, and nation, the logic of patriarchy/gender has shaped the exchanges of racialized images and power dynamics within Asian American–white interracial couples. Racialized images emerge as a critical part of mutual attraction, and then are incorporated into the gender dynamics.

Gendered immigration laws and narratives of nation and citizenship, in which white males are cast in the positions of authority, seem to continue to affect public receptions of interracial relationships and gender dynamics, particularly with regard to foreign-born Asian American women's marriages to white men. In my interviews, white men coupled with Asian American women reported little experience with negative perceptions and racism, but some white women coupled with Asian American men had negative social receptions. The Asian American women–white men couples' lack of encounters with racism could be partly due to mainstream society's acceptance of Asian American women. But the same women who reported little racism as part of a couple still offered accounts of how they suffered from racism individually. Thus, these couple's experiences may have more to do with racialized white male authority than with a lessening of racism per se. Indeed, to conflate the American public's acknowledgment of white men's choice of Asian American women with a lessening of racism serves to protect the hegemonic orders of race and gender, in which women of color continue to be seen as second-class citizens. It should be noted that, in some cases, it was precisely this authorial position of gender and race from which some white men pursued Asian women.

White men's stereotypes of Asian American women as hyperfeminine and subservient remain persistent, and some Asian American women are wary of them. In interviews, they expressed an aversion to some white men's imposition of these stereotypes, and the attendant commodification of these women. Foreign-born Asian American women who lack class mobility, language skills, and knowledge of U.S. racism and sexism were more likely to submit to such expectations and unequal marriages. In contrast, the young second-generation Asian American women in relationships with white men wanted egalitarianism. Among second-generation Asian American women who date white men, the notion of Asian American women "marrying up" by partnering with white men is considered an outdated stereotype, since many of these women have higher educational degrees and/or socioeconomic status than have their white partners. This old stereotype falsely essentializes Asian American women as inferior and naturalizes their gendered subjugation to higher-status men.

However, this study did not find sufficient evidence to determine how truly egalitarian these second-generation Asian American women's relationships were. As only one of the couples that I interviewed lived together as an engaged couple, I was unable to further discuss how American-born Asian American women's marriages to white men differ from those of foreign-born Asian American women. Such a binary generalization may not work, since factors that affect gender dynamics are women's education, income, careers, and cultural and language proficiency. But I would emphasize that, though the second-generation young Asian Americans proclaimed themselves to be upwardly mobile and independent subjects, and expressed a preference for white men for their egalitarian traits lacking in Asian American men, the women's preference for white men as protective breadwinner figures, or as liberators, remains highly traditional.

The discourse of whiteness did not simply emerge as a signifier of white supremacy or explicit white dominance, but, rather, operated more subtly through an intersection with gender. A social and cultural emphasis on multiculturalism and color-blind discourses in intimate and marital relationships obscured not solely the powers of race but also those of gender within relationships. Many white men interviewed for the study saw Asian American women as ideal partners because of their supposed racialized femininity and model minority traits. Most marriages between foreign-born Asian American women and white men followed traditional gender divisions; that is, white men were dominant. It was often the middle-class white men who were in the position to define and control their relationships, and to decide their children's racial identities. Across all generations, color-blindness (observed in such statements as "race does not matter") was a theme often voiced by white men. Perhaps from thinking of themselves as "equal to" or even "the same as" whites, many Asian Americans also conformed to color-blind views of themselves, and to the view that race is a white–black problem, not their own. On the other hand, since Asian American men had encountered negative receptions in society, they expressed color-cognizant views, such as noting how their wives had encountered negative social receptions or did not feel comfortable interacting with Asian Americans. Even though some Asian American men strove to attain the color-blind ideal of the middle-class family, they were cognizant of white communities' receptions of intermarried couples and mixed-race families, and of white women's receptions of Asian Americans.

Although young white men coupled with second-generation Asian American women were much more willing to learn the ethnic or cultural practices of their partners and partners' families than were older white men married to foreign-born (mostly Filipina American) Asian American women, the younger men's understanding of race and of their partners' experiences of racism was limited. Most of their views were filtered through a linguistic lens of color-blindness and white privilege, in which the race of an Asian American partner was understood as a matter of culture and appearance rather than as a problem of social injustice. The task of cultural crossover also emerged as gendered work, as it was more common for white women married to Asian American men to display a commitment to learning the language, cooking, and parenting styles of their partners' culture than it was for white men with Asian American partners to do sthe same.

In the cases of Asian American men–white women couples whom I interviewed, many of the successful couples emulated traditional gender dynamics centered on the logic of men's power as a result of their class status. Asian American men who possessed and displayed relatively high class status were likely to have a better chance of repudiating marginal manhood and exercising power over white women. Yet the effectiveness of such a strategy of emulation or approximation itself indicates the stability of white male role superiority. Indeed, some white women's essentialization of Asian American men through comparison of them to white men indicates a stable image of white manhood; from such a perspective, of course Asian American manhood is seen as deviant (or, at best, a model minority). With the growing income of Asian Americans, it is possible that Asian American men may increasingly view marriage with white women as a means to compete with white hegemonic masculinity. But, as seen with regard to William and Leslie, the last two men discussed in this volume, those who grow up with negative stereotypes of Asian Americans may in fact refrain from intermarriage and prefer to marry within their own race. And, as in the case of William, the ever-growing global market may offer more reasonable options for some Asian American men to exercise their transnational privileges and seek wives abroad.[1]

In the case of some professional Asian American men who sought to rebut marginalized masculinity by exercising class mobility, marriage to white women exhibited white middle-class gender dynamics; that is, white women symbolically or practically served these men as ideal wives and mothers or as liberal multicultural partners. Although the white women's experiences of race and/or views of their partners ranged from a perspective of color-blind multiculturalism, to one of race-cognizance, to one of essentialism, these women actively maintained their households and families according to white middle-class ideals and gender dynamics that upheld a system of white privilege.

Overall, my interviews uncovered far less racism, tension, and distrust toward Asian American/white couples among Asian American families and in white communities than that exhibited by black or white families toward black–white interracial relationships.[2] Asian American families often see whites as preferable partners compared to partners from other racial and ethnic minorities, even Asian-descended minorities. Further, "images of Asian Americans as perpetual foreigners and as the model minority differ markedly from that of a supposedly lazy, unintelligent, and criminal race, as African Americans are characterized."[3] Whether through Asian Americans' class mobility or stereotypes of subservience and docility, the model minority myth bolsters whites' images of Asian Americans as suitable partners. American culture's view of the model minority remains strong as a "fetishized 'ethnic dilemma'" for the purpose of "healing."[4] The *New York Times* in 2006 reported that Asian American youths' academic success derives from "the filial piety nurtured by Confucianism for 2,500 years."[5] With depictions such as this pervasive in the popular media, Asian Americans' options for dating and marrying outside their own race will continue to increase.

Logic of Gender and Multiculturalism

Susan Koshy argues that whiteness will lose its power and become only one among many ethnicities as global capitalism increasingly mobilizes new immigrants and integrates them into the U.S. economy. She writes, "Whiteness dissembles race privilege as fitness-within-capitalism and recruits highly skilled middle-class and wealthy new immigrants to endorse this narrative of American color-blind equality."[6] But, though globalization and multiculturalism may run counter to traditional ideas of racial hierarchies, they do not necessarily run counter to the logic of patriarchy. The logic of patriarchy, or the imperative of masculinity and femininity, constitutes the core idea behind the American nation, the American family, conservative politics, and religious fundamentalism, and in fact may continue to maintain and incorporate racialized masculinity and femininity in an ever-expanding global market in ways that serve to reinforce the system as it now exists. It is questionable whether whiteness, symbolically identified with national and familial patriarchy, will easily crumble, especially when American-led corporate hegemony and the imperative of U.S. democracy still govern the global economy and political system.

Koshy argues that mainstream images of Asian women have progressed from representations of the powerless sexual commodity, such as the Cho-Cho San of *Madam Butterfly*, to images of these women as the possessors of sexual capital, thanks to the pervasiveness of the model minority myth, multiculturalism, and globalization. On the other hand, she argues that Asian American women's relationships with white men betray a great degree of ambivalence, revealing "the conflict between feminist concerns and assimilationist maneuvers."[7] In other words, popular images of Asian American women have been successfully transformed "through white men's eyes," and such images are favorably received as they fulfill white male desires and images.[8]

In my study, unequal gender dynamics were pronounced among first-generation Asian American women (especially Filipina Americans) whose socioeconomic resources and language skills were limited. But, even among the more progressive and upwardly mobile young couples, gender dynamics or couples' perceptions of each other did not contest the traditional gender order. For example, Asian American women believed that white men were the most desirable or "powerful" partners; white men expected Asian American women to be hyperfeminine; and white men dominantly employed color-blind views, while Asian American women conformed to such views by staying silent about racism. It is true that the second-generation Asian American women I interviewed had better economic mobility than the foreign-born Asian American women, or even than the white men. But these women's concerns about, and hopes of, being equal to whites seem to make them strive for white men's recognition, and lead them to make compromises with white men's power over them. As a result, these women themselves may employ and even perpetuate mainstream stereotypes of Asian Americans. Further study will be necessary to analyze the psychological dimensions of this gendered and racialized submission and compromise.

When the cultural imperative of multiculturalism and color-blindness deemphasize race, the logics of white patriarchy and gender inequalities also become obscured. The logic of multiculturalism masks positions of white male authority, with their privileges of race and gender, as it serves the maintenance of gendered narratives of family and nation in America. Nicholas Kristof, a liberal columnist for the *New York Times* who often cites his wife and himself as precursors of a new future, says, "My wife is Chinese American, and our relationship would once have been felonious." He greets the recent increase in interracial marriage as "an enormously hopeful sign of progress in bridging barriers," as well as "one of the most positive fronts in American race relations today, building bridges and empathy."[9] He lists popular interracial couples with whom his readers are familiar: former defense secretary William Cohen and his African American wife; software guru Peter Norton and his African American wife; Supreme Court justice Clarence Thomas and his white wife. It is true that, compared to American society during the period of antimiscegenation laws, today's society is relatively exposed to mixed-race couples and has developed some tolerance toward these couples. Kristof's claiming his Chinese American wife as evidence of his practicing racial bridging and empathy in the multicultural age may well have positive social and cultural effects on his audience's reception of mixed-race couples. But would it be so convincing to his audience if his Chinese American wife had said the same thing? And Kristof's list of big names also shows how interracial marriage successfully maintains patriarchal order in the American family Even though these are interracial marriages, they uphold the national ideology of family and heterosexual unions consisting of hegemonic masculinities, and contribute to a form of "triumphalist multiculturalism"[10] that takes pride in "diversity as the key to America's exceptionalism and supremacy."[11]

Many Asian American–white couples in my study expressed negative views of, and concerns about, black–white relationships, but the media is portraying black–white intermarriage, as well as Asian American–white relationships, as on the rise. One recent article, a special report in the Austin *American-Statesman,* emphasizes gender, middle-class patriarchy, and the dominance of whiteness as critical elements of the "ideal" multiracial family. Titled "The Changing Faces of America," this article begins "A new generation is leading the way,"[12] and is illustrated by a picture of smiling family members: a masculine African American father, a feminine white wife, and a college-age biracial daughter. On the following page are pictures of four multiracial college students, three women and one man. The article codes these multiracial daughters and sons as the future of America. Of the four individuals pictured, two have one Asian American parent and one white parent. All four individuals have either a white mother or a white father, and the first impression these pictures convey is that the persons look "white enough." In the first big picture of the interracial family, the slim white woman sits in front with an elegant smile, her legs crossed in an extremely feminine manner. Her African American husband sits further back. As a result, the white wife's body is more prominent than her husband's; the pose thus accentuates whiteness in the family. With the woman presenting herself as a traditional feminine figure, this seems to be a safe image of a traditional upper-middle-class "good family." It is apparent that these pictures rely on a traditional ideology of family and gender roles and, most important, suggest little deviation from whiteness as a future model for interracial marriage.

The regime of gender in citizenship, marriage, and family has long governed the discourses of military brides and mail-order brides, who were given legal privileges and economic opportunities in exchange for their loyal subjugation to white male authority. Although feminists' claims that these women were victims of economic oppression and U.S. sexism are often criticized as one-sided, it is critical to note that current orders of gender in America still govern such transnational transactions of love, marriage, and sex. For example, discourses of mail-order brides are still embedded in a masculinist narrative that makes structural inequality invisible. Even after a mail-order bride from Kyrgyzstan was murdered, the media expressed sympathy for the male clients of these brokers' services by quoting brokers' comments such as "Male clients, not the women, are the most likely to be victimized in mail-order marriages." Such discourse also implicitly blames these women who "enter marriages solely to gain U.S. citizenship, then falsely complain of physical abuse as a ploy to stay in America."[13] Some mail-order bride businesses try to get around the requirement of background checks of male clients by marketing foreign women on domestic matchmaking sites, sites that appear similar to the many domestic matchmakers that primarily target American women and men.[14] But the comparison of an international matchmaking business to a local dating site is a false equation, because the domestic site commodifies partners in a more equal fashion; in other words, the women on the domestic site understand the terms of the bargain they are striking far better than do the desperate foreign brides, who are emotionally and economically vulnerable and are facing considerable potential risk.

Asian American women and men continue to struggle with racism and sexism. The media reported the story of a forty-nine-year-old white man who killed a thirty-one-year-old Chinese American woman, later telling a colleague that he "liked Asian women because they study hard, and they are very nice, and soft-spoken."[15] Helen Zia points out that, regardless of the high number of sexual assaults against Asian and Asian American women, these events rarely draw public attention and also rarely lead to prosecution as hate crimes.[16] Love and racism can coexist within relationships. Yet, as color-blindness and multicultural commodification obscure sexism or gender inequalities within interracial relationships, and many Asian Americans in the United States believe they are now equal to or are approximating to whites, such incidents reflecting the interplay of gender and race in interracial relationships may increase.

Lowe argues, "Multiculturalism is central to the maintenance of a consensus that permits the present hegemony."[17] Color-blindness in notions of intimacy, marriage, and love becomes problematic when it masks existing racial problems in America and effaces the critical work of understanding and experiencing the history and differences of the other. The logic of multiculturalism also conceals its sustenance of, and exploitation of, gender orders and inequalities. Color-blindness or multiculturalism in the context of interracial unions conforms to and protects the current structure of gender inequalities.[18] Notions of race appear to be further fragmented and marginalized in the color-blind discourses of love, sex, exoticism, pleasure, and capitalist logic, yet such fragmentation safeguards the logic of gender, family, and nation.

The Commodity of Love

Interracial intimacy and sex often raise concerns about the commodification of race and gender. Virginia L. Blum argues that the American discourse of love and intimacy is deeply embedded in consumer culture. Citing Zygmunt Bauman, who writes that "the others are valued as companions-in-the-essentially-solitary-activity of consumption,"[19] Blum argues, "Bauman might snap back that in consumer culture, fucking and shopping are pretty much the same thing—and that, once such an equivalence has fully taken over the very shape of our desires and the very foundations of our consumer-ready subjectivities, any truly emancipatory (rival) impulses have been squelched to feed the desire making-and-allaying machinery."[20] When measuring oneself and others by the yardstick of social and cultural capital becomes a critical part of our daily transactions, it is hard to argue that our desires and affections *can* be separated from consumer impulses. But it is still meaningful to argue how the logic of gender, through commodified discourses and political economy, mediates our desires for the other.

The process of living with someone and negotiating one's desire can cause great ambivalence and be rife with contradictions. Reflecting on one's desire for the other leads us to question the ethics of desire.[21] Does the other exist as a mere object of gratification, or does she/he exist as a mutually recognizable other? How do we know that our desire for the particular other is ethical? How can we demand and practice ethics in the realm of sexual desire? How does our desire for the other lead to social change? Cheng argues, "Ethics come *after* identification and complicity—that is, after immersion has already taken place."[22] In other words, there is no way to scrutinize the moment of identification with the desirable other when one's desire finally comes to the surface of one's consciousness. Arisaka says that exoticism, though it has an element of objectification, should be differentiated from objectification and commodification.[23] Exoticism may enable one to experience a self-reflective affirmation of the "ability to conceive otherwise from what is given," and it may "function as a corrective to racist or sexist attitudes."[24] Foucault argued that the ethics of the *other* are inextricably connected with one's relationship to *oneself*. He described ethics as "the kind of relationships you ought to have with yourself . . . and which determines how the individual is supposed to constitute himself as a moral subject of his own."[25]

Discussing the ethics of desire and its potential for social change go beyond the scope of this book, but asking such questions inevitably causes us to scrutinize the factors in our own culture and society that mediate our desires. Love and intimacy in American society have always been driven by two different forces—a consumer culture of "pleasure," and a discourse of "commitment" or "hard work."[26] Thus the ethics of desire is not a matter unique to interracial intimacy, but one that we must each scrutinize and contemplate in our intimate relationships.

Appendix

Couple Interviews

		Age	Marital Status	Race/ Ethnicity	Education	Occupation
1	Angelina Brown	38	Married	Filipina American	College B.A.	None
	Thomas Brown	37	Married	White	College B.A.	Consultant
2	Melissa Bennett	28	Married	Filipina American	College B.S.	Engineer
	Patrick Bennett	28	Married	White	College B.S.	Engineer
3	Amy Anderson	38	Married	Filipina American	College B.A.	Accountant
	John Anderson	38	Married	White	Ph.D	Medical researcher
4	Victoria Chen	24	Single	Chinese American	M.D. (exp)	Med. student
	Paul Hoffman	24	Single	White	High school graduate	Carpenter/
5	Vivian Kwan	25	Single	Chinese American	College B.A.	Social worker
	Peter Davis	27	Single	White	College B.A.	Multimedia designer
6	Grace Wong	23	Single	Chinese American	College B.S.	Engineer
	Jacob Lewis	26	Single	White	M.A.	Consultant
7	Rebecca Chu	21	Engaged	Chinese American	College student	Student
	Matthew Mayer	28	Engaged	White	High school graduate	Writer/ waiter

Couple Interviews (continued)

		Age	Marital Status	Race/ Ethnicity	Education	Occupation
8	Jennifer Ryu	20	Single	Chinese American	College student	Student
	Daniel Tyler	22	Single	White	High school graduate	Factory worker
9	Soonja Morris	58	Married	Korean American	High school	None
	Gary Morris	54	Married	White	Ph.D	Vice president
10	Sachiko Green	66	Married	Japanese American	High school graduate	Homemaker
	George Green	66	Married	White	College B.S.	Engineer
11	Kevin Cheung	20	Single	Chinese American	College student	Student
	Karen Smith	20	Single	White	College student	Student
12	Keith Banzon	52	Married	Filipino American	College B.S.	Engineer
	Debra Banzon	50	Married	White	College B.A.	Salesperson
13	Sothy Khim	45	Married	Cambodian American	College B.S.	Engineer
	Emily Khim	38	Married	White	College B.A.	Teacher
14	Kenji Tanaka	29	Married	Japanese American	College B.S.	Musician/ waiter
	Tracey Tanaka	26	Married	White	A.A. degree	Waitress
15	Tony Rhee	26	Married	Korean American	College student	Student/ salesperson
	Michelle Rhee	22	Married	White	College B.A.	Staff member, community college
16	Irene Huan	25	Single	Chinese American	College student	Student
	Bryan Thompson	25	Single	White	J.D. (exp)	Law student

Individual Interviews

		Age	Marital Status	Race/ Ethnicity	Education	Occupation
1	Lisa Kim	21	Single	Korean American	College student	Student
2	Julie Shin	22	Single	Korean American	College student	Student
3	Linda Miller	34	Married	Filipina American	High school	Home-maker
4	Jane Lee	52	Divorced	Korean American	College B.S.	Registered nurse
5	Mia Smith	41	Married	Filipino American	College B.S.	Distribu-tion manager
6	William Lin	35	Divorced	Chinese American	College B.A.	Media designer
7	Leslie Duong	25	Single	Vietnamese American	College B.A.	Assistant manager, media company
8	Kenneth Miyake	50	Divorced	Japanese American	College B.S.	Engineer
9	Marie Wang	45	Married	White	M.A.	Home-maker
10	Laura Martin	30	Single	White	College B.S.	Physical therapist

Notes

Introduction

1. Michel Foucault, *The History of Sexuality, Volume 1: An Introduction* (New York: Vintage, 1978).
2. Ibid., 155–156.
3. Elizabeth A. Povinelli, *The Empire of Love: Toward a Theory of Intimacy, Genealogy, and Carnality* (Durham, NC: Duke University Press, 2006).
4. Judith Butler, *Subjects of Desire: Hegelian Reflections in Twentieth-Century France* (New York: Columbia University Press, 1987), 137.
5. Michel Foucault, "Ethics of Concern for the Self as a Practice of Freedom," in *Ethics, Subjectivity, and Truth,* ed. Paul Rabinow (New York: New Press, 1997), 283–284.
6. Charles A. Gallagher, "Color Blind Privilege: The Social and Political Functions of Erasing the Color Line in Post-Race America," in *Rethinking the Color Line: Readings in Race and Ethnicity,* ed. Charles A Gallagher (New York: McGraw Hill, 2007), 130–143.
7. Erica Chito Childs, *Navigating Interracial Borders: Black-White Couples and Their Social Worlds* (New Brunswick, NJ: Rutgers University Press, 2005).
8. Patricia Hill Collins, *Black Sexual Politics: African Americans, Gender, and the New Racism* (New York: Routledge, 2004), 250.
9. Erica Chito Childs, "Looking behind the Stereotypes of the 'Angry Black Woman.'" *Gender and Society* 19, no. 4 (2005): 544–561.
10. Michael S. Kimmel, *The Gendered Society* (New York: Oxford University Press, 2000).
11. Sharon M. Lee and Marilyn Fernandez, "Trends in Asian American Racial/Ethnic Intermarriage: A Comparison of 1980 and 1990 Census Data," *Sociological Perspectives* 41, no. 2 (1998): 323–342; Sharon M. Lee and Keiko Yamanaka, "Patterns of Asian Intermarriage and Marital Assimilation," *Journal of Comparative Family Studies* 21 (1990): 287–305; Zai Liang and Naomi Ito, "Intermarriage of Asian Americans in the New York City Region: Contemporary Patterns and Future Prospects," *International Migration Review* 33, no. 4 (1999): 876–900; Rachel F Moran, *Interracial Intimacy: The Regulation of Race and Romance* (Chicago: University of Chicago Press, 2001); Larry H. Shinagawa and Gin Yong Pang, "Asian American Panethnicity and Intermarriage," *Amerasia Journal* 22 (1996), no. 2: 127–152.
12. Sue Chow, "The significance of Race in the Private Sphere: Asian Americans and Spousal Preferences," *Sociological Inquiry* 70, no. 1 (2000): 1–29.

13. Lee and Yamanaka, "Patterns of Asian Intermarriage and Marital Assimilation": 287–305; Larry H. Shinagawa and Gin Yong Pang, "Intraethnic, Interethnic, and Interracial Marriages among Asian Americans in California, 1980," *Berkeley Journal of Sociology* 33 (1988): 95–114; Shinagawa and Pang, "Asian American Panethnicity and Intermarriage": 127–152. Lee and Yamanaka find that more Asian American women than Asian American men in professional and managerial occupations are exogamous; that is, highly educated Asian American women are more likely than highly educated men to outmarry. Shinagawa and Pang point out that Asian Americans outmarry individuals "who enjoy better socioeconomic and racial status than potential Asian American mates"; see Shinagawa and Pang, "Intraethnic, Interethnic, and Interracial Marriages," 109. Correspondingly, whites tend to choose Asian Americans who are more highly educated than both the average Asian American and the average white; thus, Shinagawa and Pang view Asian American outmarriage as related to mutual upward class mobility.

14. Alfred Lopez, *Postcolonial Whiteness: A Critical Reader on Race and Empire State* (Albany: State University of New York Press, 2005), 17.

15. David L. Eng, *Racial Castration: Managing Masculinity in Asian America* (Durham, NC: Duke University Press, 2001).

16. Anne A. Cheng, *The Melancholy of Race* (New York: Oxford University Press, 2001).

17. Jane Flax, "Review Essay on Psychoanalysis and Feminism in Postcolonial Time," *Signs: Journal of Women in Culture and Society* 29, no. 3 (2004): 908–17, 912.

18. Jessica Benjamin, *Like Subjects, Love Objects: Essays on Recognition and Sexual Difference* (New Haven, CT: Yale University Press), 150.

19. Childs, *Navigating Interracial Borders*. Erica Chito Childs discusses the ways white families and individuals often opposed interracial relationships by employing discourses such as "It's not my personal preference" or " I just worry about the problems you will face in society." On the other hand, black families opposed to the interracial marriage expressed distrust of whites or concern for the individual's loss of ties with family or community.

20. Postcolonial scholars see racial hierarchy as emerging not only in the form of institutional exclusion but also in the forms of alienation, sexual desire, self-contempt, and an aversion toward certain racial and ethnic characteristics. See Homi K. Bhabha, *The Location of Culture* (New York: Routledge, 1994), and Frantz Fanon, *Black Skin, White Masks* (New York: Grove Press, 1967).

21. Karen D. Pyke and Tran Dang, "'FOB' and 'Whitewashed': Identity and Internalized Racism among Second Generation Asian Americans," *Qualitative Sociology* 26, no. 2 (2003): 151.

22. Karen D. Pyke, "Defying the Taboo on the Study of Internalized Racial Oppression," in *Global Migration, Cultural Transformation, and Social Change*, ed. Emory Elliott, Jasmine Payne, and Patricia Ploesch (New York: Palgrave MacMillan, 2007), 101–120.

23. Cheng, *The Melancholy of Race*.

24. Ibid., 26.

25. Ibid., 25.

26. Anthony Giddens, *Profiles and Critiques in Social Theory* (Berkeley and Los Angeles: University of California Press, 1982), 212.

27. Lois McNay, *Gender and Agency: Reconfiguring the Subject in Feminist and Social Theory* (Polity Press, 2000), 42–43.

28. Anthony Giddens, *Modernity and Self-Identity: Self and Society in the Late Modern Age* (Stanford, CA: Stanford University Press, 1991), 35.

29. Nancy Chodorow, *The Reproduction of Mothering: Psychoanalysis and the Sociology of Gender* (Berkeley and Los Angeles: University of California Press, 1978); Nancy Chodorow, "Gender as a Personal and Cultural Construction," *Signs: Journal of Women in Culture and Society,* 20 (1995): 516–544; Nancy Chodorow, *The Power of Feelings: Personal Meaning in Psychoanalysis, Gender, and Culture* (New Haven, CT: Yale University Press, 1999).

30. Susan Bordo, "Feminism, Postmodernism, and Gender-Skepticism," in *Feminism/postmodernism,* ed. Linda J. Nicholson (New York: Routledge, 1990), 19–38. Also, Nancy Fraser and Linda J. Nicholson, "Social Criticism without Philosophy: An Encounter between Feminism and Postmodernism," in *Feminism/postmodernism,* ed. Nicholson, 133–156.

31. Christine L. Williams, "Psychoanalytic Theory and the Sociology of Gender," in *Theory on Gender/ Feminism on Theory,* ed. Paula England (New York: Aldine de Gruyter, 1993), 131–149.

32. Robert W. Connell, *Masculinities* (Berkeley and Los Angeles: University of California Press, 1995).

33. McNay, *Gender and Agency,* 117.

34. Sigmund Freud, "Mourning and Melancholia," in James Strachey, ed. and trans., *The Standard Edition of the Complete Psychological Works of Sigmund Freud,* vol. 14 (London: Hogarth Press, 1953), 243–258.

35. Cheng, *The Melancholy of Race,* 2000.

36. Ibid., 180.

37. Walter Benjamin, *The Origin of German Tragic Drama* (London: Verso, 1985), 140.

38. Cheng, *The Melancholy of Race*; Lisa Lowe, "Heterogeniety, Hybridity, Multiplicity: Making Asian American Differences," *Diaspora* 1 (1991): 24–44.

39. Nazli Kibria, *Becoming Asian American: Second-Generation Chinese and Korean American Identities* (Baltimore, MD: Johns Hopkins University Press, 2002).

40. Yen Le Espiritu, *Asian American Panethnicity: Bridging Institutions and Identities* (Philadelphia: Temple University Press, 1992).

41. Ibid.; Nazli Kibria, "The Construction of 'Asian American': Reflections on Intermarriage and Ethnic Identity among Second-Generation Chinese and Korean Americans," *Ethnic and Racial Studies* 20 (1997): 523–544; Lowe, "Heterogeniety, Hybridity, Multiplicity."

42. Susan Koshy, "The Fiction of Asian American Literature," *Yale Journal of Criticism* 9, no. 2 (1996): 333.

43. Lingyan Yang, "Theorizing Asian America: On Asian American and Postcolonial Asian Diasporic Women Intellectuals," *Journal of Asian American Studies* 5, no. 2 (2002): 155.

44. Koshy, "Fiction of Asian American Literature," 340.

45. Lee and Fernandez define Asian Americans as "people who trace their origin to countries in Asia" (324). See Sharon M. Lee and Marilyn Fernandez, "Trends in Asian American Racial/Ethnic Intermarriage: A Comparison of 1980 and 1990 Census Data," *Sociological Perspectives* 41 (1998): 323–342.

46. Harry. H. L. Kitano, Wai-Tsang Yeung, Lynn Chai, and Herbert Hatanaka, "Asian American Interracial Marriage," *Journal of Marriage and the Family* 46, no.1 (1984): 179–190.; Lee and Fernandez, "Trends in Asian American Racial/Ethnic Intermarriage"; Lee and Yamanaka, "Patterns of Asian Intermarriage."

47. Henrietta L. Moore, *A Passion for Difference: Essays in Anthropology and Gender* (Oxford: Polity Press, 1994), 43.

48. Thomas Ogden, *Subjects of Analysis* (London: Jason Aronson Inc., 1996).

Transnational Reading of Asian Female Action Heroes," *Jump Cut: A Review of Contemporary Media, no. 48 (Winter* 2006), http://www.ejumpcut.org/archive/jc48.2006/womenWarriors/index.html (accessed October 10, 2007).

39. Rong Cai, "Gender Imaginations in *Crouching Tiger, Hidden Dragon* and the Wuxia World," *positions: east asia cultural critique* 13, no. 2 (2005): 441–472.
40. Palumbo-Liu, *Asia/America*, 396.
41. L. H. M. Ling., "Sex Machine," 296.
42. Karen Kelsky, *Women on the Verge: Japanese Women, Western Dreams* (Durham, NC: Duke University Press, 2000), 187.
43. Colleen Fong and Judy Yung, "In Search of the Right Spouse: Interracial Marriage among Chinese and Japanese Americans," *Amerasia Journal* 21, no. 3 (1995): 77–98.
44. Ibid., 90.
45. Sue Chow, "The significance of Race in the Private Sphere: Asian Americans and Spousal Preferences," *Sociological Inquiry* 70, no. 1 (2000): 12.
46. Nazli Kibria, "The Construction of 'Asian American': Reflections on Intermarriage and Ethnic Identity among Second-Generation Chinese and Korean Americans," *Ethnic and Racial Studies* 20 (1997): 523–544.
47. David L. Eng and Shinhee Han, "A Dialogue on Racial Melancholia," *Psychoanalytic Dialogue* 10, no. 4 (2000): 667–700; David L. Eng, *Racial Castration: Managing Masculinity in Asian America* (Durham, NC: Duke University Press, 2001); Ann A. Cheng, *The Melancholy of Race: Psychoanalysis, Assimilation, and Hidden Grief* (Oxford: Oxford University Press, 2001).
48. Eng, *Racial Castration*, 24.
49. Cheng, *The Melancholy of Race*, 72.
50. Eng and Han, "A Dialogue."
51. U.S. Department of Health and Human Services data cited in Elizabeth Cohen, "Push to Achieve Tied to Suicide in Asian-American Women," *CNN News*, May 16, 2007, http://www.cnn.com/2007/HEALTH/05/16/asian.suicides/index.html.
52. Karen D. Pyke and Tran Dang, "'FOB' and 'Whitewashed': Identity and Internalized Racism among Second Generation Asian Americans," *Qualitative Sociology* 26, no. 2 (2003): 152.
53. Karen D. Pyke and Denise L. Johnson, "Asian American Women and Racialized Femininities: 'Doing' Gender across Cultural Worlds," *Gender and Society* 17, no.1 (2003): 46–47.
54. Yen Le Espiritu, *Asian American Women and Men: Labor, Laws, and Love* (Walnut Creek, CA: AltaMira Press, Division of Rowman and Littlefield Publishers 2000), 91.
55. Marchetti, *Romance and the "Yellow Peril,"* 14–31.
56. Cliff Cheng, "We Choose Not to Compete: The 'Merit' Discourse in the Selection Process, and Asian and Asian American Men and Their Masculinity," in *Masculinities in Organizations*, ed. Cliff Cheng (Thousand Oaks, CA: Sage Publications 1996), 177–200.
57. Espiritu, *Asian American Women and Men*, 111.
58. Eng, *Racial Castration*.
59. Palumbo-Liu, *Asia/America*, 34.   He quotes C. M. Goethe's writing from 1931: "The Filipino tends to interbreed with near-moron white girls. The resulting hybrid is almost invariably undesirable."
60. Nguyen, *Race and Resistance*.
61. Ibid., 90.
62. Lisa Lowe, *Immigrant Acts: On Asian American Cultural Politics* (Durham, NC, and London: Duke University Press, 1996), 15.

63. Nguyen, *Race and Resistance*, 90.
64. Lowe, *Immigrant Acts*, 16–17.
65. Aihwa Ong, *Flexible Citizenship: The Cultural Logics of Transnatinality* (Durham, NC: Duke University Press, 1999).
66. Espiritu, *Asian American Women and Men*, 92.
67. James Kim, "The Legend of the White-and-Yellow Black Man: Global Containment and Triangulated Racial Desire in *Romeo Must Die*," *Camera Obscura* 19, no. 1 (2004): 150–179.
68. Kim, "Legend of the White-and-Yellow Black Man," 159.
69. Kingsley Davis, "Intermarriage in Caste Societies," *American Anthropologist* 43, no. 3 (1941): 376–395; Robert Merton, "Intermarriage and the Social Structure: Fact and Theory," *Psychiatry* 4 (1941): 361–374.
70. Jerry Jacobs and Teresa Labov, "Gender Differentials in Intermarriage among Sixteen Race and Ethnic Groups," *Sociological Forum* 17, no. 4 (2002): 621–646; Michael Rosenfeld, "A Critique of Mate Selection Theory," *American Journal of Sociology* 110, no. 5 (2005): 1284–1325.
71. Jacobs and Labov, "Gender Differentials in Intermarriage," 640.
72. Rosenfeld, "A Critique of Mate Selection Theory," 1318.
73. Lynn Chancer, *Reconcilable Differences: Confronting Beauty, Pornography, and the Future of Feminism* (Berkeley and Los Angeles: University of California Press, 1998); Dorothy C. Holland and Margaret A. Eisenhart, *Educated in Romance: Women, Achievement, and College Culture* (Chicago: University of Chicago Press, 1990).
74. Esther Pan, "Why Asian Guys Are on a Roll," *Newsweek* 135, vol. 8 (February 21, 2000), http://search.ebscohost.com.
75. Collins, *Black Sexual Politics.*
76. Margaret Hunter, "'If You're Light You're Alright': Light Skin Color as Social Capital for Women of Color," *Gender and Society* 16, no. 2 (2004): 178.
77. Michael S. Kimmel, "Masculinity as Homophobia: Fear, Shame, and Silence in the Construction of Gender Identity," in *Theorizing Masculinities*, ed. Harry Brod and Michael Kaufman (Thousand Oaks, CA: Sage Publications, 1994), 119–141.
78. Kelina M. Craig-Henderson, *Black Men in Interracial Relationships: What's Love Got To Do With It?* (New Brunswick, NJ: Transaction Publishers, 2006).
79. Jachinson Chan, *Chinese American Masculinities: From Fu Manchu to Bruce Lee* (London: Routledge, 2001), 152.
80. Milton M Gordon, *Assimilation in American Life: The Role of Race, Religion, and National Origins* (New York: Oxford University Press, 1964).
81. Harry H. L. Kitano, Wai-Tsang Yeung, Lynn Chai, and Herbert Hatanaka, "Asian American Interracial Marriage," *Journal of Marriage and the Family* 46, no.1 (1984): 179–190.
82. Randall Kennedy, *Interracial Intimacies: Sex, Marriage, Identity, and Adoption* (New York: Pantheon, 2003).
83. Rachel F. Moran, *Interracial Intimacy: The Regulation of Race and Romance* (Chicago: University of Chicago Press, 2001).
84. Joane Nagel, *Race, Ethnicity, and Sexuality: Intimate Intersections, Forbidden Frontiers* (Oxford: Oxford University Press, 2004).
85. Moran, *Interracial Intimacy*, 116.
86. Ibid., 126.
87. Collins, *Black Sexual Politics*, 249.
88. Abou Farman, "An Archeology of Inter-Racial Relations," *Fuse* 15, no. 3 (1992): 7–11.

89. Larry H. Shinagawa and Gin Yong Pang, "Intraethnic, Interethnic, and Interracial Marriages among Asian Americans in California," *Berkeley Journal of Sociology* 33 (1988): 95–114; Larry H. Shinagawa and Gin Yong Pang, "Asian American Panethnicity and Intermarriage," *Amerasia Journal* 22 (1996): 127–152.

90. Eduardo Bonilla-Silva, *Racism without Racists: Color-Blind Racism and the Persistence of Racial Inequality in the United States* (Lanham, MD: Rowman and Littlefield, 2006).

91. Sharon M. Lee and Marilyn Fernandez, "Trends in Asian American Racial/ Ethnic Intermarriage: A Comparison of 1980 and 1990 Census Data," *Sociological Perspectives* 41, no. 2 (1998): 323–342; Sharon M. Lee and Keiko Yamanaka, "Patterns of Asian Intermarriage and Marital Assimilation," *Journal of Comparative Family Studies* 21 (1990): 287–305; Zai Liang and Naomi Ito, "Intermarriage of Asian Americans in the New York City Region: Contemporary Patterns and Future Prospects," *International Migration Review* 33, no. 4 (1999): 876–900; Moran, *Interracial Intimacy*; Shinagawa and Pang, "Asian American Panethnicity."

92. Darrell Y. Hamamoto, "Kindred Spirits: The Contemporary Asian American Family on Television," *Amerasia Journal* 18 (1992): 42.

93. Ibid.

94. Maria P. Root, *Love's Revolution: Interracial Marriage* (Philadelphia: Temple University Press, 2001), 11.

95. Ibid., 61.

96. Ibid., 173.

97. Pawan H. Dhingra, "Being American between Black and White: Second-Generation Asian American Professional Racial Identities," *Journal of Asian American Studies* 6, no. 2 (2003): 117–147.

98. Ruth Frankenberg, *White Women, Race Matters: The Social Construction of Whiteness* (Minneapolis: University of Minnesota Press, 1993).

99. Frankenberg, *White Women*, 157.

100. Erica Chito Childs, *Navigating Interracial Borders: Black–White Couples and Their Social Worlds* (New Brunswick, NJ: Rutgers University Press, 2005), 42.

Chapter 2. The Good Wife

1. Nicole Constable, *Romance on a Global Stage: Pen Pals, Virtual Ethnography, and 'Mail-Order' Marriage* (Berkeley and Los Angeles: University of California Press, 2003); Paul R. Spickard, *Mixed Blood: Intermarriage and Ethnic Identity in Twentieth-Century America* (Madison: University of Wisconsin Press, 1989); Ji-Yeon Yuh, *Beyond the Shadow of Camptown: Korean Military Brides in America* (New York: New York University Press, 2002).

2. Rogelio Saenz, Sean-Shong Hwang, and Benigno E. Aguirre, "In Search of Asian War Brides," *Demography* 31, no. 3 (Aug. 1994): 549–559.

3. Caroline Chung Simpson, "'Out of an Obscure Place': Japanese War Brides and Cultural Pluralism in the 1950s," *differences: A Journal of Feminist Cultural Studies* 10, no. 3 (1999): 47–81.

4. Spickard, *Mixed Blood*; Evelyn Nakano Glenn, *Issei, Nisei, War Bride: Three Generations of Japanese American Women in Domestic Service* (Philadelphia: Temple University Press, 1989).

5. Ji-Yeon Yuh, "Out of the Shadows: Camptown Women, Military Brides, and Korean (American) Communities," *Hitting Critical Mass: A Journal of Asian American Cultural Criticism* 6, no. 1 (1999): 18.

6. Adrienne Rich, "Compulsive Heterosexuality and Lesbian Existence," *Signs: Journal of Women in Culture and Society* 5, no. 4 (1980): 631–660.

7. Karen Pyke, "'Generational Deserters' and 'Black Sheep': Acculturative Differences among Siblings in Asian Immigrant Families," *Journal of Family Issues* 26 (2005): 493. In her study of second-generation Korean and Vietnamese Americans, Pyke describes the family system shaped by Chinese Confucianism as follows: "Confucianism places priority on family interests over individual desires and needs as well as family stability and harmony. Family ties and roles are central, and family devotion is stressed. . . . Specifically, the emphasis on strong role prescriptions, family obligations, hierarchal relations, interdependence, and emotional restraint contrasts sharply with the stress on individualism, self-sufficiency, egalitarianism, expressiveness, and self-development in mainstream U.S. culture."

8. Susan Koshy, *Sexual Naturalization: Asian Americans and Miscegenation* (Stanford, CA: Stanford University Press, 2004), 137.

9. Nicole Constable, *Romance on a Global Stage: Pen Pals, Virtual Ethnography, and "Mail-Order" Marriage* (Berkeley and Los Angeles: University of California Press, 2003), 144.

10. Ibid., 222.

11. Anthony Giddens, *The Transformation of Intimacy: Sexuality, Love, and Eroticism in Modern Societies* (Cambridge, MA: Polity Press, 1992), 57.

12. Uma Narayan, " 'Male-order' Brides: Immigrant Women, Domestic Violence, and Immigration Law," *Hypatia* 10, no. 1 (1995): 106.

13. Ibid., 109.

14. Ann Laura Stoler, *Race and the Education of Desire: Foucault's History of Sexuality and the Colonial Order of Things* (Durham, NC: Duke University Press, 1995), 190.

15. Frantz Fanon, *Black Skin, White Masks* (New York: Grove Press, 1967), 63.

16. Jessica Benjamin, *The Bonds of Love* (New York: Pantheon, 1988); Jessica Benjamin, *Shadow of the Other: Intersubjectivity and Gender in Psychoanalysis* (New York: Routledge, 1998); Nancy Chodorow, *The Reproduction of Mothering: Psychoanalysis and the Sociology of Gender* (Berkeley and Los Angeles: University of California Press, 1978); Nancy Chodorow, *The Power of Feelings: Personal Meaning in Psychoanalysis, Gender, and Culture* (New Haven, CT: Yale University Press, 1999).

17. Karen D. Pyke and Denise L. Johnson, "Asian American Women and Racialized Femininities: 'Doing' Gender across Cultural Worlds," *Gender and Society* 17, no. 1 (2003): 36.

18. Patricia Hill Collins, "Like One of the Family: Race, Ethnicity, and the Paradox of U.S. National Identity," *Ethnic and Racial Studies* 24 (2001): 20.

19. Lauren Berlant, "The Face of America and the State of Emergency," in *Disciplinarity and Dissent in Cultural Studies*, ed. Cary Nelson and Dilip Parameshwar Gaonkar, 397–440 (New York: Routledge, 1996).

20. Gayatri Chakravatory Spivak, *A Critique of Postcolonial Reason: Toward a History of the Vanishing Present* (Cambridge, MA: Harvard University Press, 1999), 291.

21. Ibid.

22. Berlant, "The Face of America," 413.

Chapter 3.   A Woman Ascending

1. Pawan H. Dhingra, "Being American between Black and White: Second-Generation Asian American Professional Racial Identities," *Journal of Asian American Studies* 6, no. 2 (2003): 137.

2. Karen Pyke and Denise L. Johnson, "Asian American Women and Racialized

Femininities: 'Doing' Gender across Cultural Worlds," *Gender and Society* 17, no.1 (2003): 47.

3. Mia Tuan, *Forever Foreigners or Honorary Whites? The Asian Ethnic Experience Today* (New Brunswick, NJ: Rutgers University Press, 1998), 147.

4. Karen Pyke and Tran Dang, "'FOB' and 'Whitewashed': Identity and Internalized Racism among Second Generation Asian Americans," *Qualitative Sociology* 26, no. 2 (2003): 151.

5. David Palumbo-Liu, *Asia/America: Historical Crossings of a Racial Frontier* (Stanford, CA: Stanford University Press, 1999), 362.

6. Dorinne Kondo, *About Face: Performing Race in Fashion and Theater* (New York: Routledge, 1997), 16.

7. Michael S. Kimmel, "Masculinity as Homophobia: Fear, Shame, and Silence in the Construction of Gender Identity," in *Theorizing Masculinities*, ed. Harry Brod and Michael Kaufman, 119–141 (Thousand Oaks, CA: Sage Publications, 1994).

8. Erica Chito Childs, "Looking behind the Stereotypes of the 'Angry Black Woman,'" *Gender and Society* 19, no. 4 (2005): 544–561.

9. Lauren Berlant, "The Face of America and the State of Emergency," in *Disciplinarity and Dissent in Cultural Studies*, ed. Cary Nelson and Dilip Parameshwar Gaonkar, 397–440 (New York: Routledge, 1996), 413.

10. Berlant, "The Face of America."

11. Lauren Berlant, *The Queen of America Goes to Washington City: Essays on Sex and Citizenship* (Durham, NC: Duke University Press, 1997), 207.

12. Anthony Giddens, *Modernity and Self-Identity: Self and Society in the Late Modern Age* (Stanford, CA: Stanford University Press, 1991).

13. Robert N. Bellah, Richard Madsen, William M. Sullivan, Ann Swidler, and Steven M. Tipton, *Habits of the Heart: Individualism and Commitment in American Life* (Berkeley and Los Angeles: University of California Press, 1985).

14. Pyke and Johnson, "Asian American Women," 43–44.

15. Ji-Yeon Yuh, *Beyond the Shadow of Camptown: Korean Military Brides in America* (New York: New York University Press, 2002).

16. Charles A. Gallagher, "Color Blind Privilege: The Social and Political Functions of Erasing the Color Line in Post-Race America," in *Rethinking the Color Line: Readings in Race and Ethnicity*, ed. Charles A. Gallagher, 130–143 (New York: McGraw Hill, 2007), 133.

17. Ibid., 132.

18. Yen Le Espiritu, *Asian American Women and Men: Labor, Laws, and Love* (Walnut Creek, CA: AltaMira Press, Division of Rowman and Littlefield Publishers 2000), 94.

19. Patricia Hill Collins, *Black Sexual Politics: African Americans, Gender, and the New Racism* (New York: Routledge, 2004), 194–196.

20. Ibid., 196.

21. Pyke and Dang, "'FOB' and 'Whitewashed,'" 151.

22. Ibid., 152.

23. Ibid., 151.

24. Pyke and Johnson, "Asian American Women," 43.

25. Susan Koshy, "Morphing Race into Ethnicity: Asian Americans and Critical Transformations of Whiteness." *boundary* 28 (2001): 190.

26. Dhingra, "Being American," 137.

27. Susan Koshy, *Sexual Naturalizaton: Asian Americans and Miscegenation* (Stanford, CA: Stanford University Press, 2004), 140. Karen Kelsky also addresses this

point in the context of Japanese women's relationships with white American men (Kelsky, *Women on the Verge*).

28. Pyke and Johnson, "Asian American Women," 45–46.

Chapter 4. A Man's Place

1. Yen Le Espiritu, *Asian American Women and Men: Labor, Laws, and Love* (Walnut Creek, CA: AltaMira Press, Division of Rowman and Littlefield Publishers 2000), 92.
2. For example, Nicole Constable, *Romance on a Global Stage: Pen Pals, Virtual Ethnography, and 'Mail-Order' Marriage* (Berkeley and Los Angeles: University of California Press, 2003), and Ji-Yeon Yuh, *Beyond the Shadow of Camptown: Korean Military Brides in America* (New York: New York University Press, 2002).
3. Margaret Hunter, "'If You're Light You're Alright': Light Skin Color as Social Capital for Women of Color," *Gender and Society* 16, no. 2 (2004)": 178.
4. Richard Dyer, *White* (London: Routledge, 1997), 130.
5. Hunter, "If You're Light You're Alright," 189.
6. Patricia Hill Collins, *Black Sexual Politics: African Americans, Gender, and the New Racism* (New York: Routledge, 2004), 193.
7. Ruth Frankenberg, *White Women, Race Matters: The Social Construction of Whiteness* (Minneapolis: University of Minnesota Press, 1993), 188.
8. Ibid., 148.
9. Thomas Frank, "Why Johnny Can't Dissent," in *Commodify Your Dissent: The Business of Culture in the New Gilded Age*, ed. Frank Thomas and Matt Weiland (New York: Norton, 1997), 31–45.
10. Ibid.
11. David Palumbo-Liu, *Asia/America: Historical Crossings of a Racial Frontier* (Stanford, CA: Stanford University Press, 1999), 218.
12. Ibid., 237.
13. Ibid.
14. Ibid., 234.
15. Jose E. Munoz, "No Es Facil: Notes on the Negotiation of Cubanidad and Exilic Memory," *Drama Review* 39, no. 3 (1995): 76–82.
16. Sigmund Freud, "Mourning and Melancholia," in *The Standard Edition of the Complete Psychological Works of Sigmund Freud*, ed. and trans. James Strachey, vol. 14 (London: Hogarth Press 1917/1953), 243–258.
17. Ibid., 255.
18. Robert W. Connell, *Masculinities* (Berkeley and Los Angeles: University of California Press, 1995), 189.

Chapter 5. Playing the Man

1. Patricia Hill Collins, *Black Sexual Politics: African Americans, Gender, and the New Racism* (New York: Routledge, 2004), 186.
2. Feminist scholars have argued that men are influenced in their selection of women by other men's approval and recognition. Sharon Bird, "Welcome to the Men's Club: Homosociality and the Maintenance of Hegemonic Masculinity," *Gender and Society* 10, no. 2 (1996): 120–132; Jean Lipman-Blumen, "Toward a Homosocial Theory of Sex Roles: An Explanation of the Sex Segregation of Social Institutions," in *Women and the Workplace*, ed. Martha Blaxall and Barbara B. Reagan, 15–31 (Chicago: University of Chicago Press, 1976); Heidi Hartmann,

"The Unhappy Marriage of Marxism and Feminism: Towards a More Progressive Union," in *Women and Revolution: A Discussion of the Unhappy Marriage of Marxism and Feminism*, ed. Lydia Sargent, 1–41 (Boston: South End Press, 1981); Gayle Rubin, "The Traffic in Women: Notes on the 'Political Economy' of Sex," in *Toward an Anthropology of Women*, ed. Rayna R. Reiter, 157–210 (New York: Monthly Review Press, 1975); Eve Sedgwick, *Between Men: English Literature and Male Homosocial Desire* (New York: Columbia University Press, 1985).

3. Anthony S. Chen, "Lives at the Center of the Periphery, Lives at the Periphery of the Center: Chinese American Masculinities and Bargaining with Hegemony," *Gender and Society* 13, no. 5 (1999): 584–607.

4. Robert Connell argues that the notion of hegemonic femininity is inappropriate. Traits of femininity are globally constructed in relation to the dominance of masculinities; thus, femininities signify the subordination of women to men, a subordination in which women's domination of men rarely occurs. See Robert W. Connell, *Masculinities* (Berkeley and Los Angeles: University of California Press, 1995). However, Pyke and Johnson suggest that the notion of hegemonic femininities critically addresses the hierarchy among women of differing classes and races. They write, "However, this discounts how other axes of domination, such as race, class, sexuality, and age, mold a hegemonic femininity that is venerated and extolled in the dominant culture, and that emphasizes the superiority of some women over others, thereby privileging white upper-class women." In Karen D. Pyke and Denise L. Johnson, "Asian American Women and Racialized Femininities: 'Doing' Gender across Cultural Worlds," *Gender and Society* 17, no.1 (2003): 35.

5. Gina Marchetti, *Romance and the "Yellow Peril": Race, Sex, and Discursive Strategies in Hollywood Fiction* (Berkeley and Los Angeles: University of California Press, 1994).

6. Jessica Benjamin, *The Bonds of Love* (New York: Pantheon, 1988), 78.

7. Ibid., 82.

8. Elizabeth Grosz, *Jacque Lacan: A Feminist Introduction* (New York: Routledge, 1990), 129–130.

9. Ibid., 129.

10. Arlie R. Hochschild, *The Second Shift: Working Parents and the Revolution at Home* (New York: Viking, 1989); Lillian Rubin, *Intimate Strangers: Men and Women Together* (New York: Harper and Row, 1983).

11. Ibid.

12. Michael Messner, "'Changing Men' and Feminist Politics in the U.S.," in *Theory and Society* 22, no. 5 (1993): 723–737.

13. Mary C. Waters, *Ethnic Options: Choosing Identities in America* (Berkeley and Los Angeles: University of California Press, 1990).

14. Ji-Yeon Yuh, "Moved by War: Migration, Diaspora, and the Korean War," *Journal of Asian American Studies* 8, no. 3 (2005): 288.

15. David L. Eng, *Racial Castration: Managing Masculinity in Asian America* (Durham, NC: Duke University Press, 2001), 213.

16. Pierrette Hondagneu-Sotelo and Michael Messner, "Gender Displays and Men's Power: The 'New Man' and the Mexican Immigrant Man," in *Theorizing Masculinities*, ed. Harry Brod and Michael Kaufman, 200–218 (Thousand Oaks, CA: Sage Publications, 1994), 215.

17. Bird, "Welcome to the Men's Club"; Michael Messner, *Power at Play: Sports and the Problem of Masculinity* (Boston: Beacon, 1992).

18. Pyke and Johnson, "Asian American Women."

Chapter 6.   Men Alone

1. Asian American men in this study often used the term "American" to mean "white" American. This conflation is a common practice and is observed among Filipino Americans, Korean Americans, Chinese Americans, and Japanese Americans. See Yen Espiritu, "'We Don't Sleep around Like White Girls Do': Family, Culture, and Gender in Filipina American Lives," *Signs: Journal of Women in Culture and Society* 26, no. 2 (2001): 415–440; Stacey J. Lee, *Unraveling the "Model Minority" Stereotype: Listening to Asian American Youth* (New York: Teachers College Press, 1996); Mia Tuan, *Forever Foreigner or Honorary Whites? The Asian Ethnic Experience Today* (New Brunswick, NJ: Rutgers University Press, 1998). However, when Asian Americans describe *themselves* as "American" instead of "Asian," they may be implying that they "are assimilated to the white world and no longer ethnic." See Pyke and Johnson, "Asian American Women," 51.
2. David L. Eng and Shinhee Han, "A Dialogue on Racial Melancholia," *Psychoanalytic Dialogue* 10, no. 4 (2000): 678.
3. Karen D. Pyke and Tran Dang, "'FOB' and 'Whitewashed': Identity and Internalized Racism among Second Generation Asian Americans," *Qualitative Sociology* 26, no. 2 (2003): 151.
4. Ibid.
5. Ibid., 157.
6. Ann A. Cheng, *The Melancholy of Race: Psychoanalysis, Assimilation, and Hidden Grief* (Oxford: Oxford University Press, 2001).
7. Ibid., 16.
8. Ibid., 17.
9. Erica Chito Childs, "Looking behind the Stereotypes of the 'Angry Black Woman.'" *Gender and Society* 19, no. 4 (2005): 544–561.
10. Nazli Kibria discusses how parents' preferences for marrying within the same ethnicity play critical roles in second-generation Chinese and Korean Americans' choice of marital partner. See *Becoming Asian American: Second-Generation Chinese and Korean American Identities* (Baltimore, MD: The Johns Hopkins University Press, 2002), 171.

Conclusion

1. For example, Hung Cam Thai, "Clashing Dreams: Highly Educated Overseas Brides and Low-Wage U.S. Husbands," in *Global Woman: Nannies, Maids, and Sex Workers in the New Economy*, ed. Barbara Ehrenreich and Arlie R. Hochschild, 230–253 (New York: Metropolitan Books, 2003).
2. Erica Chito Childs, *Navigating Interracial Borders: Black-White Couples and Their Social Worlds* (New Brunswick, NJ: Rutgers University Press, 2005).
3. Pawan H. Dhingra, "Being American between Black and White: Second-Generation Asian American Professional Racial Identities," *Journal of Asian American Studies* 6, no. 2 (2003): 120.
4. David Palumbo-Liu, *Asia/America: Historical Crossings of a Racial Frontier* (Stanford, CA: Stanford University Press, 1999), 396.
5. Nicholas D. Kristof, "The Model Students," *New York Times*, May 14, 2006, Lexis-Nexis.
6. Susan Koshy, "Morphing Race into Ethnicity: Asian Americans and Critical Transformations of Whiteness." *boundary* 28 (2001):193.

7. Susan Koshy, *Sexual Naturalizaton: Asian Americans and Miscegenation* (Stanford, CA: Stanford University Press, 2004), 140.
8. Ibid., 148.
9. Nicholas D. Kristof, "Love and Race," *New York Times*, December 6, 2002, A-33.
10. Kim Claire Jean, "Imagining Race and Nation in Multiculturalist America," *Ethnic and Racial Studies* 27, no. 6 (2004): 987–1005.
11. Ibid., 991.
12. Donna J. Nakazawa, "A New Generation Is Leading the Way," *Parade Magazine*, July 6, 2003, 4–5.
13. David Crary, "Lawmakers Hope to Inform, Protect Americans' Foreign Would-be Brides," *The Austin American-Statesman*, July 6, 2003, A-9.
14. Jane O. Hansen, "Mail-Order Bride Business Is Popular, Controversial," Cox News Service, December 7, 2004, Lexis-Nexis.
15. Oren Dorell, "Man Got Gun Permit on Day of Killing," *Raleigh News and Observer*, October 14, 2002; Ellen Sung, Cindy George, and Dawn Wotapka, "Note Is Clue," *Raleigh News and Observer*, October 14, 2002, http://modelminority.com/modules.php?name=Newsandfile=articleandsid=181
16. Helen Zia, "Racism, Hate Crime, and Pornography," in *Race, Class, and Gender: An Anthology*, ed. Margaret Andersen and Patricia H. Collins (Belmont, CA: Wadsworth, 2004), 502–506.
17. Lisa Lowe, *Immigrant Acts: On Asian American Cultural Politics* (Durham, NC, and London: Duke University Press, 1996), 86.
18. Eng points to international adoption as an example of the family challenging current orders of gender, race, and nation and negotiating with "ethical multiculturalism." See David L. Eng, "Transnational Adoption and Queer Diasporas," *Social Text* 76, no. 3 (2003): 1–37.
19. Zygmunt Bauman, *Liquid Love: On the Frality of Human Bonds* (Oxford: Polity Press, 2003), 75.
20. Virginia L. Blum, "Love Studies: Or, Liberating Love," *American Literary History* 17, no. 2 (2005): 339–340.
21. Jessica Benjamin, *Shadow of the Other: Intersubjectivity and Gender in Psychoanalysis* (New York: Routledge, 1998); Jacques Derrida, "Violence and Metaphysics: An Essay on the Thought of Emmanuel Levinas," in *Writing and Difference* (Chicago: University of Chicago Press, 1978); Emmanuel Levinas, *Emmanuel Levinas: Basic Philosophical Writings*, ed. Adriaan Theodoor Peperzak, Simon Critchley, and Robert Bernasconi (Bloomington: Indiana University Press, 1996).
22. Anne A. Cheng, *The Melancholy of Race* (New York: Oxford University Press, 2001), 188.
23. Yoko Arisaka, "Exoticism and the Phenomenology of Racial Desire," in David Kim, ed., *Passions of the Color Line* (Albany: State University of New York Press, forthcoming).
24. Ibid., 7.
25. Michel Foucault, *The Foucault Reader*, ed. Paul Rabinow (London: Penguin, 1984), 352.
26. Blum notes Ann Swidler's findings on the cultural discourse of love, a discourse that consists of contradictory ideas of love: 1) romantic love as a way of personal satisfaction; 2) love as a process of commitment and hard work.. See Ann Swidler, *Talk of Love: How Culture Matters* (Chicago: University of Chicago Press, 2001); Blum, "Love Studies," 342–346.

Bibliography

Anderson, Kathryn, Susan Armitage, Dana Jack, Judith Wittner Anderson. "Beginning Where We Are: Feminist Methodology in Oral History." In *Feminist Research Methods: Exemplary Readings in the Social Sciences*, edited by Joyce M. Nielsen, 94–112. Boulder, CO: West View Press, 1990.

Arisaka, Yoko. "Exoticism and the Phenomenology of Racial Desire." In *Passions of the Color Line*, edited by David Kim. Albany: State University of New York Press, forthcoming.

Bauman, Zygmunt. *Liquid Love: On the Frailty of Human Bonds*. Oxford: Polity Press, 2003.

Bellah, Robert N., Richard Madsen, William M. Sullivan, Ann Swidler, and Steven M. Tipton. *Habits of the Heart: Individualism and Commitment in American Life*. Berkeley and Los Angeles: University of California Press, 1985.

Benjamin, Jessica. *The Bonds of Love*. New York: Pantheon, 1988.

————. *Love Objects: Essays on Recognition and Sexual Difference*. New Haven, CT: Yale University Press, 1998.

————. *Shadow of the Other: Intersubjectivity and Gender in Psychoanalysis*. New York: Routledge, 1998.

Benjamin, Walter. *The Origin of German Tragic Drama*. London: Verso, 1985.

Berlant, Lauren. "The Face of America and the State of Emergency." In *Disciplinarity and Dissent in Cultural Studies*, edited by Cary Nelson and Dilip Parameshwar Gaonkar, 397–440. New York: Routledge, 1996.

————. *The Queen of America Goes to Washington City: Essays on Sex and Citizenship*. Durham, NC: Duke University Press, 1997.

Bernerd, Jessie S. *The Future of Marriage*. New York: World Pub, 1972.

Bhabha, Homi K. *The Location of Culture*. New York: Routledge, 1994.

Bird, Sharon. "Welcome to the Men's Club: Homosociality and the Maintenance of Hegemonic Masculinity." *Gender and Society* 10, no. 2 (1996): 120–132.

Blum, Virginia L. "Love Studies: Or, Liberating Love." *American Literary History* 17, no. 2 (2005): 335–348.

Bonilla-Silva, Eduardo. *Racism without Racists: Color-Blind Racism and the Persistence of Racial Inequality in the United States*. Lanham, MD: Rowman and Littlefield, 2006.

Bordo, Susan. "Feminism, Postmodernism, and Gender-Skepticism." In *Feminism/postmodernism*, edited by Linda J. Nicholson, 19–38. New York: Routledge, 1990.

Butler, Judith. *Subjects of Desire: Hegelian Reflections in Twentieth-Century France*. New York: Columbia University Press, 1987.

Cai, Rong. "Gender Imaginations in Crouching Tiger, Hidden Dragon, and the Wuxia World." *positions: east asia cultural critique* 13, no. 2 (2005): 441–472.

Chan, Jachinson. *Chinese American Masculinities: From Fu Manchu to Bruce Lee.* London: Routledge, 2001.

Chancer, Lynn. *Reconcilable Differences: Confronting Beauty, Pornography, and the Future of Feminism.* Berkeley and Los Angeles: University of California Press, 1998.

Chen, Anthony. "Lives at the Center of the Periphery, Lives at the Periphery of the Center: Chinese American Masculinities and Bargaining with Hegemony." *Gender and Society* 13, no. 5 (1995): 584–607.

Cheng, Anne A. *The Melancholy of Race.* New York: Oxford University Press, 2001.

Cheng, Cliff. "We Choose Not to Compete: The 'Merit' Discourse in the Selection Process, and Asian and Asian American Men and Their Masculinity." In *Masculinities in Organizations,* edited by Cliff Cheng, 177–200. Thousand Oaks, CA: Sage Publications, 1996.

Childs, Erica C. "Looking Behind the Stereotypes of the 'Angry Black Woman.'" *Gender and Society* 19, no. 4 (2005): 544–561.

———. *Navigating Interracial Borders: Black–White Couples and Their Social Worlds.* New Brunswick, NJ: Rutgers University Press, 2005.

Chodorow, Nancy. *The Reproduction of Mothering: Psychoanalysis and the Sociology of Gender.* Berkeley and Los Angeles: University of California Press, 1978.

———. "Gender as a Personal and Cultural Construction." *Signs: Journal of Women in Culture and Society* 20, no. 3 (1995): 516–544.

———. *The Power of Feelings: Personal Meaning in Psychoanalysis, Gender, and Culture.* New Haven, CT: Yale University Press, 1999.

Chow, Sue. "The Significance of Race in the Private Sphere: Asian Americans and Spousal Preferences." *Sociological Inquiry* 70, no. 1 (2000): 1–29.

Cohen, Elizabeth. "Push to Achieve Tied to Suicide in Asian American Women," *CNN News,* May 16, 2007, http://www.cnn.com/2007/HEALTH/05/16/asian.suicides/index.html.

Collins, Patricia Hill. "Like One of the Family: Race, Ethnicity, and the Paradox of US National Identity." *Ethnic and Racial Studies* 24 (2001): 3–28.

———. *Black Sexual Politics: African Americans, Gender, and the New Racism.* New York: Routledge, 2004.

Connell, Robert W. "A Very Straight Gay: Masculinity, Homosexual Experience, and the Dynamics of Gender." *American Sociological Review* 57, no. 6 (1992): 735–751.

———. *Masculinities.* Berkeley and Los Angeles: University of California Press, 1995.

Constable, Nicole. *Romance on a Global Stage: Pen Pals, Virtual Ethnography, and 'Mail-Order' Marriage.* Berkeley and Los Angeles: University of California Press, 2003.

Craig-Henderson, Kelina M. *Black Men in Interracial Relationships: What's Love Got to Do With It?* New Brunswick, NJ: Transaction Publishers, 2006.

Crary, David. "Lawmakers Hope to Inform, Protect Americans' Foreign Would-be Brides," *The Austin American-Statesman,* July 6, 2003, A9.

Davis, Kingsley. "Intermarriage in Caste Societies." *American Anthropologist* 43, no. 3 (1941): 376–395.

Derrida, Jacques. "Violence and Metaphysics: An Essay on the Thought of Emmanuel Levinas." In *Writing and Difference.* Chicago: University of Chicago Press, 1978.

Dhingra, Pawan H. "Being American between Black and White: Second-Generation

Asian American Professional Racial Identities." *Journal of Asian American Studies* 6, no. 2 (2003): 117–147.

Dorell, Oren. "Man Got Gun Permit on Day of Killing," *Raleigh News and Observer,* October 14, 2002. *http://modelminority.com/modules.php?name=News&file=article &sid=181.*

Dyer, Richard. *White.* London: Routledge, 1997.

Eng, David L. *Racial Castration: Managing Masculinity in Asian America.* Durham, NC: Duke University Press, 2001.

———. "Transnational Adoption and Queer Diasporas." *Social Text* 76, no. 3 (2003): 1–37.

Eng, David L., and Shinhee Han. "A Dialogue on Racial Melancholia." *Psychoanalytic Dialogue* 10, no. 4 (2000): 667–700.

Enloe, Cynthia. *Bananas, Beaches, and Bases: Making Feminist Sense of International Politics.* Berkeley and Los Angeles: University of California Press, 1990.

Espiritu, Yen L. *Asian American Panethnicity: Bridging Institutions and Identities* Philadelphia: Temple University Press, 1992.

———. *Asian American Women and Men: Labor, Laws, and Love.* Walnut Creek, CA: AltaMira Press, Division of Rowman & Littlefield, 2000.

———. "'We Don't Sleep Around Like White Girls Do': Family, Culture, and Gender in Filipina American Lives." *Signs: Journal of Women in Culture and Society* 26, no. 2 (2001): 415–440.

Fanon, Frantz. *Black Skin, White Masks.* New York: Grove Press, 1967.

Farman, Abou. "An Archeology of Inter-Racial Relations." *Fuse* 15, no. 3 (1992): 7–11.

Flax, Jane. "Review Essay on Psychoanalysis and Feminism in Postcolonial Time." *Signs: Journal of Women in Culture and Society* 29, no. 3 (2004): 908–917.

Fong, Colleen, and Judy Yung. "In Search of the Right Spouse: Interracial Marriage among Chinese and Japanese Americans." *Amerasia Journal* 21, no. 3 (1995): 77–98.

Foucault, Michel. *The History of Sexuality, Volume 1: An Introduction.* New York: Vintage, 1978.

———. *The Foucault Reader,* edited by Paul Rabinow. London: Penguin, 1984.

———. "Ethics of Concern for the Self as a Practice of Freedom." In *Ethics, Subjectivity, and Truth,* edited by Paul Rabinow, 281–301. New York: New Press, 1997.

Frank, Thomas. "Why Johnny Can't Dissent." In *Commodify Your Dissent: The Business of Culture in the New Gilded Age,* edited by Thomas Frank and Matt Weiland, 31–45. New York: Norton, 1997.

Frankenberg, Ruth. *White Women, Race Matters: The Social Construction of Whiteness.* Minneapolis: University of Minnesota Press, 1993.

Fraser, Nancy, and Linda J. Nicholson, "Social Criticism without Philosophy: An Encounter between Feminism and Postmodernism." In *Feminism/postmodernism,* edited by Linda. J. Nicholson, 133–156. New York: Routledge, 1990.

Freud, Sigmund. "Mourning and Melancholia." In *The Standard Edition of the Complete Psychological Works of Sigmund Freud,* edited by James Strachey, vol. 14, 243–258. London: Hogarth Press, 1953.

Gallagher, Charles A. "Color Blind Privilege: The Social and Political Functions of Erasing the Color Line in Post-Race America." In *Rethinking the Color Line: Readings in Race and Ethnicity,* edited by Charles A Gallagher, 130–143. New York: McGraw Hill, 2007.

Giddens, Anthony. *Profiles and Critiques in Social Theory.* Berkeley and Los Angeles: University of California Press, 1982.

———. *Modernity and Self-Identity: Self and Society in the Late Modern Age*. Stanford, CA: Stanford University Press, 1991.

———. *The Transformation of Intimacy: Sexuality, Love, and Eroticism in Modern Societies*. Cambridge, MA: Polity Press, 1992.

Glenn, Evelyn N. *Issei, Nisei, War Bride: Three Generations of Japanese American Women in Domestic Service*. Philadelphia: Temple University Press, 1989.

Gordon, Milton M. *Assimilation in American Life: The Role of Race, Religion, and National Origins*. New York: Oxford University Press, 1964.

Grosz, Elizabeth. *Jacque Lacan: A Feminist Introduction*. New York: Routledge 1990.

Hamamoto, Darrell Y. "Kindred Spirits: The Contemporary Asian American Family on Television." *Amerasia Journal* 18 (1992): 35–53.

Hansen, Jane O. "Mail-Order Bride Business Is Popular, Controversial," *Cox News Service*, December 7, 2004. *Lexis-Nexis*.

Hartmann, Heidi. "The Unhappy Marriage of Marxism and Feminism: Towards a More Progressive Union." In *Women and Revolution: A Discussion of the Unhappy Marriage of Marxism and Feminism*, edited by Lydia Sargent, 1–41. Boston: South End Press, 1981.

Henderson, Robert. *The Secret of Dating Asian Women*. Mango Press, 1995.

Hochschild, Arlie R. *The Second Shift: Working Parents and the Revolution at Home*. New York: Viking, 1989.

Holland, Dorothy C., and Margaret A. Eisenhart. *Educated in Romance: Women, Achievement, and College Culture*. Chicago: University of Chicago Press, 1990.

Hondagneu-Sotelo, Pierrette, and Michael Messner. "Gender Displays and Men's Power: The 'New Man' and the Mexican Immigrant Man." In *Theorizing Masculinities*, edited by Harry Brod and Michael Kaufman, 200–218. Thousand Oaks, CA: Sage Publications, 1994.

Hunter, Margaret. "'If You're Light, You're Alright': Light Skin Color as Social Capital for Women of Color." *Gender and Society* 16, no. 2 (2004): 175–193.

Jacobs, Jerry, and Teresa Labov. "Gender Differentials in Intermarriage among Sixteen Race and Ethnic Groups." *Sociological Forum* 17, no. 4 (2002): 621–646.

Kang, Laura Hyun Y. *Compositional Subjects: Enfiguring Asian/American Women*. Durham, NC: Duke University Press, 2002.

Kaplan, Caren. "Resisting Autobiography: Out-law Genres and Transnational Feminist Subjects." In *De/colonizing the Subject: The Politics of Gender in Women's Autobiography*, edited by Sidonie Smith and Julia Watson, 115–138. Minneapolis: University of Minnesota Press, 1992.

Kelsky, Karen. *Women on the Verge: Japanese Women, Western Dreams*. Durham, NC: Duke University Press, 2000.

Kennedy, Randall. *Interracial Intimacies: Sex, Marriage, Identity, and Adoption*. New York: Pantheon, 2003.

Kibria, Nazli. "The Construction of 'Asian American': Reflections on Intermarriage and Ethnic Identity among Second-Generation Chinese and Korean Americans." *Ethnic and Racial Studies* 20 (1997): 523–544.

———. "The Contested Meanings of 'Asian American': Racial Dilemmas in the Contemporary U.S." *Ethnic and Racial Studies* 21 (1998): 939–958.

———. *Becoming Asian American: Second-Generation Chinese and Korean American Identities*. Baltimore, MD: Johns Hopkins University Press, 2002.

Kim, Claire J. "Imagining Race and Nation in Multiculturalist America." *Ethnic and Racial Studies* 27, no. 6 (2004): 987–1005.

Kim, James. "The Legend of the White-and-Yellow Black Man: Global Containment and Triangulated Racial Desire in *Romeo Must Die*." *Camera Obscura* 19, no. 1 (2004): 150–179.

Kim, L. S. "Crouching Tiger, Hidden Dragon: Making Women Warriors: A Transnational Reading of Asian Female Action Heroes." *Jump Cut: A Review of Contemporary Media*, no. 48 (Winter 2006). *http://www.ejumpcut.org/archive/jc48.2006/womenWarriors/index.html.*

Kimmel, Michael S. "Masculinity as Homophobia: Fear, Shame, and Silence in the Construction of Gender Identity." In *Theorizing Masculinities*, edited by Harry Brod and Michael Kaufman, 119–141. Thousand Oaks, CA: Sage Publications, 1994.

Kitano, Harry H. L., Wai-Tsang Yeung, Lynn Chai, and Herbert Hatanaka. "Asian American Interracial Marriage." *Journal of Marriage and the Family* 46, no. 1 (February 1984): 179–190.

Kondo, Dorinne. "Gripe 'Miss Saigon' is a Celebration of Stereotypes," *The Los Angeles Times*, February 18, 1995. *http://pqasb.pqarchiver.com/latimes/advancedsearch.html.*

———. *About Face: Performing Race in Fashion and Theater.* New York: Routledge, 1997.

Koshy, Susan. "The Fiction of Asian American Literature." *Yale Journal of Criticism* 9, no. 2 (1996): 315–346.

———. "Morphing Race into Ethnicity: Asian Americans and Critical Transformations of Whiteness." *boundary* 28 (2001): 153–194.

———. *Sexual Naturalizaton: Asian Americans and Miscegenation.* Stanford, CA: Stanford University Press, 2004.

Kristof, Nicholas D. "Love and Race," *New York Times*, December 6, 2002, A-33.

———. "The Model Students," *New York Times*, May 14, 2006. *Lexis-Nexis.*

Lee, Sharon M., and Marilyn Fernandez. "Trends in Asian American Racial/Ethnic Intermarriage: A Comparison of 1980 and 1990 Census Data." *Sociological Perspectives* 41, no. 2 (1998): 323–342.

Lee, Sharon M., and Keiko Yamanaka. "Patterns of Asian Intermarriage and Marital Assimilation." *Journal of Comparative Family Studies* 21 (1990): 287–305.

Lee, Stacey J. *Unraveling the "Model Minority" Stereotype: Listening to Asian American Youth.* New York: Teachers College Press, 1996.

Levinas, Emmanuel. *Emmanuel Levinas: Basic Philosophical Writings.* Edited by Adriaan Theodoor Peperzak, Simon Critchley, and Robert Bernasconi. Bloomington: Indiana University Press, 1996.

Liang, Zai, and Naomi Ito. "Intermarriage of Asian Americans in the New York City Region: Contemporary Patterns and Future Prospects." *International Migration Review* 33, no. 4 (1999): 876–900.

Ling, L. H. M. "Sex Machine: Global Hypermasculity and Images of the Asian Women in Modernity." *positions: east asia cultures critique* 7, no. 2 (1999): 277–306.

Lipman-Blumen, Jean. "Toward a Homosocial Theory of Sex Roles: An Explanation of the Sex Segregation of Social Institutions." In *Women and the Workplace*, edited by Martha Blaxall and Barbara B. Reagan, 15–31. Chicago: University of Chicago Press, 1976.

Lopez, Alfred. *Postcolonial Whiteness: A Critical Reader on Race and Empire State.* Albany: University of New York Press, 2005.

Lowe, Lisa. "Heterogeniety, Hybridity, Multiplicity: Making Asian American Differences." *Diaspora* 1, no. 1 (1991): 24–44.

———. *Immigrant Acts: On Asian American Cultural Politics.* Durham, NC: Duke University Press, 1996.

Liu, William M. "Sex Tour Narratives: Narcissism and Fantasy in Determining Asian American Sexuality." *Hitting Critical Mass: Journal of Asian American Cultural Criticism* 4, no. 2 (1997): 87–110.

Marchetti, Gina. *Romance and the "Yellow Peril": Race, Sex, and Discursive Strategies in Hollywood Fiction.* Berkeley and Los Angeles: University of California Press, 1994.

McNay, Lois. *Gender and Agency: Reconfiguring the Subject in Feminist and Social Theory.* Oxford: Polity Press, 2000.

Merton, Robert. "Intermarriage and the Social Structure: Fact and Theory." *Psychiatry* 4 (1941): 361–374.

Messner, Michael. *Power at Play: Sports and the Problem of Masculinity.* Boston: Beacon, 1992.

———. "'Changing Men' and Feminist Politics in the U.S." *Theory and Society* 22, no 5. (1993): 723–737.

Moore, Henrietta L. *A Passion for Difference: Essays in Anthropology and Gender.* Oxford: Polity Press, 1994.

Moran, Rachel F. *Interracial Intimacy: The Regulation of Race and Romance.* Chicago: University of Chicago Press, 2001.

Munoz, Jose E. "No Es Facil: Notes on the Negotiation of Cubanidad and Exilic Memory." *Drama Review* 39, no. 3 (1995): 76–82.

Nagel, Joane. *Race, Ethnicity, and Sexuality: Intimate Intersections, Forbidden Frontier.* Oxford: Oxford University Press, 2004.

Nakazawa, Donna J. "A New Generation Is Leading the Way." *Parade Magazine,* July 6, 2003. *(As seen in the Austin American-Statesman.)*

Narayan, Uma. "'Male-order' Brides: Immigrant Women, Domestic Violence, and Immigration Law." *Hypatia* 10, no. 1 (1995): 104–119.

Nguyen, Viet Thanh. *Race and Resistance: Literature and Politics in Asian America.* Oxford: Oxford University Press, 2002.

Ogden, Thomas. *Subjects of Analysis.* London: Jason Aronson, 1996.

Ong, Aihwa. *Flexible Citizenship: The Cultural Logics of Transnatinality.* Durham, NC: Duke University Press, 1999.

Palumbo-Liu, David. *Asia/America: Historical Crossings of a Racial Frontier.* Stanford, CA: Stanford University Press, 1999.

Pan, Esther. "Why Asian Guys Are on a Roll," *Newsweek* 135, vol. 8, February 21, 2000. *http://search.ebscohost.com.*

Povinelli, Elizabeth A. *The Empire of Love: Toward a Theory of Intimacy, Genealogy, and Carnality.* Durham, NC: Duke University Press, 2006.

Pyke, Karen D. "'Generational Deserters' and 'Black Sheep': Acculturative Differences among Siblings in Asian Immigrant Families." *Journal of Family Issues* 26 (2005): 491–517.

———. "Defying the Taboo on the Study of Internalized Racial Oppression." In *Migration and Immigration, Social Change, and Cultural Transformation,* edited by Emory Elliott, Jasmine Payne, and Patricia Ploesch, 101–120. New York: Palgrave McMillan, 2007.

Pyke, Karen D., and Tran Dang. "'FOB' and 'Whitewashed': Identity and Internalized Racism among Second Generation Asian Americans." *Qualitative Sociology* 26, no. 2 (2003): 147–172.

Pyke, Karen D., and Denise L. Johnson. "Asian American Women and Racialized Femininities: 'Doing' Gender across Cultural Worlds." *Gender and Society* 17, no. 1 (2003): 33–53.

Rich, Adrienne. "Compulsive Heterosexuality and Lesbian Existence." *Signs: Journal of Women in Culture and Society* 5, no. 4 (1980): 631–660.

Ricoeur, Paul. *From Text to Action.* Evanston, IL: Northwestern University Press, 1991.

Root, Maria P. *Love's Revolution: Interracial Marriage.* Philadelphia: Temple University Press, 2001.

Rosenfeld, Michael. "A Critique of Mate Selection Theory." *American Journal of Sociology* 110, no. 5 (2005): 1284–1325.

Rubin, Gayle. "The Traffic in Women: Notes on the 'Political Economy' of Sex." In *Toward an Anthropology of Women*, edited by Rayna R. Reiter, 157–210. New York: Monthly Review Press, 1975.

Rubin, Lillian. *Intimate Strangers: Men and Women Together*. New York: Harper and Row, 1983.

Saenz, Rogelio, Sean-Shong Hwang, and Benigno E. Aguirre. "In Search of Asian War Brides." *Demography* 31, no. 3 (August 1994): 549–559.

Sedgwick, Eve. *Between Men: English Literature and Male Homosocial Desire*. New York: Columbia University Press, 1985.

Shimizu, Celine P. "The Bind of Representation: Performing and Consuming Hypersexuality in *Miss Saigon*." *Theatre Journal* 57, no. 2 (2005): 247–265.

———. *The Hypersexuality of Race: Performing Asian/American Women on Screen and Scene*. Durham, NC: Duke University Press, 2007.

Shinagawa, Larry H., and Gin Yong Pang. "Intraethnic, Interethnic, and Interracial Marriages among Asian Americans in California, 1980." *Berkeley Journal of Sociology* 33 (1988): 95–114.

———. "Asian American Panethnicity and Intermarriage." *Amerasia Journal* 22, no. 2 (1996): 127–152.

Simpson, Caroline C. "Out of an Obscure Place: Japanese War Brides and Cultural Pluralism in the 1950s." *differences: A Journal of Feminist Cultural Studies* 10, no. 3 (1999): 47–81.

Spickard, Paul R. *Mixed Blood: Intermarriage and Ethnic Identity in Twentieth-Century America*. Madison: University of Wisconsin Press, 1989.

Spivak, Gayatri C. *A Critique of Postcolonial Reason: Toward a History of the Vanishing Present*. Cambridge, MA: Harvard University Press, 1999.

Stoler, Ann L. *Race and the Education of Desire: Foucault's History of Sexuality and the Colonial Order of Things*. Durham, NC: Duke University Press, 1995.

Sung, Ellen, Cindy George, and Dawn Wotapka. "Note Is Cute." *Raleigh News and Observer*, October 14, 2002. *http://modelminority.com/modules.php?name=News&file=article&sid=181*.

Swidler, Ann. *Talk of Love: How Culture Matters*. Chicago: University of Chicago Press, 2001.

Thai, Hung Cam. "Clashing Dreams: Highly Educated Overseas Brides and Low-Wage U.S. Husbands." In *Global Woman: Nannies, Maids, and Sex Workers in the New Economy*, edited by Barbara Ehrenreich and Arlie R. Hochschild, 230–253. New York: Metropolitan Books, 2003.

Ty, Eleanor. "Welcome to Dreamland: Power, Gender, and Post-Colonial Politics in *Miss Saigon*." *Essays in Theatre* 13, no. 1 (1994): 15–27.

Waters, Mary C. *Ethnic Options: Choosing Identities in America*. Berkeley and Los Angeles: University of California Press, 1990.

Williams, Christine L. "Psychoanalytic Theory and the Sociology of Gender." In *Theory on Gender/Feminism on Theory*, edited by Paula England, 131–149. New York: Aldine de Gruyter, 1993.

Yang, Lingyan. "Theorizing Asian America: On Asian American and Postcolonial Asian Diasporic Women Intellectuals." *Journal of Asian American Studies* 5, no. 2 (2002): 139–178.

Yu, Henry. "Tiger Woods Is Not the End of History: Or, Why Sex across the Color Line Won't Save Us All." *American Historical Review* 108 (2003): 1406–1414.

Yuh, Ji-Yeon. "Out of the Shadows: Camptown Women, Military Brides, and Korean

(American) Communities." *Hitting Critical Mass: A Journal of Asian American Cultural Criticism* 6, no. 1 (1999): 13–33.

———. *Beyond the Shadow of Camptown: Korean Military Brides in America.* New York: New York University Press, 2002.

———. "Moved by War: Migration, Diaspora, and the Korean War." *Journal of Asian American Studies* 8, no. 3 (2005): 277–291.

Zane, Kathleen. "Reflections on a Yellow Eye: Asian I (\Eye/) Cons and Cosmetic Surgery." In *Talking Visions: Multicultural Feminism in a Transnational Age,* edited by Ella Shohat, 161–191. Cambridge, MA: MIT Press, 1998.

Zia, Helen. "Racism, Hate Crime, and Pornography." In *Race, Class, and Gender: An Anthology,* edited by Margaret Andersen and Patricia H. Collins, 502–506. Belmont, CA: Wadsworth, 2004.

Index

About the Author

Kumiko Nemoto is an assistant professor of sociology at Western Kentucky University. She received her Ph.D. in sociology from the University of Texas at Austin. Her research interests include gender, race, sexuality, family, and work. She has conducted research both in the United States and in Japan.

HQ 1031 .N45 2009
Nemoto, Kumiko, 1970-
Racing romance

DATE DUE

DEMCO 38-296

Printed in the United States
219506BV00001B/3/P

9 780813 545332